The Essence of Managing Groups and Teams

THE ESSENCE OF MANAGEMENT SERIES

PUBLISHED TITLES

The Essence of Managing Groups and Teams

HANK WILLIAMS

Hank Williams is a director of **Learning Curve**, a network of
management consultants specialising in people and team development.
For further information, contact:
Learning Curve (Lancaster)
60 Regent Street
Lancaster LA1 1SH
tel/fax: +44 (0)1524 846750

Prentice Hall

London   New York   Toronto   Sydney   Tokyo   Singapore
Madrid   Mexico City   Munich

First published 1996 by
Prentice Hall Europe
Campus 400, Maylands Avenue
Hemel Hempstead
Hertfordshire, HP2 7EZ
A division of
Simon & Schuster International Group

© Prentice Hall Europe, 1996

Typeset in 10/12pt Palatino
by Keyset Composition, Colchester

Printed and bound in Great Britain by
T.J. Press (Padstow) Ltd, Padstow, Cornwall.

Library of Congress Cataloging-in-Publication Data

Williams, Hank.
    The essence of managing groups and teams/Hank Williams.
      p. cm. — (The essence of management series)
    Includes bibliographical references and index.
    ISBN 0-13-356528-9 (alk. paper)
    1. Work groups. 2. Supervision of employees. I. Title.
II. Series.
HD66.W537   1996
658.4' 02 — dc20   95–26374
                                             CIP

British Library Cataloguing in Publication Data

A catalogue record for this book is available from
the British Library

ISBN 0-13-356528-9

---

1 2 3 4 5   00 99 98 97 96

Contents

Introduction

The aim

The Essence of Managing Groups and Teams is a handbook for managers which helps you to think about and improve the way you manage the groups of people you lead.

It is the companion book to *The Essence of Managing People*, which focuses on the management of individuals and the one-to-one interaction. *The Essence of Managing Groups and Teams* focuses on the management of groups and the one-to-group interaction. The two books complement and build on each other. Together they provide you with an invaluable resource for developing your people-management skills.

The management of groups is a large subject which can be addressed in many different ways. Most of my involvement with groups and teams now is in the capacity of an external facilitator, brought in to help groups achieve specific tasks or to improve their effectiveness generally and to help teams to work well together or to resolve specific difficulties. So in this book, the approach I am taking is to explain the processes I use when I am facilitating groups and teams. There are two reasons for this choice:

1. It provides a coherent and immediate structure for exploring the central issues which underpin effective teamwork.
2. It encourages and enables you to think of yourself as an *internal* facilitator, and this is the role that managers and team-leaders are increasingly being expected to perform.

One consequence of this approach is that this book is only concerned with the *management* of groups and teams. There is nothing here about selection, for example, because I am never involved in deciding the composition of the teams I facilitate. And it is possible that there are other issues which you might expect this book to address which in fact it does not. I hope that there is enough in what is here to compensate for these omissions.

Another consequence is that I am describing *my* processes for facilitating groups and teams. There are other processes and other ways of working. I lay no claim to my way being better than any other. It is just the way I know best because I developed it myself, on the job. So this book will not describe any other processes that exist, not because I disagree with them, but simply because I don't use them. There may be other models and approaches that you are familiar with which are not referred to directly. Having said that, the differences between the various processes and models that exist are often much slighter than I like to imagine and I am sometimes distressed to realize that what I thought of as an original idea is actually only my way of expressing someone else's model!

The focus

The Essence of Managing Groups and Teams focuses on two key aspects of group management and explores these aspects in detail. They are:

□ **Group process:** Understanding the processes which determine group behaviour and effectiveness; actively facilitating these processes to ensure that groups work well together.
□ **Interactive skills:** Understanding the verbal behaviours which underpin interaction; managing your own behaviour and influencing the behaviour of others to ensure effective communication.

The book is based on the principle that we make choices all the time about how we manage and interact with others. Some of these choices are conscious decisions. Many are not: they are instinctive responses to people and situations which are influenced by our needs, values, preferences and habits. The work you will be doing as you read the book is to:

□ Reflect on and evaluate the choices you make.
□ Explore alternatives.
□ Identify practical steps you can take at work that will make you a more effective manager and leader.

The reader

The Essence of Managing Groups and Teams will be most relevant and useful to you if you are currently leading a team or managing a group of people. The exercises and activities are based on the assumption that this is the case. It is appropriate for all managers, whatever their experience: you will find it helpful if you have been managing groups for six months or for twenty years.

The book will also be useful to you if you are preparing to become a supervisor or manager for the first time. It will help you to think through the kind of manager you want to be and to reflect on your likely strengths and weaknesses. Although many of the exercises and activities will be impractical unless you know the people you will be managing, you can use them when you become a manager to help you decide your leadership style and behaviour.

The book will also be of use to people who, although they don't lead or manage groups, spend some or all of their time facilitating groups and teams led by others.

The issues addressed in the book apply to almost all situations where someone is responsible for leading a group or team. This might be a multinational corporation, a small company, a local government department or a voluntary organization. Although your work setting has an impact, many of the underlying issues of group management are the same.

The reading

The Essence of Managing Groups and Teams covers a wide range of issues in a lot of detail. It also has a large number of exercises and activities which could take up a substantial amount of your time. So you need to think carefully about how best to use it in order to meet your needs. Here is some information that might help you to do this.

Sequence

The book is divided into three Parts:

Part 1. Identity: Looks at some of the key identity issues of group management: the strategic choices you make about how you maximize the resources within the group and the style of leadership you provide.

Part 2. Process: Helps you to understand the ways in which the group you manage works together (group process), to identify areas of current or potential problem and to manage group process effectively. The exercises and activities in Part 2 help you to reflect on and improve your skills as a 'process manager'.

Part 3. Behaviour: Helps you to improve the way you interact with your people. It focuses on the behavioural skills required to effectively manage formal and informal group discussion. The exercises and activities in Part 3 give you the opportunity to reflect on how you manage interactions at the moment and to identify how to develop your skills further.

The three Parts are interlinked, building on and referring back to each other. So, unless you have a strong reason not to, it will probably be better for you to work through the book in the sequence in which it has been written. However, each Part is free-standing, so if you have a particular interest in behaviour, for example, you could read that part of the book first.

Activity

There are two kinds of activity in the book. These are:

□ **Exercises,** which ask you to reflect on your experience to date, either as a way of introducing a concept or as a way of helping you to relate the concept to real life.

□ **Activities,** which ask you to plan steps or actions you will take at work to apply concepts that have just been covered or generally to improve your performance.

You must decide the extent to which you want these exercises and activities to become integral to your reading of the book. You may prefer not to do them at all, in order to get through the book more quickly. You may prefer to devise your own ways of actively using the book.

A word of warning: it is easy to assume that because we have understood something we are able to apply it. This is rarely the case. The development of your skills and abilities as a manager will only happen if you consciously reflect on and practise applying the things you have learnt from this book that you find valuable.

The words

There are some words that are used frequently which need some explanation. They are:

□ **Leader** and **manager** have been used interchangeably, mainly to avoid repetition. They have been used to describe anyone who is responsible for managing the performance of a group of other people. This includes people who may not be referred to as managers in their organization, such as supervisors.

□ **Group** and **team** have been used interchangeably to describe the group of people that you manage, even though you may not regard them as a team in the strict sense of the word. The distinction between group and team is explored in Chapter 1.

□ **Organization** has been used to refer to the setting in which you work, even though you might not use that word to describe it.

□ **Them/they** has been used frequently to avoid specific gender-referencing.

My background

I am a director of the Learning Curve network and a management consultant who works with commercial organizations to help them develop the performance of their people, both as individuals and as groups and teams. This involves consultancy interventions to develop values and systems and training and coaching managers to develop skills and capabilities. I work with multinationals and with UK companies.

I have been facilitating groups and teams for the past fourteen years: this has involved both team-building and crisis intervention. I have worked closely with several companies to help them develop the capability of their managers to manage groups and teams effectively. This has brought me into contact with hundreds of managers and the issues they face. *The Essence of Managing Groups and Teams* is based on these experiences.

I have also managed people myself, recruiting and developing a team of training consultants for a consultancy company. Before joining the private sector, I worked extensively with local government and voluntary organizations.

Influences

There have been two key influences that have informed the writing of this book and that I would like to acknowledge:

□ The material on motivation and self-management in Parts 1 and 2 is based on the work of the Pellin Institute, run by Peter Fleming. In a broader sense, my involvement with Pellin has contributed significantly to my own development as a person and as a people worker.

☐ Much of Part 3 is based on the work of Huthwaite Research Group and their behavioural approach to interactive skills. I worked for Huthwaite for four years, developing interactive skills training programmes for managers. Although I have not used their systems or research explicitly, they underpin the sections of Part 3 which deal specifically with behaviour.

Part 1

———

Identity

———

Part 1 explores issues of identity. It helps you to reflect on your role and contribution as manager and team-leader from three perspectives: the requirement of the group or team; your own strategic choices; and the aspects of your personality that influence these choices. The exercises and activities in Part 1 enable you critically to review the way you currently lead your group or team.

1

Groups and teams: What is the difference?

I once worked for a training consultancy, made up of several business units, plus an administrative support group. Each business unit consisted of three to five consultants. The management felt that the relationship between these different units could be improved and decided to send us on a team-building event – a week in the Lake District doing a series of outdoor activities which would help us to discover more about ourselves and each other and thus hopefully generate the awareness and motivation to manage relationships within the company more positively and constructively.

I refused to go. Team-building was not what we needed. We were not teams. We were a bunch of individual contributors with overripe egos (like most consultants) grouped together in loose affiliations whose only function was to determine the scope of our activity. The problems being experienced were partly an inevitable feature of a consultancy organization, partly the consequence of the way this organization was structured – in particular its system of reward and remuneration, and partly the management's inability to tackle and resolve issues with specific individuals and relationships.

Not only did I think team-building was inappropriate, I felt that it was actively counter-productive, fostering a misplaced belief in a corporate identity which had never actually existed and which only served to mask the real issues and responsibilities within the company. I advocated instead that these real issues be clearly and openly articulated and then addressed directly with interventions by the relevant people in the most appropriate way. There was little interest shown in either my analysis or my proposal. There *was* a ready criticism of my refusal to go to the Lakes, which was seen as a refusal to be part of the team.

I use this story to illustrate two things: the need to distinguish between groups and teams; and the way in which the 'team myth' can be used to disguise the work that a group of people needs to undertake in order to improve its effectiveness. I am often asked by clients to run team-building sessions for groups of people within their organization. My first question now is always: 'Are you a team or are you a group?' The answer to this question will help me to determine the client's actual needs and to plan how best to meet them.

What makes a team a team?

There are two factors that I look for when I am trying to distinguish teams from groups. These are:

☐ The level of dependency.
☐ The degree of commonality.

The level of dependency

In my previous organization, the consultants each worked independently: they were set their own revenue target, they sold their own business, they delivered most of their training programmes on their own. They only occasionally needed to work together. They were expected to be able to achieve their targets through their own effort. The level of dependency on each other was virtually zero. A certain amount of their revenue would be earned through servicing other consultants' accounts, but to all intents and purposes, they were independent contributors.

This is true of many working groups. The work of one individual within the group is not dependent for its successful execution on the work of its other members. A department of school teachers, for example, is likely to share the same profile as my consultancy organization; the times when they depend on their colleagues will be few and far between. A group can share the same office space, day in, day out, but the nature of the activity they do in that space means that the level of dependency is very low. And so the output of the group is not dependent on its members working effectively as a team. Consequently the group does not *need* to work together as a team.

There are groups where the level of dependency is high – where the work of each person is totally interlinked with the work of others so that they cannot achieve their output unless other members of the team achieve theirs. Project teams often fall into this category. The high level of dependency requires people to collaborate with each other, to adapt their activity and behaviour so that it dovetails with the activity of others and is subordinated to the overriding needs of the group. The group has to work together as a team if it is to be successful.

Most working groups fall somewhere in between the two extremes. There is some dependency but it is not necessarily high. Some of the work done can be carried out by individuals working on their own, but some of the work requires the group to cooperate with each other, support each other, coordinate their activity. Such groups are somewhere on the line between 'collection of individuals' at one end of the continuum and 'close-knit team' at the other.

EXERCISE 1.1

Spend a few minutes now reflecting on the level of dependency in some of the groups that you are involved with at work. If the level varies from group to group, consider how this affects the identity of each group and the way its members work with and relate to each other.

The degree of commonality

The other factor that distinguishes groups from teams is the degree to which the goals of the team override the goals of its individual members. In the example of the consultancy company I used to work for, it was a fact that our individual revenue targets were more important to us than our team targets. This was only partly because of the way we were rewarded – we received bonuses for meeting both of these targets. It was mainly because the values of the organization gave status to those consultants who exceeded their individual target. We measured our success and compared ourselves to our colleagues with this yardstick. And because of this, it was an essentially competitive environment: not only did our individual performance matter more to us than our team performance but our motivation was to ensure that our own performance exceeded those of our colleagues.

It was because of these two reasons, the low level of dependency and the low degree of commonality, that I felt that team-building was an inappropriate strategy. There was no requirement on us to work effectively in teams; in fact the requirement was exactly the opposite: for us to be successful individual contributors. It is true that the lack of collaboration sometimes created problems, but this was usually caused by the weak management of strong individuals. To attempt to impose a team identity onto a culture which was essentially and necessarily individualistic and competitive was doomed to failure.

EXERCISE 1.2

Spend a few minutes now reflecting on the level of commonality in some of the groups that you are involved with at work. If the level varies from group to group, consider how this affects the identity of each group and the way its members work with and relate to each other.

Only when the degree of commonality is high is it relevant to think of the group as a team and to treat it accordingly. As with the level of dependency, there are many positions on the line between low and high commonality, and most groups will fall somewhere in between. The degree of commonality will depend on a number of elements: the values of the organization; the nature of the work; the motivations and personalities of the people involved. It can be manipulated to a certain extent, in that you can generate a higher degree of commonality of purpose than naturally exists, and much team-building activity tries to do this by working on vision and mission statements and the like. Often the effect of such an intervention is short-lived because the constructed commonality generated is undermined by the constraints that exist naturally within the group.

A high degree of commonality is only appropriate and only possible in certain situations. In some cases, like my consultancy company, it will be more effective to have a high degree of individual purpose – and a group of highly motivated individuals – than to try to impose a superordinate common purpose which nobody is *actually* committed to or motivated by. Such a group, with such an identity, will require a particular style of management, but it is no less worthy or effective than a genuine team which shares a common purpose that is its main motivating force.

CASE STUDY 1.1

Gavin has asked me to run a team-building session with his group: five people who help senior managers to manage large-scale change projects in a major UK organization that is in a state of rapid growth and constant change. He is concerned that they don't operate as a team at all: they go off and do their own thing; they don't communicate effectively; they don't share information and experience; they are more focused on their clients within the organization than on their membership of the team.

I separate out the two different issues that Gavin describes to me. The first is one of identity: we should be a team but nobody wants to be. The second is one of communication systems: we don't communicate effectively together. Gavin has lumped these two issues together, using the second to reinforce the first: we are not a team and therefore we don't communicate well together and if we were more of a team we would communicate better. The two issues are entirely unconnected. The group could communicate more effectively together whether they are a team or not.

My first piece of work with Gavin is to decide whether his group needs to be a team in order to work effectively. The situation he describes to me is one where the level of dependency is low – his people are individual contributors spending almost all their time on their own with their internal clients, and one where the degree of commonality is also low – there is no meaningful team goal, other than generalities about improving project management in the organization. His people are motivated by the need to ensure that the projects they personally are involved in are successful. That's what turns them on and so it should be. There is no requirement for them to work together as a team. They are a loose affiliation of specialists dispersed within the organization who are working individually. 'Wonderful,' says Gavin when he recognizes this. What a relief not to have to try to forge a team out of this group of strong-willed individuals. What a relief not to feel like a bad manager for failing to do so.

My second piece of work with Gavin is to understand the actual requirement for communication within the group and to identify the reasons why this requirement is not being met naturally. There are several causes: some are pragmatic – it is difficult to get everybody in the same room for half an hour – some are to do with personality clashes, and some are to do with Gavin's style of management. Having stripped away the diversion of team identity, my work with the group is to address these issues directly and to generate specific and practical solutions for developing an appropriate and well-managed communication process.

The 'team myth'

Case study 1.1 provides another illustration of the power of the mythology that has built up around the team concept. The word 'team' is used to describe an idealized state. It is representative of a shift from one way of working to another, a paradigm shift away from the linear hierarchies of the industrial era to the more empowered, circular structures of the post-industrial era. But as well as this generalized meaning, it is a specific description of how people should work together, with the implication that if they do not, there is something wrong with them. This was Gavin's concern: because his group did not live up to the idealized team state he felt that they were failing and that he was failing them as their team-leader. The power of the myth overrides the reality of the situation.

I do believe that the team structure is an effective way of organizing people so that they achieve their objectives. But I become concerned when 'team' becomes an ideological rather than a merely structural concept in organizations, because then it becomes harder to assess the natural forces within a group and the actual requirement for its effective working. The language and processes of teamwork can be applied willy-nilly, in the naive belief that artificially constructed dependency and commonality will make a team out of any group. It is more important to decide whether the group needs to operate as a team first, before identifying strategies for developing the appropriate identity and the structures, processes and skills required for operating effectively within that identity.

Figure 1.1 The group-team continuum.

The group–team continuum

By using the concepts of dependency and commonality, it is possible to locate a working group on what I call the 'group–team continuum'. This is illustrated in Figure 1.1.

At one end of this continuum, the working group is actually a loose federation of individuals with little requirement to work together effectively. They are grouped together for purely organizational reasons: such as ease of identification, management structures, allocation of space. They don't need to communicate with each other much, they don't make many group decisions, they don't need to get on that well with each other (although of course it would be nicer if they did). A group of field engineers who don't actually spend much time together, apart from meeting each morning for their day's work to be allocated, could be such a group.

At the other end is the close-knit team, whose success is dependent on their ability to work closely and effectively with each other. The contribution of the individual is worthless if taken outside the team setting. The people in such a group do not necessarily spend a lot of time together, and may not be located in the same room or even the same country, but they have to ensure that their activity is coordinated, that they communicate effectively and that they resolve any tensions within the group that may impact negatively on the performance of the team. A design team will typically fall into this category, for example.

In the middle of the continuum is the collaborative working group – where exactly it should be placed between the two extremes will be determined by the extent to which its members need to collaborate. Collaboration is necessary if a level of dependency exists. The higher the level of dependency, the further the group should be placed to the right-hand end of the continuum. In my experience, most groups fall somewhere between the two extremes. Senior management groups will typically exist in the middle-ground of the continuum. Although they like to think of themselves as teams, they are in many cases groups of individuals who are most preoccupied with running their own departments. The extent of the collaboration required will depend on the specific scenario, but can sometimes be quite low. Senior managers usually need to operate effectively as a decision-making body, but this is not the same as having to operate as a team. You don't have to be a team to make good decisions.

EXERCISE 1.3

Spend a few minutes now reflecting on where you would place the group you lead on the group–team continuum, bearing in mind your responses to the previous two exercises.

The differences between groups and teams

So far, I have given two examples of mistaken identity. In both examples, my old consultancy company and Gavin's group in Case Study 1.1, a group was being mistaken for a team. In the first example, as a result of this misperception, an inappropriate intervention was made. It was not just that a team-building event in the Lakes was the wrong solution; the intervention was being made at the wrong level in the organization. The real cause of the problems was weak management and it was this that needed addressing. In the second example, Gavin's anxiety regarding his group's identity was generating unnecessary pressures and dissatisfactions for him and the team as a whole. The gap between image and reality was confusing to the extent that people didn't know what to expect of each other and were therefore unsure about how to behave towards each other. This was particularly true of Gavin, who was unclear about what people expected of him and confused in his own expectations of himself. Freed from the sense that he should be a team-leader, Gavin was free to perform more effectively the coordinating role that was actually required of him. **It is usually the case that whereas teams need leaders, groups need managers.**

I have mentioned the different requirements of group and team. These differences can be summarized under four headings: expectations, communications, process and intimacy. I will now explore each of these in turn.

Expectations

The team concept carries with it a number of expectations regarding the nature of the relationships among team members. These revolve, in particular, around aspects such as involvement, commitment, cooperation and support. A true team requires high levels of all these qualities from its members and it is legitimate for people to expect to give and receive these high levels. If someone doesn't receive what they feel to be sufficient, they can legitimately feel let down by the team. If they are perceived not to give sufficiently, it is legitimate for other members of the team to challenge them and demand that they change their attitude and behaviour for the good of the team.

As we move leftward down the group–team continuum, expectations around involvement, commitment, cooperation and support diminish. They are not required so intensely. If the group is simply a federation of individuals sharing the same workspace and doing similar tasks, the requirement can be simply to coexist comfortably with each other, with minimal levels of support and cooperation.

In the company I used to work for, the desire to define itself as a close-knit team shaped expectations in particular, dysfunctional ways. For example, when we weren't out working with clients, we were expected to come to the office in order to foster the team identity (one of the conditions of employment was that we lived within a forty-mile radius of the office). Consequently, when the organization expanded in the early 1990s, it moved to larger premises to accommodate its workforce. But because the reality was that we weren't a team, the benefits of consultants being in the office were minimal. The disadvantages were considerable – especially for the consultants, who spent large amounts of time away from home anyway. If the organization had shaped its expectations around an accurate placement on the group–team continuum, this would have affected its recruitment strategy, its accommodation strategy (and therefore its over-heads), the morale and the productivity of its consultants. It would have completely redefined the organization.

This example shows how the difference in expectations between groups and teams can have quite profound effects on an organization. In most cases, the effects won't be so widespread, as with Gavin's 'team', where wrong expectations generated a tension within the group and within Gavin. It was this tension, in fact, that became one of the barriers that stopped them communicating effectively.

Communications

Unless your group is at the extreme left of the group–team continuum, there will be a requirement to communicate with each other in order to ensure that you work effectively together. The difficulty usually is identifying what that requirement consists of: the level of formality, the forum, the frequency, the function, the parameters. Together, these make up the 'communication structure' of a group. Regardless of whether it is a team or not, each group has its own specific requirements and these need to be clearly defined if an appropriate structure is to be developed.

Many of the groups I work with complain initially that they don't communicate effectively, in the same way that they complain about not being as much of a team as they would like to be. These are loose terms, laden with many possible meanings. We have seen that it is necessary to ask first: 'Are you a team or are you a group?' as this will help to set appropriate expectations within the group. A similar question needs to be asked in response to complaints about poor communication. It is this: 'What do you actually need to communicate to each other?' I have sat in too many meetings in my life where it becomes apparent that this question has not been fully thought through. I imagine you could say the same.

Before I worked with Gavin's team, their communication structure was as follows: a weekly meeting first thing on a Monday morning and a monthly meeting to put together a monthly report of their activity. And it wasn't working. Because it was low priority for people, they didn't protect the time in their diaries and so often didn't turn up, including Gavin. They couldn't remember the last time that everybody had attended a Monday morning meeting. One reason why the group were not committed to the existing structure was that the meetings were too informal – and therefore seemed low priority. Also, people were unclear about the function of the two meetings, particularly the weekly one.

My initial work with Gavin's team was to help them to clarify what their requirement to communicate with each other was and develop a suitable communication structure for meeting that requirement – by 'suitable', I mean a structure that they were all committed to and which they were going to be able to carry out given the nature of their work. They defined a series of needs and then identified appropriate forums for meeting those needs. The Monday morning meeting stayed, now as a short, formal business meeting to communicate the week's work. Everybody had to attend it, including Gavin. In addition, there were quarterly development meetings which the group used to share experiences, to learn from each other and to discuss general issues regarding the work they did, after which they went out for a meal in order to spend time together socially. The writing of the monthly report didn't require a full group meeting; one person was charged with collecting and collating all the relevant information and people committed themselves to getting the relevant information to him in time.

This is an example of what I mean by a communication structure. Each group, wherever they are on the group–team continuum, will need to identify the structure that works best for them. This may involve one-to-one and small group meetings as well as full group ones, inside or outside of work hours, off site or on site. Many groups develop their communication structure instinctively – especially when the requirement is straightforward and access to each other is easy. When the requirement is more complex and people's availability is problematic, then the process of defining the requirement and identifying the structure is clearly more difficult. In my experience, many groups develop communication structures by default and assume that their structure is inevitable – regardless of the degree to which it is effective. Such assumptions need checking out and structures need to be constantly reviewed to take into account changes in the requirement.

EXERCISE 1.4

Spend a few minutes now reflecting on the communication structure of your group by answering the following questions:

- ☐ What are the communication requirements?
- ☐ What is the current communication structure?
- ☐ How was this established?
- ☐ Does the current structure meet the requirements?
- ☐ How satisfied do you think people are with the current structure?
- ☐ Are there ways in which it could be improved?

In general, teams need more sophisticated communication structures than groups, because the need for exchanging information, group decision-making, developing openness and building relationships is usually higher. In either case, the driving principle should be to keep the structure as lean as possible so that it takes up as little time as possible.

Process

Another reason why teams require more sophisticated communication structures is that they usually need to focus more on their *process*: the ways in which they work together and manage their relationships. Although this will be an issue for all groups, it is a key issue for teams – one that is integral to their success. I will be exploring the issue of group process in detail in Part 2 of this book.

Because of the greater dependency, teams need people to work well together. And because working well together is difficult to achieve for most of us, the process by which this is achieved needs careful attention. It is sometimes the case that a team works well together naturally (although I am instantly mistrustful if any team tells me that this is the case!). More often, teams have to work hard at it: consciously reflecting on and deciding how they want to work together to ensure that they collaborate effectively. And if they don't pay enough attention to their process, it is likely that serious problems will arise that will interfere with their effectiveness as a working unit. The greater dependency on each other generates both a need for the process to work well and also great frustration if it doesn't.

Groups, because they are less dependent on each other, are less dependent on their process. They will work better if they manage it well, but the management requirement is less and it is less likely to lead to crisis if they don't.

Intimacy

One of the reasons why I want to distinguish whether a group I am working with is a genuine team or not is because the distinction helps me to decide the appropriate level of intimacy that I should be trying to generate. By intimacy, I am referring to how well people need to get to know each other and therefore how open they need to be with each other. If I am working with genuine teams, I will design events that generate a high level of contact between the members which enables them to understand more about their colleagues and to disclose more about themselves – particularly in terms of their preferences regarding their sense of purpose, their sources of motivation and their feelings of accomplishment. We will look at each of these factors in more detail in Chapter 4.

Because this level of intimacy involves disclosure, it involves risk and therefore I will only try to generate it if I feel it is necessary for the team's effectiveness. For most working groups it won't be – the level of intimacy required is relatively low. In such cases, people need to understand each other's preferences: their style of working and interacting. But they do not generally need to go beyond this. Their work doesn't depend on it.

The greater the level of intimacy, the greater the potential volatility within the team. This is one of the factors that makes teams such exciting places to work. As a result of the heightened level of openness and disclosure, as well as being more dependent on each other, team-members are more vulnerable to each other. There is the potential for the abuse of intimacy – especially when the team is under pressure or when things start to go wrong. People can misuse the information thay have gained about each other in hurtful and destructive ways. And there is the possibility that teams can generate too much intimacy, so that the closeness between some or all of the members interferes with their ability to evaluate objectively and ultimately to work effectively together.

The level of intimacy between group members should be dictated by the degree and nature of their interdependency. It should, as much as possible, be directly relevant to the nature of the group's identity and activity. I am thinking here of team-building events I have had described to me where the level of intimacy generated had been to a large extent an end in itself. This can be exciting and produce a group 'high' which can be dangerously self-deluding. In most cases, when the high has worn off, the intimacy generated is seen to be transient and even misdirected. This is because it has not been driven by the requirement of the group but by the preferences of the trainer – for whom the generation of intimacy can be a very satisfying outcome. One of the attachments of the 'team myth' is that openness is unequivocally good. This has become dogma. I have come to realize that it is more useful to regard openness as a strategy, and to handle it with care.

Summary

In this chapter, I have explored the distinction between group and team and provided two measures for locating your group on the 'group–team continuum': the level of dependency and the level of commonality. I have stressed the importance of being clear about the extent to which your group needs to operate as a team, and the dangers of misapplying the team myth. Teamwork is hard work, requiring a high degree of awareness, commitment, skill and time. It is best to make sure that teamwork is required before committing any of these valuable resources.

I have also indicated the key differentials between groups and teams and in so doing have briefly introduced the four concepts that underpin effective teamwork: expectations, communications, process and intimacy. These are themes which will be returned to continually in this book, especially the concept of process. In the next chapter, we are going to look at the composition of groups in terms of three factors: resources, roles and responsibilities.

ACTIVITY 1.1

Before moving on, spend a few minutes reflecting on Chapter 1. Remember the thoughts, insights or ideas that have occurred to you about you or your group as you have read this chapter. Note down in the space below (or on a separate sheet of paper if you prefer) any of these that you feel it would be useful to record so that you can refer back to them in the future. Some may have helped you to identify things you could do to manage your group more effectively and a space has been provided to record these separately.

Thoughts and insights   **Actions arising**

2

Resources, roles and responsibilities

Resources

There are several tools that exist which help to define the qualities that people have and how this affects the roles they play in teams. I am thinking in particular of the different types of psychometric testing that I have come across, and also of Belbin's work on team roles. These tools are usually based on information collected through questionnaires; the way people answer the questions indicates the type of person they are, their preferences, their ways of working. I am often asked to use these tools by clients who want me to run team-building events and I have always said no, for the simple reason that I have never been trained to use them. And for the same reason, I won't be talking about them here. Instead, I will be describing my own approach to assessing the resources within a team and the impact this has on the roles people play.

In truth, I have shied away from mechanical, questionnaire-based tools. This is not because I think there is anything wrong with them. I am sure that they can produce interesting data and a framework or language for discussing issues in teams. The problem is one of style. I like to work subjectively and intuitively. I prefer to watch a group in action and see what is happening with my own eyes and to work with the group based on my empirical observations. All I need to know is presented for me by the group in action.

In this book, I am going to describe several ways in which I look at groups in action, what I look for and the interpretations I make based on what I see. These structures for observation relate to different aspects of a group's life. In this chapter, I am going to describe how I gather information which is fundamental to decisions I make about how to work with a group. It

21

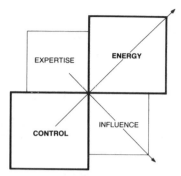

Figure 2.1 The Key Resources.

is concerned with the group's **resources**: their abundance and their availability.

I look for four resources which I believe a group or team needs if it is going to operate effectively. These are: energy, control, expertise and influence. Figure 2.1 illustrates their relationship to each other. I will talk about each in turn and then use a case study to illustrate how they operate and how I use them.

Energy

The resource that I am most interested in and look for most keenly when I work with groups is **energy**. I want to know how much energy the group has at its disposal, what kind of energy it is, where it is coming from, how it is being channelled, what is blocking it and what is required to release it and channel it more effectively, for the good of the group. For me, energy is a group or team's key resource, for it is the driver which generates momentum and achievement.

Energy has many forms, and is represented in many different ways. Some of these are clearly visible, others less so. Generally you can sense the level of energy in a group of people soon after you come into contact with them, but it can be difficult to articulate clearly what formed the basis of your intuitive assessment. The signs I tend to look for are:

□ **Initiative:** Does the group generate ideas, is it creative, does it think positively, does it look for solutions, does it recognize opportunities and take risks?

□ **Enthusiasm:** Does the group enjoy working together, is it excited by the work it is doing, does it want to achieve results, is it motivated by success?

□ **Contact:** Do members of the group respond well to each other, encourage and support each other, have fun together, challenge each other, take risks with each other?

When these qualities are in abundance, the group hums with energy, you can almost reach out and touch it. It may or may not be being put to good use, but the high level of energy is a wonderful resource which makes all kinds of things possible. If the energy is being channelled well, the group will be an attractive one – literally – I will feel that I want to be a part of the group myself, included in the excitement and pleasure of co-working. If the energy is not being well channelled, then the group can be potentially dangerous, hurtful to its own members or to those who come into contact with it. The energy is expressed as a tension which generates anxiety and this anxiety feeds the energy of the group, making it harder to channel. But the fact that there is energy there is encouraging. I would rather have negative energy than no energy – for it is easier to channel energy and redirect it positively than to generate it from scratch.

If the qualities of initiative, enthusiasm and contact are scarce, then the group sags, limp and weary, dissatisfied and confused. Their work and their relationships tend to be perfunctory. They tend to repel rather than attract: I am reluctant to get involved, I don't want to be sucked into their apathy or dissatisfaction, I feel that what energy I have will be swallowed up. I will need to find out the causes of this lack of energy, and in particular to establish whether the causes are internal – to do with the personalities and relationships within the group – or external – to do with the nature of their activity or their relationship to the wider organization.

EXERCISE 2.1

Spend a few minutes now reflecting on the level of energy in your group or team by answering the following questions:

□ Are you satisfied with the level of energy in the group?
□ How would you describe that energy in terms of initiative, enthusiasm and contact?
□ Do you feel that the energy of the group is being well channelled?

Control

The necessary corollary to energy is control. This is the second resource I look for when I am observing groups, for I want to know the extent to which the group is able to control and channel the energy at its disposal. I want to know what forms this control takes, who is exercising it, how effectively they are exercising it and the ways in which the group responds to it. Control can be harder to identify than energy, for it often involves quieter and more discreet behaviour. I look for three indicators. They are:

- □ **Self-control:** The extent to which people control their own energy and emotions so that they retain awareness of the needs of the group and its other members (as opposed to letting themselves get out of control – see the section in Chapter 7, Managing the pendulum).

- □ **Process control:** The extent to which the group is able to manage its own process – its way of working together – so that it can achieve its tasks and objectives effectively and efficiently. Part 2 focuses on process in detail.

- □ **Evaluation:** The extent to which the group evaluates before identifying solutions and making decisions – analyzing the issues and exploring options before reaching conclusions.

Energy and control exist in relation to each other and groups work well when the balance between the two is appropriate. The greater the energy in the group, the greater the need for control to channel the energy. High energy without sufficient control will lead to high momentum and low achievement. If there is a low level of energy in the group, the need for control will also be lower. Many of the groups I observe these days have more energy than control, and they suffer from this imbalance. Some groups, and I have worked in one, had more control than there was energy and this is a deadly combination: control should never have the upper hand because it will turn energy sour and erode goodwill. Control must work in harmony with the energy that is available. **One of the essences of effective teamwork and team leadership is to achieve this harmony.**

EXERCISE 2.2

Spend a few minutes now reflecting on the level of control in your group or team by answering the following questions:

- □ Are you satisfied with the level of control in the group?
- □ How would you describe that control in terms of self-control, process control and evaluation?
- □ Do you feel that the level of control is in proportion to the level of energy?

Expertise

The resources of expertise and influence are less significant to me as a facilitator because in most cases I can have less impact on them than I can have on energy and control. This is especially true of expertise, which is down to the composition of the team, something I rarely have any influence over. Nevertheless it is clearly a crucial resource for the team. In general, there are three kinds of expertise that a group or team will need if it is to be successful. These are:

☐ **Technical:** The expertise necessary to perform the group's core activities. These may be literally technical, such as engineering, but could also be expertise in marketing, personnel, business strategy, etc. This is the baseline expertise required.

☐ **Process:** The expertise required to manage group process effectively. This underpins the control resource, in that it enables the group to maximize its technical expertise by sharing it and using it effectively.

☐ **Political:** The expertise required to identify the context for the team's work and incorporate the demands of this context into the team's output. This partly underpins the influence resource, in that it enables the group to produce work which will be acceptable to the wider organization and therefore more likely to be implemented effectively.

Most groups and teams have high levels of technical expertise. Their shortfall is more likely to occur with the other kinds of expertise. Their ability to manage process and therefore provide the level of control necessary to interact with their level of energy might be low. And their political awareness, their ability to understand and manipulate the change processes within their organization, might be low (understandably so, as change management requires a level of sophisticated political expertise that eludes most of us!).

Expertise can be developed if the group has the potential to learn and there is time for them to do so. But in general, the level of expertise is determined by the composition of the group and so it is vital, when deciding the composition, to cater for all three kinds of expertise if at all possible (often technical expertise is the only criterion used). The other three resources also need to be considered, but because expertise underpins much of control and influence, and because it is so difficult to address once the team is in place, it is the key resource for deciding the composition of groups and teams.

EXERCISE 2.3

Spend a few minutes now reflecting on the level of expertise in your group or team by answering the following questions:

☐ Are you satisfied with the level of expertise in the group?

☐ How would you describe that resource in terms of technical, process and political expertise?

☐ Do you feel that the expertise of the group is being well utilized?

Influence

Although, like expertise, influence is not a primary resource for me, as a facilitator, it is a crucial resource for the team itself. It is secondary to me, because, like expertise, it is harder for me to have any impact on, but it is a key factor in the team's ability to make decisions and to have those decisions implemented. There are two aspects to influence which I look for when I am observing groups. These are:

☐ **Internal influence:** Who are the influential members of the group? Does their expertise match their influence? How is their influence exercised? How is it received? Are there people who should be more influential? Why aren't they? Could they be?

☐ **External influence:** Who does the group need to be influencing in the wider organization? Does the group know this? Does it have strategies for influencing them? Does it take the needs/attitudes of the wider organization into account in its work? If not, why not? Are there people in the group who have the potential to do this?

There is some overlap between internal influence and control, and if there are issues with internal influence, I will often address them indirectly through work on control. But influence is one of the ways in which we exercise power, and there are times when the distribution of power within the group needs to be addressed directly. Because this tends to be difficult and potentially explosive, I will usually explore the control option first, to see if there are ways in which influence can be moderated through stronger control of the group's energy and processes (see the section on power, control and domination in Chapter 3).

There is some overlap too between external influence and political expertise. The most common cause of low external influence is low political expertise and the solution in such cases is development, through training usually, to increase the level of expertise in skills such as networking and persuasion. But there are times when the low external influence is caused by inappropriate internal influence: when, for example, the key influencers within the group want to challenge the wider organization in ways that are unlikely to succeed and are overriding the people with political expertise within the group. In such cases, it is necessary to work on the internal influence issues in the ways described above.

EXERCISE 2.4

Spend a few minutes now reflecting on the level of influence in your group or team by answering the following questions:

☐ Who are the most powerful internal influencers in the group and are they who you want them to be?
☐ Do they influence the group appropriately?
☐ Does the group have as much external influence within the wider organization as you would like?

I have briefly introduced the four key resources that I look for and work on with the group and teams that I facilitate. I hope that they have given you a framework to start reflecting on the groups you are involved with. These four resources are the fundamental building-blocks for much of this book and I will be returning to them constantly. By so doing, I will be expanding on the introduction I have given here through the different practical ways in which I apply the key resources in my work.

ACTIVITY 2.1

Spend a few minutes now thinking about the resources that exist in the group that you manage. Use the matrix in Figure 2.2 to assess each member of the group against the four resources discussed above. Give them a rating from 1 to 5: for example, if you think they bring a lot of energy to the group, put a 5 in the appropriate box; if you think they don't exert any influence, put a 1 in the appropriate box.

Energy						
Control						
Expertise						
Influence						

Figure 2.2

The available resource

The resources available to any group will depend on the people who belong to it. They each bring with them their individual mix of energy, control, expertise and influence. When I am assessing the group's resources, I am looking at its members to see which of them have expertise, which bring energy, which provide control, which exert influence. I look for signs that will show me the kind of resources individuals are capable of and want to bring to the group. Here are some examples:

☐ **Energy:** Physical activity; high contribution in meetings; humour; optimism; desire for solutions; desire for achievement; creativity; encouraging of others; preparedness to take risks. And also impatience; lack of awareness of others; interrupting others; impulsiveness; recklessness.

☐ **Control:** Listening to and watching others carefully; aware of own and others' behaviour; asking questions; evaluating; aware of and intervening in the group process; patience; ability to keep perspective; thoroughness. And also cautious and risk-averse, over-clarifying; slowing things down, pedantic, repetitive.

☐ **Expertise:** Expressing opinions and providing information; wanting to get things right; analytical; prepared to challenge and disagree. And also opinionated; argumentative; abstract; non-pragmatic; more interested in own ideas than other people's; doesn't ask questions or listen well; tends to think they are always right.

☐ **Influence:** Assertive; persuasive; decisive; solution-centred. Possibly watchful, subtle, strategic, questioning; possibly forceful, direct; single-minded. And also possibly dominating; insensitive; uninterested in the views of others; wilful; petulant.

This is not an exhaustive list, nor is it always an accurate one. I make mistakes: I make an assessment of somebody based on their behaviour in a particular meeting and later find that the assessment is wrong, or that I have misunderstood their behaviour. I am not preoccupied with objective accuracy, which is one of the reasons why I don't use psychometric testing. I want to generate hypotheses that I can experiment with, and the indicators above are what I use to generate these hypotheses.

If a group is made up of people who all have high energy then it is likely that the group will have high energy. But this won't always be the case: it depends on the extent to which people make their natural resources available to the group. They may be generous with their energy, for example, or they may withhold it. Their decision will be influenced by five factors:

☐ **Relationships:** The nature of the relationships that form between people in the group will affect the extent to which individuals are prepared to make their resources available. The relationships alone can encourage or discourage people's generosity.

☐ **Activity:** The nature of the activity that the group is engaged in will have a significant impact on the extent to which individuals are prepared to make their resources available. If the activity meets people's needs (for stimulation, for example) then it will encourage generosity, if it doesn't then it can encourage the reverse.

☐ **Environment:** The nature of the environment that the group is working in will also have a significant impact. The environment, physical or cultural, can present frustrations which inhibit generosity and distort the effective channelling of energy.

☐ **Achievement:** The extent to which the group achieves its goals successfully, and to which it feels it is able to do this, will have a significant impact on resource availability. Lack of meaningful achievement generates self-doubt which saps energy. Without energy, there is no momentum for the other resources to be usefully applied.

☐ **Recognition:** The extent to which individuals and the group as a whole receive the recognition they need for their efforts and achievements is a key factor in keeping the resources within the group available. Lack of meaningful recognition demotivates and leads people to withhold their resource. We will look at recognition in more detail in Chapters 4 and 7.

EXERCISE 2.5

Spend a few minutes now reflecting on the extent to which these five factors – relationships, activity, environment, achievement and recognition – affect the availability of resources within your group.

The resource requirement

The five factors that determine the availability of resource also shape the nature of the resource required of the group. The mix of relationships, the nature of the activity and the environment, the potential for significant achievement, the availability of meaningful recognition are pressures which make particular demands of a group and determine the balance of its internal resources. For example:

☐ A group full of experts, each with a strong belief in the value of his/her own expertise, is likely to produce a requirement for control.

☐ A highly political organizational culture will require the group to have and use a high level of influence if it is to be effective.

☐ A lack of recognition may require high levels of energy if momentum is to be sustained (those of you in the voluntary sector will know exactly what I am talking about).

Groups and teams need to understand their available resource, their strengths with regard to energy, control, expertise and influence. They also need to understand the resource requirement that is determined by relationships, activity, environment, achievement and recognition. This may not be the requirement they would like – in my experience it rarely is. In the consultancy organization I used to work for, the level of political expertise and influence required of me was far higher than I wanted it to be – this was one of the reasons why I left and why I now work freelance. It was a requirement that absorbed too much of my energy and became one that I was no longer prepared to meet.

Groups need to acknowledge the constraints within which they operate and explore the ways in which they can mobilize their resources to meet the requirement. This is a simple description of a complex and difficult process. It is one, however, that is at the heart of effective teamwork. The quality of the available resources is important. But it is no guarantee of success.

EXERCISE 2.6

Spend a few minutes now reflecting on the resource requirement that your group faces by answering the following questions:

☐ What requirement is generated by the five factors – relationships, activity, environment, achievement and recognition – i.e. what demands does it make of the group in terms of energy, control, expertise and influence?

☐ To what extent do the group's resources match these requirements, i.e. does the group have the level of energy required to carry out the activity effectively?

Roles

The matching of the available resource to the resource requirement is the process that a group goes through in order to allocate roles to its members. In other words, a person's role within the group is determined partly by the resources they bring, and partly by the adjustment they make in order to align their personal resources to the needs of the group in terms of both internal balance and external requirement.

When I started working for my previous company, for example, there were initially two of us in my 'team'. I had just joined the company. I was full of energy and enthusiasm, bounding around like Tigger, wanting to do well, wanting to be liked, optimistic, creative, excited. My boss had been there a long time and had far less energy but he did bring the other resources in abundance: expertise, control and influence. We were an ideal combination: he shared his expertise with me and I shared my energy with him. We dovetailed perfectly – it was a very satisfying and rewarding relationship for both of us.

As my expertise grew, the pattern of resources within the 'group' changed. I naturally exerted more influence as I became more knowledgeable and experienced and my boss was happy to share that influence with me, whilst still retaining and providing a high level of control. This too worked well. I was happy for him to provide the control as this gave me the security to learn, take risks, be creative – and bound around like Tigger. He was happy for me to be more influential because he came to recognize and value the expertise that I brought with me from my previous work and experience.

The team grew: over time we recruited three more people. My boss started to move out of the group to become involved in other aspects of the organization, increasingly leaving the leadership of the team in my hands. My role changed: now I was having to provide more of the control, as well as having to adjust to the presence of others and to the resources that they brought. Now I was the one with the expertise and the influence, and I still had a high level of energy and commitment for the work. In fact, I was so resource-full that I don't doubt that I was overpowering – disabling some of the people who joined the team. One of them complained to me that she felt deskilled. I see now what she meant: I wasn't giving her the room to bring her resources into the group – I was taking up all the available space myself.

I use this example to illustrate how we can use the four key resources to define our own – and other people's – roles within groups and teams. When I am assessing a group's resource, I am also identifying the roles people play. I look for the energizers, the controllers, the experts and the influencers. These are crude role descriptions, and there are many other, more sophisticated ways of characterizing group roles. But these four descriptors are enough for me. They help me to understand how the available resources are distributed among the group members, and the extent to which people are satisfied with this distribution. If there are several influencers, for example, it is likely that some of them will be dissatisfied with the amount of influence they are able to exert; if there are several controllers, there is likely to be competition over control of the group; and so on.

EXERCISE 2.7

Spend a few minutes now reflecting on the roles people play in your group or team in terms of energizers, controllers, experts and influencers. If you did Activity 2.1, the matrix you filled in will help with this exercise. Does the distribution of resources meet the needs of the group? How satisfied do you think people are with the roles they have taken on?

Our role within a group or team is defined partly by our own resources and partly by the resource preferences of other members. There is often a tension between these two defining factors and it is this tension that makes teams so difficult, demanding, challenging and potentially rewarding to be part of – for the resolution of the tension and the successful distribution of roles is an immensely satisfying experience – one of the ways that we transcend self and subsume it within a greater whole. To achieve this, we need to be aware enough to understand the role make-up of our groups and teams and flexible enough to adjust in order to accommodate the resource preferences of others.

Responsibilities

The distribution of resources within a group determines the members' roles and these roles provide the group with a structure that helps to shape the contributions and behaviour of its members. This structure often bears no relation to the formal roles, or responsibilities, that people have. The team-leader, for example, may not be an influencer; the chairperson may not be a controller. These formal responsibilities also provide the group with a structure that helps shape the contributions and behaviour of its members. Whereas the formal responsibilities provide the *official* structure of the group, the roles provide the *unofficial* structure. The relationship between these two structures is crucial to the effectiveness of the group.

With some teams, the official and the unofficial structure are the same: the team leader is the most influential member of the team, for example; the person in charge of resources is the person who naturally provides control. Such teams are likely to function effectively. The problems occur when there is a mismatch: when the official structure is not supported by the unofficial structure. This creates a tension in the team that can be destabilizing, causing divided loyalties, destructive competition, even open conflict.

In the last year I worked with two groups who were experiencing problems caused by mismatches between official and unofficial structures. In both cases, the problem centred on the official team-leader/senior manager. Neither person was a natural leader: one, Gavin from the earlier case study, could not provide the energy and internal influence that his team needed; the other had such a high control resource that he used it to subvert the group as a way of dealing with two team-members, either of whom would have made a better team-leader than himself. In these cases, people's natural roles became distorted by the pressure of the official structure – or rather, by the group's adherence to the official structure.

EXERCISE 2.8

Spend a few minutes now reflecting on the match between the official and unofficial structures in your group. Is there an official structure, with clearly defined positions for key people? If so, how does this compare with the unofficial structure, in terms of the distribution of key resources?

Balancing roles and resources

In the early stages of a group or team's life (sometimes called the 'forming' stage) its members are engaged in the process of balancing resources and allocating roles in order to learn how to work together and to develop effective working practices. This process is often unconscious, going on under the surface as people find out about each other and adjust their behaviour to fit into the emerging group norm. There are two resolutions that, in my opinion, need to be made. These are:

□ Resolving role clashes.
□ Resolving structural differences.

Neither is easy to achieve and, once achieved, both need constant attention and review. We will look briefly at each of them in turn here. We will look at them in more detail in Part 2 when we look at managing process.

Resolving role clashes

It is possible to hand-pick teams in order to bring together the right mix of personalities and resources, thus ensuring that the well-endowed team produces high performance. But in my experience, the opportunities to do this are rare, either because there are other, more powerful, criteria which decide team selection, or because the people needed to provide the ideal mix are not all available. And even if it can be done, there is always the likelihood that the dream team on paper does not perform to expectations – for the very reason that it is hard to anticipate the ways in which different personalities will respond to each other in a group setting. The dynamics set in motion by bringing a group of people into close proximity tends to trigger underlying responses which can reveal aspects of someone's personality that you will never have imagined existed.

It is also almost always the case that a successful and effective team tends to have a good balance of the four key resources, distributed appropriately among its membership: there will be the people who bring energy and others who provide control; there will be a good spread of expertise of all three kinds (technical, process and political); and the right people will be most influential within and without the team. This happy allocation of roles allows people freedom to contribute according to their strengths and ensures that they get the recognition they need for the contribution they have made (see Chapter 4).

But this happy allocation rarely occurs at the beginning of the forming stage. Usually it marks the end of a period of negotiation and adjustment. For what do we do if the resources with which our personality is well endowed are the ones that other members of the group also bring in abundance? If, for example, our dominant resource is our energy, and this is also the dominant resource of the other members of the group, then there are choices to be made: Do we hold onto our preferred role and throw our energy into the ring with the rest of them? Or do we look for another role, perhaps seeing the need for control in this high-energy group and tapping our control resource to take on the role of process manager? Again, it depends. First, in this instance, it depends on whether we have a control resource to tap; second, it depends on whether the rest of the group allow us to adopt such a role; and most importantly, it depends whether we have the maturity to recognize the problem and exercise our options. It can take great strength of character to resist competition over roles and to adapt for the benefit of the group. I didn't have this maturity in my first leadership role. I'm not too sure that I would have it now if the opportunity came round again.

Sometimes the adjustments happen organically as people decide whether to compete with each other over roles or not. We can often recognize that we have met our match, that this person has more energy than us or is likely to win in a battle over influence or control; we bow to someone's superior expertise, relinquish control, stop straining to be the most energetic, enthusiastic, committed, funny, creative. We look for other ways in which we can contribute, sometimes happily playing second fiddle, sometimes drawing on other resources, depending on the space that is available and on the needs of the group.

These organic resolutions may not be perfect, may not completely resolve the tensions, but they provide a sufficiently stable base for the team to operate effectively. They may calm the turbulence of the dynamics, but often the potential for disruption in the future remains, usually brought to the surface when external changes affect the team's life, or external pressures put people under stress and they revert to their natural preferences, forgetting temporarily the unwritten agreements that have been made.

Sometimes there has to be more overt negotiation, even conflict, before the clashes and competition can be resolved. When people are equal in strength of resource and are not prepared to give way – they both want to be the key influencer, the one with most expertise, the energizer, the controller – then the competition for these places is sustained. I might see two people chairing the same meeting, vying for the control position. I might hear two or more people engaging in fruitless and arcane debate as each tries to demonstrate the superiority of their expertise, or in unnecessary and increasingly irrational argument as two influencers slug it out, each trying to get his/her own way. Competition of this kind clearly has a negative impact on the performance of the group, interfering with its ability to manage process, evaluate rationally and make quality decisions. In such cases, when people are not prepared to adjust, then the clashes have to be brought into the open, identified clearly for what they are, and the whole team needs to be involved in a process of mediation in which the needs of the team are placed above the needs of the individuals. Adjustments have to be negotiated until some agreement can be reached which allows the group to move forward and work together with some degree of effectiveness.

In many cases, this open mediation does not occur and the group continues unhappily, operating as best it can under the constraints it is placing upon itself. It won't happen unless people within the team recognize the need and are influential and energetic enough to bring the issues to the surface. The problem is that people with high energy and influence resources are often the protagonists in role clashes and also often have a low awareness of the impact of their own behaviour. And even when the issues are brought to the surface, it can be difficult for a group to manage their resolution on its own, and usually someone with a skilled control resource is required. If such a person doesn't exist within the group, it will have to look for help from outside, from, for example, a facilitator such as myself.

EXERCISE 2.9

Spend a few minutes now reflecting on the extent to which your group has acknowledged and resolved personality differences that exist between its members. If there have been differences which have been resolved, how did this resolution come about? Did people adjust instinctively? Who made the adjustments? How happy do you think they are with the adjustments they have made?

Resolving structural differences

Structural differences often involve the issue of leadership, usually because the leader is appointed from without rather than elected by the team itself. Problems arise when there are people in the team who have the resources to be a better team-leader than the official holder of the position. This difference between official and unofficial structures can wreak havoc, especially if the official leader is weak, and the unofficial leader is ambitious. The conflict between the two can make life miserable for the rest of the team.

We will look at leadership in the next chapter and this will provide some possible solutions to such difficulties, but it generally takes a mature person to allow their officially defined responsibility within the team to be moderated by the unofficial structure, and to accept the prospect that the team will be more effective if people are free to perform roles rather than responsibilities. For, in most cases, the unofficial structure that emerges organically within teams as people adopt roles is more powerful and more effective than the official structure that is designed and imposed from without.

Groups and teams often allocate responsibilities as a way of sorting out their roles, thus generating an official structure from within. If the two are compatible this can be an excellent way of creating space and definition for people to make the most effective and rewarding contributions. I have seen groups appoint someone with high control resource to manage their meetings for example, even though she wasn't the official team-leader. But sometimes this strategy is a way of avoiding issues – of focusing on responsibilities instead of roles because the role clashes are too difficult or threatening – and in such cases, the structures are unlikely to be compatible, and can even exacerbate the tensions that already exist. Structural changes often only serve to relocate the problem.

For example, I once facilitated a project team in which one member was a representative from their main supplier, i.e. an employee of a different organization from the rest of the team. In order to involve and empower this outsider, the team-leader asked him to chair all the team meetings, one of which I came along to observe. The man was clearly uncomfortable in this position, mainly because he was a hopeless chairperson, which he readily admitted. The team-leader had acted intelligently in terms of the official structure: by giving the outsider clear responsibility he had also freed himself to be an influencer without being a controller as well (a dominating combination as we will see in the next chapter). But he had ignored the issue of role and how this is shaped by the resources we bring to the group: the supplier's representative was high in expertise – not in control. When I pointed this out, the whole team sighed with relief. The team-leader resumed control of the meetings which were far more effective as a result. Another solution would have to be found to resolve the issue of the domination of the leader and ensure the involvement of the client as part of the team.

This example indicates that one of the keys to resolving structural differences is to be clear about the distinction between roles (the unofficial structure determined by the distribution of resources) and responsibilities (the official structure determined by the organization). It is necessary first to understand the resources that exist within the team and to recognize the way that the team has organized itself in managing the allocation of these resources and thus the definition of roles. When this is clear, the roles can be compared to the responsibilities as defined by the official structure in order to see the level of compatibility. If the two structures are incompatible, then, as before, there is the need for open – and often very difficult – negotiation to try to resolve the differences. As before, if the team doesn't have the resources to manage such negotiations themselves, it is best to bring in someone from outside to facilitate the process.

Summary

In this chapter, I have described how I assess the resourcefulness of groups and teams and their effectiveness at managing their resources so that people are given appropriate roles and responsibilities. There are four key resources that I look for:

☐ Energy.
☐ Control.
☐ Expertise.
☐ Influence.

The group's resourcefulness is made up of the individual contributions of its members. They bring their natural resources, but have to adjust on joining the group to accommodate the resources and preferences of others. Through this process of adjustment, people adopt roles within the group. I look out for the energizers, the controllers, the experts and the influencers. I want to know whether people are happy with their roles and whether they are contributing effectively.

There are several points of tension that will frustrate people in groups.

One of these is the relationship between the roles that emerge within the group – its unofficial structure – and the responsibilities that people have – the group's official structure.

The work for all groups and teams is to mobilize and release their resources effectively. This requires groups to be aware of their resources, roles and responsibilities and to manage any tensions that emerge so that they don't become blocks, preventing the free flow of resources towards the achievement of the team's goals. This is a grand way of describing what teams are doing all the time, but often not consciously or effectively.

ACTIVITY 2.2

Before moving on, spend a few minutes reflecting on Chapter 2. Remember the thoughts, insights or ideas that have occurred to you about you or your group as you have read this chapter. Note down in the space below (or on a separate sheet of paper if you prefer) any of these that you feel it would be useful to record so that you can refer back to them in the future. Some may have helped you to identify things you could do to manage your group more effectively and a space has been provided to record these separately.

Thoughts and insights   **Actions arising**

3

Leadership

In looking at roles in the previous chapter, the issue of leadership has, unsurprisingly, cropped up a number of times. Leadership is one of the key considerations with groups and teams and an issue that has occupied the whole content of books much larger than this one. What I want to do in this chapter is to look at some of the choices that leaders have to make and some of the options that are available to them. I will be looking at three aspects of this mega-topic. They are:

- □ Defining the responsibility.
- □ Selecting strategies.
- □ Selecting styles.

Defining the responsibility

I use the four key resources to help me identify the roles that people prefer and that teams require. I also use them as a way of reflecting on leadership, both in terms of how the team-leader is choosing to operate and what a team needs from its leader. This has helped me to identify two broad strategies that a manager has to choose between, which I now refer to as leadership models. I call the first of these the **vanguard model** and the second the **deficit model**. Each describes one way of defining the responsibilities of the leader in relation to the team.

The vanguard model

The vanguard model is what I regard as the traditional leadership model, in which the leader leads from the front, inspiring their team to follow them. The leader will focus on their own resource preferences. They do this regardless of the resources available in the rest of the team. They focus on their own strengths, hoping to instil through example similar qualities in the team-members.

Looking back, I was a vanguard leader. I saw myself as a pioneer, forging a new way forward, having to hack ruthlessly through the jungle of old customs and practices of the organization. I expected my fellow team-members to follow me, fight alongside me, have my energy, share my vision, work to my standards. And I became frustrated and disappointed if they didn't. I felt isolated. I tended to blame them for not following me, rather than exploring the choices I was making and the expectations that they placed on others.

I'm not saying that I was a self-obsessed and uncaring leader. Well, self-obsessed maybe, but I was also caring of the other people, supportive of them, investing time and effort in their development. I got a lot of satisfaction out of this aspect of leadership. But I had another drive, at least as big, which was to influence the organization, to change what I saw as outmoded and limited ways of working, and it was this vision that shaped my key choice about my leadership role, and made me a vanguard leader.

Nor am I saying that the vanguard model is wrong. Vanguard leaders can be very effective, both in terms of achieving objectives and generating a good team identity and morale and establishing positive and caring relationships with individual team-members. But there are circumstances when the vanguard model will not be appropriate or effective. In these cases, the leader alienates their team, not providing them with the kind of leadership they need, causing frustration and disaffection or competition and conflict. I am working with a manager at the moment, for example, whose control resource is so high that he can't let go, interfering, intervening, overcontrolling, to an extent where people have become resentful, mistrustful and rebellious.

The deficit model

The deficit model is what I regard as the modernist leadership option, in which the leader leads from behind, assessing the resources available within the team and defining the contribution required from the leader according to the areas of weakness – plugging the gaps. If a team lacks energy, the leader provides the energy. If the team lacks control, the leader provides the control and so on.

If, for example, the team is packed with energy resource and the leader too has high energy, they can first see that the team won't necessarily require their energy, and second that that amount of energy will need to be channelled and controlled. They recognize that their most useful contribution is likely to be to provide that control, even if this goes against their natural role preferences. The deficit model leader curbs their personal needs for the benefit of the team. Not only does this ensure that the required control is there, it also frees the other team-members to contribute from their strengths, creating more space and less competition on the energy front.

Sometimes the team's deficit is their leader's preference (e.g. they are low on control and the leader is a high controller). This is a happy combination and one that should work well. In such cases, it can be hard to tell the difference between the two models, so let me emphasize what the essence of this difference is. Whereas the vanguard leader seeks to *inspire*, the deficit leader seeks to *maximize* the resources at their disposal, giving people the space to operate from their strengths and the support to use those strengths effectively. If they are flexible, they are able to adapt their contribution according to the resources of the different teams they lead, providing high energy for one, for example, and high control for another. **Where the vanguard leader is preoccupied with what he or she needs from their team, the deficit leader is preoccupied with what the team needs from its leader.**

EXERCISE 3.1

Spend a few minutes now reflecting on your own leadership style. Do you feel you tend towards the vanguard model or the deficit model? How appropriate is this choice given the group you manage?

The deficit model will not always be appropriate, but in my experience, it is increasingly becoming the required option, as the role of the manager and the team-leader changes along with the major organizational changes of the past ten to twenty years. Increasingly, team-leaders are being appointed because of their leadership qualities and skills rather than their expertise. They are often leading teams who have more technical expertise than they do, and this creates a momentum towards deficit leadership – if you are sitting back to assess the expertise available to you, you are in a position to assess the other resources at the same time and therefore to identify the weaknesses that need to be compensated for. The emphasis is shifting from managing tasks and activities to managing people and processes, and this shift is also generating a momentum towards deficit leadership – an awareness of the strengths and weaknesses of people and the way they work together as the basis for a strategy of development and facilitation – i.e. maximizing the resources.

But although there is a trend towards deficit leadership, this does not mean that it is always the right option. Shifts in ethos should never override flexibility: the ability to evaluate and select the appropriate option according to circumstances. I have worked with teams over the past year who are crying out for a vanguard leader, just as I have worked with some who are struggling because their leader has not recognized the need to choose the deficit model. I will briefly discuss the main criteria that affect which model is appropriate and then use a couple of case studies to illustrate them.

Conditions of use

There are three criteria which need to be taken into consideration when deciding which model of leadership is appropriate. These are:

- ☐ **The available resource:** The deficit model is possible only if there is a substantial resource available to the leader. If the team is inexperienced, for example, so that there is little expertise, control, or influence, it is likely that leading from the front is the only option. If the deficit in resources is too big, the vanguard model is necessary. On the other hand, if there are high levels of energy, expertise and control within the team, it would be foolish for the leader to try to lead from the front. It will probably be more useful for them to provide influence both within and without the team in ways that were acceptable to its members.

- ☐ **The nature of the work:** As we have seen in Chapter 2, the resources available within the team have to be ones that match the requirements of the nature of the work it is engaged in. If the work involves innovation, for example, energy will be a far more important resource than control. Even if the group has a high energy resource, it may be necessary for the leader to supplement it in order to meet the requirement.

- ☐ **The organizational context:** The third consideration is the context in which the team is operating: the kind of organization it is part of and the requirement this places on the way the team and its leader operate. I have known teams use their high amounts of energy to run very fast into the brick walls of organizational conservatism and indifference or, worse, get lost in a maze of political in-fighting, back-watching and empire-building. I have made such mistakes myself: energy tends to believe it is irresistible! In such cases, the need for a high influence resource may define the responsibility of the leader above any other consideration. On the other hand, the team may be operating in an organization becalmed by inertia and loss of direction, in which case energy may be the imperative which overrides the available resources of the team.

CASE STUDY 3.1 Gavin's team

We have looked at Gavin's team before, when we explored the difference between groups and teams. I am going to revisit it now, applying the three criteria just discussed to see what choice of leadership model would have been most appropriate for Gavin:

☐ **Resources:** A moderate-to-high level of expertise in the group; high energy – one person in particular; low control – although one person had potential; low in internal influence, although Gavin provided some external influence.

☐ **Work:** A service group who helped other teams within the organization to manage projects effectively by providing project management expertise.

☐ **Context:** The organization is high energy, fast moving, constantly changing, highly political, with a relatively inexperienced management population.

Because of the nature of the work and the organization, most of Gavin's time and effort were applied outside the team, servicing his clients and trying to influence the organization. He left the management of the team to the person with high energy, although energy was not the key requirement. This was internal influence: the team were crying out for clear direction and purpose, given their fragmented and reactive existence. Control was less of an issue, as people were self-regulating. The team consistently asked Gavin to lead from the front, which he rejected because he equated this with vanguard leadership – which he didn't feel he could provide. In fact, what they needed was for Gavin to be more influential internally – a role that he forsook when he delegated the leadership to the person with high energy. This frustrated the team, which in turn frustrated the person with high energy and created a very unhealthy dynamic.

CASE STUDY 3.2 Ivana's team

Ivana's team was a senior management group working within the same organization as Gavin's team. We shall see how the differences in resources and work affected the leadership responsibility required of Ivana.

☐ **Resources:** A moderate level of expertise – some people were new to management positions; moderate energy – one person in particular had high energy, but energy was dampened by the dynamics within the group; moderate control – two people had high control skills; high influence within the team – four people, including Ivana, were high influencers.

☐ **Work:** The group managed one of the organization's main financial operations.

☐ **Context:** As before, high energy, fast moving, constantly changing, highly political, with a relatively inexperienced management population.

The resource issue is the key one with this group, but the picture is complicated. Ivana had a high level of expertise, but was using it to exercise high levels of control and influence which were frustrating the other members of the group – partly because her control resource was not being used well and was having a disruptive effect. Ivana was a classic vanguard leader of the old school, leading with her strengths regardless of the resources and requirements of the team. They actually had adequate levels of control, energy and influence resources. Their main deficit was expertise, which Ivana would be able to supply more effectively if she was less controlling, i.e. let the other, more skilled people in the group take responsibility for controlling the group process. That was likely to have a positive effect on the energy of the group and allow Ivana to exercise internal influence when she needed to (rather than excessively), because it would free the other influencers. If Ivana had opted for the deficit model, using her considerable expertise to help people maximize their own resources, the group would have been far more effective and a lot happier. As it was, much of their energy was wasted resisting and coping with Ivana's excessive control and influence. (When vanguard leadership doesn't work, it can absorb and waste a lot of the team's energy resource.)

These two case studies show how complex the choices facing the leader can sometimes be. It is easier for an outsider like me to assess the situation and see what is required, but much harder for people within the team, whose perception is influenced by their own needs and emotions and the often intractable dynamics of the group. I found both these groups complex and difficult to work with, but analyzing them in the way I have illustrated above helped me to think through what was going on and identify the principles on which a solution needed to be based.

In many cases, however, the choices are more straightforward and the dynamics are less complex. The key, in my view, is for team leaders to identify the available resources and assess their suitability given the nature of the work and the organizational context. If the resources are generally low or the organization is inert, vanguard leadership is likely to be appropriate. But if there are substantial resources within the team, it is likely that the deficit model will be more effective. You will be making better use of the resources available to you, including yourself, and that is likely to have a motivational effect on the team's energy and a positive effect on its group dynamic.

Selecting strategies

The four key resources can help you define your responsibilities as a leader. They will also influence the strategic choices you make about how you manage your own time and effort and the activity of your people.

Doers, delegators and developers

There are three basic strategic choices which characterize the way managers prioritize their time and effort, and therefore the kind of manager they are: doing, delegating and developing. When I observe managers and team-leaders in action, I look to see whether they fall into one of these three broad categories:

☐ **The 'doer':** 'Doers' see their job primarily in terms of performing tasks and achieving targets. They don't like delegating, preferring to lead by example, taking as much responsibility for the team's workload themselves as they can and for this reason they tend to opt for the vanguard model of leadership. For the 'doer', management of people focuses on ensuring that they do the tasks they are given in the agreed timescale. 'Doers' don't invest much time in developing the capabilities of their people.

☐ **The 'delegator':** Like 'doers', delegators are still task-focused, but their strategy for achieving tasks and objectives is different. They will delegate as much of their workload as they can, ensuring that they don't get bogged down in activity which prevents them from performing their more strategic management role, such as influencing the organization on behalf of their department or team. Good 'delegators' make sure that their people are able to perform the tasks that they delegate to them, but because they are still primarily task-focused, they are not investing much time in developing their people.

☐ **The 'developer':** 'Developers' see their job primarily as enabling their team to perform tasks and achieve its targets. Like 'delegators', they delegate as much of the workload as possible, so that they have the time to take a strategic role inside and outside the team. Unlike 'delegators', however, they use delegation as part of a wider plan for developing the performance and potential of their people. They invest considerable time in this aspect of their work, in order to motivate and support people to take increasing responsibility. For this reason, they are more likely to opt for the deficit model of leadership or, at least, to have the awareness to opt for it if it is appropriate.

These three labels are crude caricatures. Most managers are preoccupied with achieving their targets, most managers delegate to some extent, just as most are concerned, to some extent, with developing their people. The labels are more useful if laid out on a continuum which stimulates you to think about where you would locate yourself.

EXERCISE 3.2

Spend a few minutes now reflecting on how you see yourself as a manager: are you mainly a 'doer', 'delegator' or 'developer'? How flexible are you in adapting your strategic choices to the demands of the situation. Focus on how much you:

☐ Delegate work when possible.

☐ Invest time in developing your people.

If helpful, place a mark on the line below to indicate where you think you are on the continuum between the two.

doer_____delegator_____developer

There will be circumstances when you need to be near the left-hand end of the continuum and there will be circumstances when it is more appropriate to be at the other end. Your choice about where to be on the 'doer–developer' continuum will be influenced by several factors. Some of these factors are external, concerning the nature of the work, the capabilities of the people, the culture of the organization. Others will be internal, concerning your own preferences – your willingness to take risks, for example.

External factors

Just as the momentum in leadership ethos is currently towards the deficit model, the external factors prevalent in many organizations in the 1990s are putting increasing pressure on managers to be 'developers'. This is expressed in different ways in phrases like: manager as coach, the facilitative manager, the learning organization. There are several reasons for this trend:

☐ The flattening of hierarchies – there are fewer management levels, so managers have broader spans of control.
☐ The increase in matrix and project management structures.
☐ The separation of management and technical career ladders.
☐ The promotion of managers for their management rather than technical capabilities.
☐ The dependence of managers on technical experts within their teams because of the rate of technological change.

But as with the team ethos, there are risks that ideology overrides reality.

Although the trend rightly encourages managers to be 'developers', this will only be an appropriate strategy in the right conditions, which will need to include some, if not all, of the following factors:

☐ The people who work for you will need to have the potential and the desire to develop their performance, and preferably their career. This is an absolute prerequisite to any investment of your time and energy in helping them to fulfil their potential.

☐ The nature of the team's work will need to have the scope for people to develop their capabilities and expand their role and responsibilities. If there isn't scope, it is unlikely that there will be significant pay-off in investing in their development.

☐ Your workload as manager will need to have elements that can be delegated and that will be of benefit to you if they are. If, for example, your job involves strategic, long-term planning and decision-making and you are constantly prevented by short-term issues from focusing on the wider aspects of this role, delegating more will be crucial to your overall effectiveness.

☐ The culture and values of your organization will need to encourage development as a viable strategy. If your organization expects you to be a 'doer', it will be hard for you to buck the trend. If it expects you to be a 'developer', it will be easier for you to be one, and riskier for you not to be!

EXERCISE 3.3

Spend a few minutes now reflecting on the following three questions in order to help you evaluate where you should be on the 'doer'–'developer' continuum. If you invested more time in 'developing', would there be significant benefit to be gained in terms of:

☐ The performances of individual team-members?
☐ The team's performance overall?
☐ Your performance as manager?

Having reflected, you may feel that your instinctive choices about whether to be a 'doer', 'delegator' or 'developer' were appropriate to your external circumstances. On the other hand, you may feel that you ought to change the strategic choices you have been making up till now. In most cases, this is likely to involve a move towards the 'developer' end of the continuum.

Internal factors

Most managers tend naturally towards being 'doers' – particularly in the early stages of their career in management. This is not surprising: 'doing' is what they know best and it is usually through their success at 'doing' that they have earned their promotion. As you become more experienced and comfortable at being a manager, it is likely that you will gravitate naturally towards being a 'developer'. Having said that, I have met many managers at all levels who do not invest significant time and effort in developing the people they manage. Rationally, they will accept the need to do so. But there are factors which stop them from actually doing it.

These factors are often internal – to do with the kind of person we are – and as such, we tend to be unaware of the impact they have on the choices we make. Some of the aspects of our personality which will affect the extent to which we are prepared to be 'developers' are:

☐ **Trust:** 'Doers' typically are people who only trust themselves to do a job well. They don't like to delegate work because they don't trust the other person to do it to the required standard. 'Developers' are more likely to trust people to do things well.

☐ **Risk:** 'Developers' tend to be more comfortable with taking risks. As a result they will give their people opportunities to develop even though there are risks attached to them failing. 'Doers' are more likely to avoid such risks, preferring to do it themselves.

☐ **Control:** 'Doers' often feel uncomfortable unless they are in close control of every aspect of their team's performance. For them, delegation means loss of control. 'Developers' are better able to control from a distance, interfering less with their people's work.

☐ **Satisfaction:** 'Doers' get their feelings of accomplishment out of doing things. They tend not to get the same satisfaction from seeing people grow and develop, which is a less tangible achievement. 'Developers' enjoy the process of helping people learn and get satisfaction from enabling them to fulfil their potential.

EXERCISE 3.4

Spend a few minutes now reflecting on the internal factors listed above (trust, risk, control and satisfaction) and the extent to which they affect your choices about being a 'doer', 'delegator' or 'developer'.

I have met very few people for whom the issues of trust and control particularly don't act as inhibitors which have to be overcome to some extent. I see myself as a developer, and have invested significant time and effort following that strategy, but I also know that I don't delegate as much as I should, preferring to do it myself because I don't trust people to do it as well as I will, and as a result I put myself under unnecessary pressure and deny others the opportunity to take on new responsibilities and learn new skills.

Delegation

Your strategic choice as a manager or leader is often most accurately identified by the extent to which you delegate work to your people. Extreme 'doers' will try to avoid delegating unless they have to. Extreme 'developers' will delegate as much as they can.

ACTIVITY 3.1

Identify three tasks or responsibilities within your current workload that you could delegate. If you struggle to think of three – struggle: unless you are a high 'developer' already, I don't believe that they don't exist. When you have identified them, answer the following questions for each of the tasks/responsibilities you have identified:

☐ Why haven't you delegated them already?

☐ How will you benefit from successfully delegating each task or responsibility?

☐ Who will gain from the experience of doing them?

☐ What steps do you need to take to ensure that they carry out the task or responsibility adequately?

The trouble with delegation is that it creates work! It creates work for the manager – it is nearly always going to be easier to do it yourself (if you had the time). It creates work for the person you delegate to – and you may feel that they are already overloaded. So, if you are going to delegate, it is important to have a clear objective and to recognize the value of it being achieved. There are several possible objectives, each with their place on the 'doer'–'developer' continuum, as illustrated in Figure 3.1.

Your objective will determine the way that you delegate, and in particular the amount of control you need to retain. If your objective is to get the job done, you may need to give more input to make sure that the person understands what is required of them and is able to meet those requirements. The further down the continuum you go, your role will be to enable the person to manage the task and their own learning themselves.

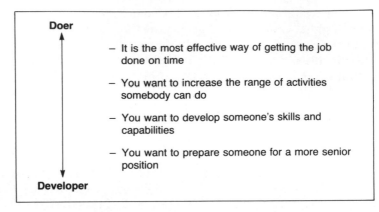

Figure 3.1 Objectives for delegation.

The other problem with delegating is that they will never do it as well as you! You will have a picture of how the task should be done – which is the way that you would do it. You will also have a picture of how the person you delegate the task to will do it – and the difference between these two pictures can be distressing, which is why we often decide to do it ourselves. So your objective must also shape your expectations. The price paid in lowered standards must be offset by the benefit gained from the time you have saved yourself and from the person's development.

Selecting styles

There are two basic styles which characterize the way managers manage their people and their interactions with them. They are: to be directive or to be consultative. When I observe managers and team-leaders in action, I look to see which style they tend to use and how flexible they are at moving between styles according to the situation.

Being directive: Being directive is in many ways the most straightforward leadership style. The manager or leader makes the decisions and tells their people what to do, why, how and by when. They make sure that the tasks are accomplished and give positive or negative feedback depending on performance. There is little scope for people to become involved in decision-making or planning. It is done for them and their role is to be end-users, accepting and implementing their manager's decisions. 'Doers' tend to use this style frequently, for it reflects their task-focused attitude to their work.

Being consultative: Being consultative is the opposite of being directive.

It is a more complex style, more difficult to do well, and therefore less common. It is, however, the style that best suits the deficit model and the 'developer' strategy, and so managers are now being expected to use this style of leadership more frequently. The manager involves their people in the decision-making and planning process by seeking their views and ideas, incorporating these whenever possible into the final decision, which is still in their hands. Whereas the behaviour of the directive manager involves a high level of telling, the consultative manager uses a high level of questioning as a way of not just eliciting views and ideas, but also of influencing the way people perceive issues and their relationship to them.

EXERCISE 3.5

Spend a few minutes now reflecting on your leadership style. Which is your natural style: directive or consultative? Are you aware of using both styles? Do you consciously decide which style to use? If so, what criteria influence that decision?

Both styles have their place and will be effective depending on the specific circumstances in which they are used. Successful leaders tend to be able to use both styles comfortably, choosing wisely and adapting flexibly to suit the needs of the situation. For most of us, being directive is our natural style, the one we adopt most readily and fall back on in times of pressure and crisis. For some of us it will be our only style. Some people develop a consultative style naturally. Others will have learnt to be consultative, either through painful experience or through training or, sometimes, through having been managed themselves by a manager who uses a consultative style.

The key is to select the appropriate style, both in terms of the general leadership of your team – which style is going to work best; and also with specific interactions, particularly persuasive ones, when it will be necessary to select the approach which will work best with that issue and that individual. The following five considerations need to be taken into account. I will describe them in terms of general leadership style, but they also apply to specific interactions, which we will explore in more detail in Part 3.

People: The extent to which your people want to be consulted or not and can contribute meaningfully when they are. Some people are happier to be directed and may even see consultation as grounds for a demarcation dispute (that's your job, you're the manager, etc.). Some people want to be consulted, but don't have the knowledge or experience to contribute usefully, although this can be a dangerous assumption to make. But some people both want to be consulted and can contribute to a significant extent if they are – and will feel greater ownership and motivation as a result.

Relationship: The nature of the relationship you have with your people. A directive style will be more appropriate if your team-members acknowledge and respect your power and authority as leader and trust your ability to make the right decisions on their behalf. If they don't, the use of the directive style will lead to resentment, resistance and possibly open conflict. It may still be appropriate to use a consultative style if you have their respect, but it will be even more necessary if you don't!

Workload: Often your workload will make the decision about which style to use for you. Being consultative takes longer and it may be that you are simply too busy. It is not only easier to tell people what to do, it can be a lot quicker – unless it backfires, in which case it can take up a lot more of your time in the long run. When decisions need to be made quickly and incisively, using a consultative style can seem like an avoidance of responsibility.

Resistance: The extent to which your people resist or are likely to resist the decisions you have made. If people are going to be resistant, a directive style will be high risk, creating a win–lose scenario in which they either carry out your wishes grudgingly or reject your authority. A consultative style will be lower risk, but only if you can use it to persuade them that your wishes are in their interest. If that is not possible, then it may be necessary to take the risk of using the directive style and making sure that you win in such a way that it doesn't alienate people for too long.

Quality: Depending on the knowledge and experience of your people, it is possible to achieve higher-quality results using a consultative style for two reasons: first, by getting other ideas and perspectives to compare with your own; second, because it tends to generate a higher level of commitment as people feel involved in the process and that they have some ownership over the outcome.

EXERCISE 3.6

Spend a few minutes now reflecting on your choices regarding leadership style, using the five criteria listed above – people, relationship, workload, resistance and quality – to assess whether your choices are appropriate. You might want to focus on your leadership style generally, or on specific instances when you have had to gain commitment to decisions or exert your authority.

Empowerment, development and the consultative style

I want to spend a few minutes now discussing empowerment in the context of the consultative style. Empowerment – a buzzword of the 1990s – is essentially a management ethos which suggests that managers should empower their people by giving them increased responsibility over their own time and effort. The intended benefits are greater initiative, greater commitment and greater accountability. It challenges the traditional relationship between manager and subordinate by taking some of the power that goes with the position of manager and transferring it to the traditionally powerless subordinates. This is a sensible and laudable ethos, which is at the heart of the change that is taking place in the relationship between organizations and individuals.

But it is an ethos, not a strategy. And shifts in ethos take time to take root. Strategies need to be identified, according to the specific circumstances, that will enable that ethos shift to be established over a period of time, and in a way that truly respects the needs and wishes of the people being empowered. I have been in too many factories and office buildings where the principle of empowerment has been *imposed* on people in a way that is counter to the very ethos that it embodies.

If empowerment is to be established, it is likely that the strategic choice required to do so will be development and that the style needed to implement this strategy will be consultative, specifically to enable people to understand the consequences of this shift in ethos and to use the power that is being transferred to them responsibly and effectively. If managers are truly to empower people, they need to understand these strategic and style requirements and, if necessary, acquire the skills that go with them. They will also need to understand the requirements of the deficit model, because it is the logical corollary of the ethos of empowerment.

Power, control and domination

Whilst we are on the subject of power, I want briefly to use the key resources that I described in Chapter 2 to highlight a common problem with leadership: the thin line between power and domination. The people who come on my training programmes often complain that their manager or team-leader is too dominating. This suggests that the manager is likely to have a high level of two key resources: control and influence. And this is often because he or she sees these two resources as one and the same thing. In other words, they don't make the distinction between power and control.

Put simply, leaders who are high influencers usually want to be powerful within their group or team, influencing discussions and decisions so that they conform to their own way of thinking. They want power over the team's *product*. Leaders who are high controllers usually want to manage closely the ways in which people work together to achieve their product. They want control over the team's *process*.

Each of these resource profiles on their own will not necessarily be dominating, although excessively high levels of influence can be over-powering. It is when the two are combined – high influence *and* high control – that leadership is likely to turn into domination in ways that can demotivate and alienate people. The combination of power and control, where both process and product are determined by the leader, can leave little room for other team-members to have a sense of their own power or value.

Domination may be appropriate, particularly if the rest of the team is low in the resources of influence and control – in which case they will need the leader to provide those resources for them. And if the leader uses those resources well, skilfully and sparingly, then they can make an invaluable contribution. But domination is often unnecessary and counter-productive and, as I say, a result more of the leader's failure to distinguish between power and control than of their assessment of their responsibilities according to the deficit model.

By separating power into its two component parts – influence over product and control over process – it is possible for managers to resist the tendency for the natural power that goes with their position as leader to become domination. By focusing on one aspect rather than both, it is possible either to retain power and share control, or to retain control and share power. Which option is appropriate will depend on the resources available within the group. If there is a reliable control resource, then responsibility for controlling process can be shared; if there is a reliable influence resource, then so can responsibility for influencing product.

This concept of separating power and control is easier to understand when applied to specific relationships and interactions, which we will be doing later in this book. I have introduced it here at a general level, because recognizing and understanding the difference between power and control is an essential prerequisite to many of the choices that leaders have to make on a daily basis.

Summary

In this chapter, we have looked at leadership in three ways: how you define what kind of leader you are – the vanguard and deficit models; your strategic choices regarding the ways you manage activity – doing, delegating and developing; and your style choices regarding the way you manage interactions and decision-making – directive or consultative. Figure 3.2 illustrates how these three different aspects of leadership align themselves against each other.

How you lead your group or team is essentially a matter of choice. You

Definition	vanguard .... deficit
Strategy	doer .... delegator..developer
Style	directive ....consultative

Figure 3.2 Leadership – definition, strategy and style choices.

will have strong natural tendencies towards particular choices and these will probably work well for you in some situations. But they won't work well in every situation and the key these days is to be flexible: to be able to exercise as many options as possible. Which option is appropriate will depend on the circumstances: the nature of the group, the activity and the environment. Being able to understand these factors, assess their implications and adapt accordingly is the new leadership paradigm.

ACTIVITY 3.2

Before moving on, spend a few minutes reflecting on Chapter 3. Remember the thoughts, insights or ideas that have occurred to you about you or your group as you have read this chapter. Note down in the space below (or on a separate sheet of paper if you prefer) any of these that you feel it would be useful to record so that you can refer back to them in the future. Some may have helped you to identify things you could do to manage your group more effectively and a space has been provided to record these separately.

Thoughts and insights   **Actions arising**

4

Self-identity

So far, we have looked at the different identities of groups and teams; our personal resources and the way they influence the roles we adopt in teams; our choices about the kind of leader we are. Now we are going to look more closely at self-identity and, in particular, the aspects of our self which shape our contribution as a team member or leader. There are four concepts that I am going to describe, all derived from my contact over the years with the Pellin Institute and their work on contribution training. As well as providing ways of understanding yourself, these concepts also provide tools which help you to apply that understanding by managing your contribution more effectively. The four concepts are:

☐ Feelings of accomplishment.
☐ Recognition.
☐ Authority.
☐ Purpose.

Feelings of accomplishment

My neighbour washes his car every Saturday morning. Not only that – he enjoys it. He does it lovingly, and when he's finished, he stands back, breathes in, admires his work, and clearly feels good about himself. He is getting feelings of accomplishment – a basic human need that is crucial to our ability to make it through the day: the feeling that we have accomplished something. The emphasis here is on the *feeling* rather than the actual accomplishment. A clean car is an accomplishment, but it is more than this that gives my neighbour a sense of well-being. This derives from the feeling of gratification that he has gained from cleaning the car. A feeling of accomplishment is the feeling we get when we have done something that gives us satisfaction, that allows us to feel pleased with ourselves and to feel fulfilled.

I wouldn't gain that feeling from washing my car. I would like my car to be clean but I get no feelings of accomplishment from washing cars. I hate it. It does nothing for me. I would rather pay to take my car through a car wash than do it myself. We each have our own sources of feelings of accomplishment.

Feelings of accomplishment are the fuel that keeps us going through the day. They generate energy. Before I start writing each morning, I will find some small, often absurdly trivial, tasks to accomplish, to cross off my tick list, because I need feelings of accomplishment to 'rev' me up for the far harder and often frustrating task of writing. Feelings of accomplishment is a tool that we can use to manage our energy at work, to plan our day so that we get the satisfaction we need to fuel our activity.

If people are not getting enough feelings of accomplishment, they are in trouble. If this is the case at work, they will become demotivated, they will not care about what they are doing or how well they are doing it. They will look for feelings of accomplishment in secondary activity which can be counter to their objectives and detrimental to their relationships: they may seek feelings of accomplishment, for example, from a form of guerrilla warfare against the management, subverting tasks in order to triumph over their perceived oppressor – the manager who is 'forcing' them to work in such an ungratifying environment.

EXERCISE 4.1

Spend a few minutes now reflecting on your own feelings of accomplishment at work. What are the sources of your feelings of accomplishment? Do you actively manage your workload so that you use feelings of accomplishment in order to sustain your motivation? Do you get enough feelings of accomplishment? If not, how does this affect your performance and behaviour at work?

In Chapter 3, we looked at some of the internal factors that affect the strategic choices managers make about their leadership style, with regard to the 'doer–developer' continuum. One of these factors was satisfaction, which is closely connected to feelings of accomplishment. One of the problems for people in their early managerial career is that the feelings of accomplishment they are accustomed to are connected to the activity they have been doing. Salespeople, for example, get their buzz from selling. It is often a mistake to promote a successful seller into sales management because the risk is that you will be cutting them off from their sources of feelings of accomplishment. Unless they are likely to get feelings of accomplishment from the activity of managing others, they will probably stay at the 'doer' end of the 'doer–developer' continuum, and are unlikely to manage their team well as a result.

Many people want to move into management because they perceive it as the only way of getting the recognition they feel they deserve, whether that be status, power or money. But although such recognition can be gratifying, it is no substitute for daily feelings of accomplishment. Which is why many people in management positions are unhappy with their new role, or say they were happier before they became managers. They talk about the hassle and grind of their management job. What they are saying, in effect, is that they don't get enough feelings of accomplishment from it, because it is feelings of accomplishment that make the hassle and grind bearable. They miss the feelings of accomplishment they got when it was legitimate for them to be 'doers'.

Just as we can use feelings of accomplishment as a tool to manage our daily workload, we can also use them to help ourselves and others to plan their career development. Some people get the same feelings of accomplishment now from activity that they were doing twenty years ago. I know a joiner whose life is still enriched by his daily activity of turning wood into furniture. I envy him. I don't get the same buzz now from running training programmes that I did ten years ago. In five years' time, maybe there won't be any buzz at all – I can sense this now. And if I let that happen, if I am still doing the same kind of work in five years' time, and there is no buzz, then I know it will affect the quality of my work – not only will I be dissatisfied, I will be unsuccessful, and my lack of success will feed my dissatisfaction. Recognizing this, anticipating it, is the beginning of a process of identifying what I want to be doing in the future and planning how to make that possible.

EXERCISE 4.2

Spend a few minutes now reflecting on your career development in terms of feelings of accomplishment. First, look back and consider how your sources of feelings of accomplishment have changed over your career to date. Then look forward and try to anticipate whether and how they may change in the future. Consider the implications this may have for your career development.

Recognition

My neighbour gets feelings of accomplishment from cleaning his car. I don't. We each derive feelings of accomplishment from what we do in the world and we do what gives us feelings of accomplishment. But why is it that we choose and derive feelings of accomplishment from different activity? One answer to this lies in our need for recognition: we do things in order to get recognition and the kind of recognition we need will influence what it is that we do and how we do it. My neighbour wants his car to be clean because he wants to be thought of as someone who has a clean car. He washes it himself (rather than go to a car wash) because he gets feelings of accomplishment from the activity. My attitude is very different. I prefer to be thought of as someone who doesn't care about the state of his car.

Both of us are motivated by a need for recognition. But the type of recognition we seek is very different. Dave Pellin suggested that there are three kinds of recognition that act as motivating forces. These are the need for:

- **Admiration:** When we are motivated by our vanity, our need to be admired by others.
- **Respect:** When we are motivated by our need for material control and reward.
- **Acceptance:** When we are motivated by our need to be liked and accepted by others, our need for closeness and intimacy.

My neighbour is motivated by the need for respect: he is looking after his material assets and wants to be respected both for having them and looking after them. I am motivated by the need for admiration: I want to be admired for not caring about material things, for defying social norms. Pathetic, I know, but it is the rebel in me that refuses even to take my car to the car wash however filthy it gets!

This is not to say that my neighbour is just motivated by a need for respect, just as I am not motivated only by my need for admiration. Everyone has needs for all three kinds of recognition to some extent. Some people are clearly driven by one of them in particular, others by an equal measure of all three. You will probably know people whose behaviour is dominated by their need for admiration, for example. You will know others where it is hard to identify one need as being any more dominant than the others. And we change over time. In their youth, for example, someone may be driven almost exclusively by the need for love and acceptance. As they grow older their need for material reward may become an increasingly strong motivation which determines the decisions they make about their lives.

EXERCISE 4.3

Spend a few minutes now reflecting on your own need for recognition in terms of admiration, respect and acceptance. Is your need spread equally between the three, or is it dominated by one in particular? This is a hard question to answer on your own. It may be useful to get feedback from others to compare with your own assessment.

Our need for particular kinds of recognition shapes the contribution that we make in the world. People who seek high levels of acceptance, for example, often follow careers in caring professions: nursing, teaching, social work. People who need a lot of admiration often have high-profile careers, in the theatre, for example, or politics. Accountants tend to be motivated by a need for respect, and their contribution, literally the control of material things, is likely to give them the respect they need. Our work is the main arena for making the contributions we need to make in order to get the recognition we seek.

This is true on a daily basis: each day, our work provides an arena for recognition. We might get it directly through the activity we do: I present some of my material well on a training programme and get feedback from participants which feeds my need for admiration. I help someone to see how they could manage a relationship better and the contact I have made with them meets my need for acceptance. I make the group laugh – I bask in the admiration. I send off the invoice a week later and I am getting the respect I need! In these direct and indirect ways, work, for most of us, will provide the recognition we need, and the recognition we need will shape the way we do our work.

Some people can't get their need for recognition met through their work. They might feel they should have a more senior position (respect), or that they aren't allowed to take any risks or initiatives of their own (admiration), or that they don't have enough contact with other people (acceptance). If this is the case, their motivation and commitment will suffer. They may lose interest in their work; they may become disillusioned or cynical; they may try to get their needs met in inappropriate ways – such as the manager who wants to be liked, or the joker who doesn't know when to stop.

EXERCISE 4.4

Spend a few minutes now reflecting on the extent to which you get the recognition you need from your work, and particularly from your role as team-leader.

Admiration and respect are generally more appropriate forms of recognition for team-leaders and managers, and often represent different resources and styles. A need for admiration tends to be congruent with high levels of energy and influence. A need for respect tends to fit with high levels of expertise and control. This is not always the case – someone can want admiration for their expertise, for example, but I use it as a rule of thumb when I am trying to understand what motivates a manager to behave in particular ways. Someone with a high need for admiration will probably find it easier to be a 'vanguard' leader; someone with a high need for respect is likely to find it easier to be a 'deficit' leader. It also helps me to understand why people might be behaving inappropriately.

It is usually unwise, however, for team-leaders and managers to try to get their need for acceptance met from their team. A desire to be liked by your team-members will impede your ability to manage them fairly and authoritatively, and is likely to cause confusion and resentment. This is not to say that you shouldn't be liked by them, just that it is dangerous to *need* to have their acceptance. I have worked with countless managers over the years who have experienced this difficulty: they will tend to avoid a difficult decision for fear of alienating someone – the opposite of acceptance.

When people aren't getting the recognition they need from the work that they do, their motivation suffers. So does their effectiveness. There are ways in which my need for admiration is met by my work as a trainer: I am the centre of a group's attention for long periods. But if my need for applause is too dominant, it could make me insensitive – I will be using the group to feed my needs rather than helping them to meet their own. As I have got older, however, the level of fulfilment I get from being a trainer has decreased. I need applause of a different kind, from a bigger audience and it is this need that motivates me to write books. Similarly, if a manager isn't getting their needs met through their leadership of the group, this will have a significant impact on their effectiveness as a leader, and in particular, on the development of their authority.

Authority

Authority is one of the great intangibles: What is it? Where does it come from? How do you develop it? Why are some people so apparently full of authority whereas others lack it completely? Authority is a key leadership quality. Is it just a matter of personality: you've either got it or you haven't? Or is it something that you can learn, develop, build over time?

One way of understanding authority is in terms of a combination of feelings of accomplishment and appropriate recognition. We develop our authority through doing things which give us feelings of accomplishment and for which we get the recognition we need. I have developed authority as a trainer because I have delivered a lot of training programmes, because I have gained feelings of accomplishment from this activity and because I have received the admiration and acceptance that I needed: admiration of the strength of my material and my ability to manage groups; acceptance from the care I show people in wanting to help them learn and develop. My work in management development has provided a sustained and structured arena in which I can make an appropriate and effective contribution that will help me get the recognition I need.

Authority develops through the combination of doing activity and receiving recognition. My neighbour will not develop authority through the activity of washing his car even though he does it every weekend, because he will not receive enough meaningful recognition for that activity. Similarly, I have not developed my authority as a manager because I haven't done it for long enough, even though I got positive recognition when I did it. Because it wasn't the kind of recognition I wanted, I chose to stop doing it, and so chose not to develop my authority in that area.

EXERCISE 4.5

Spend a few minutes now reflecting on your own authority and how it has developed, using the framework of feelings of accomplishment and recognition.

One of the problems for first-time managers is that the authority they have painstakingly developed over the years is not necessarily going to apply to their role as leader. The authority that a salesperson develops through selling will not give them authority as a sales manager. They will have to develop that through managing groups and individuals well over a period of time and getting the feelings of accomplishment and recognition they need from doing so. If the activity of management doesn't give them the kind of recognition they need, then they are unlikely to do the job well and so are unlikely to develop their authority. And this is what happens to many sales managers: they can't stop selling, because this is where their authority lies, and where they get the recognition they need. Because they can't stop selling, they don't start managing well and so don't learn to develop their authority as a manager.

Managers have to have authority in the eyes of the people they manage. This authority can only be developed through doing and being seen to do. Each time you give one of your people feedback about their work and do it to your satisfaction, so that you get feelings of accomplishment from doing it, then you will be developing your authority. The feelings of accomplishment provide the motivation to do it again. If, by doing it, you feel you gain the respect of the other person and this meets your need for respect, then this recognition reinforces your growing sense of authority, encourages you to do it again, do it better, take more risks. Each time you manage an interaction with your people successfully, your authority will develop. Each time you avoid interactions which you know you should have, your authority diminishes.

ACTIVITY 4.1

Spend a few minutes now identifying an opportunity for developing your authority. This might be a task or an interaction with someone that you have been putting off because it feels difficult – something which you know you need to do, something which instinctively you know that, if you did it, it would help you to develop your authority. Now do it!

Purpose

So far we have looked at three concepts: feelings of accomplishment, the need for recognition and the development of authority. They are inextricably linked: what we do is shaped by our need for recognition; doing it gives us feelings of accomplishment; the combination develops our authority. These three concepts lead us towards a fourth: **purpose**. It is our sense of purpose that sustains us through our lives. We need it to get out of bed in the morning, to get us through the day, to help us survive the bad times, to give us the energy to go on, to give our lives meaning. Purpose is our primary source of energy. When we lack purpose, we lack energy, direction, confidence, fight. When our sense of purpose is strong, it provides a framework which gives our lives meaning: we know why we do what we do, we have a sense of our future, we have vision.

Feelings of accomplishment are the building-blocks of purpose. When my neighbour washes his car, the feelings of accomplishment that he knows he will get from this activity give him some small sense of purpose. In this case, it is isolated, superficial, temporary. It does not provide a framework for his life. It generates the energy to get the job done and that is all. When the window-cleaner comes round to wash my windows, however, it is different. The activity is essentially the same, but the sense of purpose is different. He may not get huge feelings of accomplishment from cleaning windows any more, but the activity enables him to earn a living, provide for himself and his family. This is his underlying purpose, as it is for many of us, and it is what gives him the energy, day after day, to get out there with his ladders, doing work which, of itself, I imagine he doesn't enjoy that much.

But the window-cleaner is also an environmentalist. He campaigns against nuclear power with an energy and commitment that puts me to shame. This is the true passion of his life, in the way that religion is for some, or politics, or sport, or healing, or teaching. And it is this passion that is his deep and sustaining purpose: it explains his job, which provides him with enough money without using up too much of his time, energy or commitment. His passion will provide him with focus throughout his life, it will enrich his life with shape and meaning, it will sustain him.

These examples have illustrated three distinct levels of purpose:

- **Superficial:** Superficial purpose is the accumulation of isolated feelings of accomplishment. It is enough to get us through the day, but little more. Many unemployed people only have superficial purpose in their lives – because there is nothing that binds their feelings of accomplishment together into meaningful patterns. They literally take each day as it comes.

- **Underlying:** Underlying purpose is more substantial and longer term. We derive it from the desire to build our career, home, family, social life through a coherent effort which provides us with a sense of fulfilment and significance. Underlying purpose supports our lives, week in, week out, but it is finite: projects are completed; careers end; children leave home; relationships finish. Family and work are the most common sources of underlying purpose.

- **Sustaining:** Sustaining purpose is what gives meaning to our lives over and above our work and family. It is not finite, and will survive and outlast the end of a career or the departure of children or the breakdown of a relationship. It might be a cause, a passion, a vocation which transcends the daily realities and responsibilities of our lives and is our main source of energy, enrichment and self-identity.

Each form of purpose is constructed from the building-blocks of feelings of accomplishment. The difference between the three is the extent to which our feelings of accomplishment are gathered from within a coherent framework which gives meaning to our activity and so deepens our sense of fulfilment. For most of us, work provides a source of underlying purpose, the means by which we provide a home and security for our families, a direction for ourselves, a sense of what the future will hold. This may be the stability of doing the same activity or the challenge of developing a career, of exploring and fulfilling our potential. Even if the work is not in itself gratifying, the fact that it provides the money to pay for the aspects of our lives that are important to us gives it meaning and value.

But, especially now, as patterns of employment are changing so radically, it is important to recognize that our underlying purpose is essentially outside our control. If we do not acknowledge this, then we are vulnerable to the devastating consequences of its removal. If we are dependent on our underlying purpose for our life's meaning, the loss of our job can feel like the end of the world; just as when our children leave home we can feel dazed and confused and without purpose in life.

For some people, their work provides more than their underlying purpose. It is more than a career, it is a vocation: to heal, to educate, to invent, to design, to repair. It is their life's work. For them, work is fulfilling both their underlying and sustaining purpose – and this is a powerful and energizing combination. They are not dependent on their job to fulfil their purpose. They will find ways of continuing such activity when they retire. Sustaining purpose gives them the resilience to survive shocks such as redundancy. These people tend to have enormous energy and great authority.

For some people, like my window-cleaner, their sustaining purpose lies outside their work. Their relationship to their job will be dependent on the extent to which it helps them fulfil their underlying purpose. But if their job demands too much time or energy, or doesn't provide them with enough money, then their motivation will suffer and they will be more reluctant to commit the time and energy required.

EXERCISE 4.6

Spend a few minutes now reflecting on your own sense of purpose. To what extent does your work provide you with your sustaining purpose as well as your underlying purpose? Or does your sustaining purpose lie outside your work? If so, does your work help or hinder you to fulfil your sustaining purpose?

There are times when a team's objectives can bond people together in a shared underlying purpose, where membership of the team as well as the activities it is engaged in becomes a defining aspect of our lives. If these objectives tie into people's sustaining purpose, the bonding is even more intense. If everyone wants to generate the ultimate marketing strategy, the next scientific or technological leap forward, then this common deep purpose will generate an extraordinary level of team identity and affiliation.

Far more frequently, in my experience, groups and teams are made up of people with different levels of and senses of purpose. Some are passionate in their belief in the value of the work; others are in it for the money; others are seeking to develop their career; some are more preoccupied with a sustaining purpose that lies outside their work, which consumes their real passion and interest. Seeing things in this way helps me to be more accepting and less judgemental about people. It is unrealistic to expect that work will provide the sustaining purpose for all of them.

The problem with a strong sense of purpose is that it creates its own lack of awareness. We tend to believe that it is the activities we are engaged in that give us the drive, the energy, the commitment, the enthusiasm; and we think that if only other people engaged in the same activities they would feel the same drive as we do. But it is the fact that our purpose is being fulfilled that gives us our drive, and if the activities do not fulfil the purpose of other people they will not feel the same. How many parents have felt frustrated because their children don't share their enthusiasms? How many managers have felt frustrated because their people don't share their commitment? It is not that those children and those people necessarily lack purpose, it is just that their purpose is different.

For team-leaders especially, it is important to recognize that your commitment to the project stems from your purpose being fulfilled, rather than the intrinsic qualities of the project. When I was leading my team, my energy and vision and passion stemmed from my deep and sustaining purpose as a teacher. I wanted my colleagues to share this and became frustrated with them when they didn't; I wanted them to share my commitment to helping people to learn and develop, because that was the only reason I could see why people would want to do this work. Purpose creates its own lack of awareness: of course there are other reasons why people want to do this work; for some of them it was just a job, an interesting way of paying the bills. When I came to accept that, and not just accept but respect it, then I became a more effective leader.

EXERCISE 4.7

Spend a few minutes now reflecting on your level of awareness and acceptance of sustaining purpose of each of your team-members. Do you expect everyone to share your commitment to the work? Does your commitment blind you to the sustaining purpose of others? To what extent do you accept these differences?

Summary

In this chapter, we have looked at four concepts which help us to understand our own identity as people and as managers and team-leaders. These are:

☐ Feelings of accomplishment.
☐ Types of recognition (the motivating forces).
☐ The development of authority.
☐ The three types of purpose.

These four concepts are each complex in their own right, and even more complex in the way that they relate to each other. Figure 4.1 shows one way

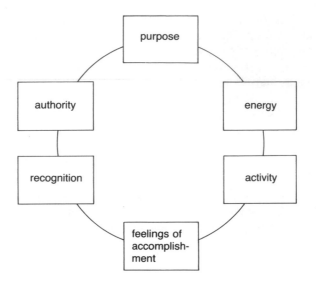

Figure 4.1 The self-identity cycle.

ACTIVITY 4.2

Before moving on, spend a few minutes reflecting on Chapter 4. Remember the thoughts, insights or ideas that have occurred to you about you or your group as you have read this chapter. Note down in the space below (or on a separate sheet of paper if you prefer) any of these that you feel it would be useful to record so that you can refer back to them in the future. Some may have helped you to identify things you could do to manage your group more effectively and a space has been provided to record these separately.

Thoughts and insights   **Actions arising**

in which you could understand their interconnectedness. I use this circle as a diagnostic tool to help me understand where the issues might be for some of the people that I work with. There is no one starting-point in the circle – the concepts flow continually into each other: purpose generates the energy to act, which gives us feelings of accomplishment and creates the opportunity for recognition which together develop our authority, which helps us find our purpose, which provides the energy and so on.

If people are experiencing problems with their energy or motivation, I use the circle to help them think through where the block might lie: Is it lack of purpose or lack of recognition for example? Are they not developing their authority? Are they not getting enough feelings of accomplishment? When the causes of the problem are clearer, it is easier to identify possible solutions. Not easy – only easier. Sometimes, knowing where the block lies is all that can be achieved for the moment.

Part 2

Process

Part 2 explores group process: the ways in which people work together. It helps you to reflect on how you manage your group on a daily basis by examining four levels of process in detail. The exercises and activities in Part 2 help you critically to review the way your group or team currently works together and provide you with possible interventions you could make to improve your group process.

5

Product and process

When we looked at leadership in Chapter 3, we defined domination as being a high level of involvement in both the team's *product* and the team's *process*. In this chapter, we are going to look at these two concepts in more detail, particularly process; we are also going to look at the need for groups and teams to establish an appropriate balance of focus between the two.

First, let me give you a fuller definition of the two terms:

- **Product:** Product is the output the team achieves, as determined by its objectives and activities. To focus on product is to concentrate on the tasks that you (and the other members of the team) have to do to achieve that output.
- **Process:** Process is the ways in which people work together in order to achieve their output. It includes the ways in which people allocate tasks, organize their activity, communicate with each other and make decisions. To focus on process is to make conscious choices about these issues, and to involve other team members in the making of those choices.

Put simply, product is *what* we do; process is *how* we do it. The two are inextricably linked. The minute we start to do something, we adopt a process for doing it. We may not adopt it consciously, it may not be very effective, but it is there – underpinning our activity in the same way that foundations underpin the structure of a house. Like foundations, process is often invisible, and we can be completely unaware of its presence. And like foundations, if the process is weak, the activity and its product are likely to suffer as a result.

71

Product v process

The difference between product and process is a crucial distinction to make in the way that you manage yourself, your activity and other people. Having an appropriate balance of focus on each of them is crucial to the effective management of groups and teams. This balance, however, can be extremely difficult to achieve. The pressure to focus on and achieve product is very strong and also very seductive. It often prevents us from focusing sufficiently on process. The pressure is twofold:

☐ **External:** Most people these days work under considerable time constraints: they have to achieve results within tight deadlines, and there are never enough hours in the day. The targets get tougher, the resources shrink. We don't have enough time to do everything, let alone think about how to do it.

☐ **Internal:** Most people have a tendency to want to get on with things. They prefer not to spend time beforehand thinking about how, they want to get on and *do*. Achieving product is far more interesting and rewarding than thinking about process.

The combination of these two pressures can be overwhelming. Process frequently doesn't get a look in! People dive straight into the task, whether it be writing a sales proposal, solving a technical problem, a discussion with somebody, a meeting. They spend no time thinking through or talking about how best to go about writing the proposal, tackling the problem, handling the discussion or managing the meeting. The pressure to get on and do consistently overrides the need to plan, and this has consistently problematic consequences.

Focusing on process does take time and, because of the internal pressure to get on with things, people don't feel they can afford to spend any time on anything but the task in hand. And if people aren't used to focusing on process, or aren't very good at managing it, they will be reluctant to waste time talking about it. But if you don't focus on process, ironically, you usually end up wasting time: the sales proposal takes longer to write because it has to go through several drafts; the solution quickly identified doesn't resolve the core problem, only the symptoms; the discussion doesn't deal with the key issues you wanted to raise; the meeting wanders off down a series of attractive but irrelevant side roads. Ignoring process, although very tempting, is not efficient. The knack is to invest just enough time in process to achieve product efficiently.

EXERCISE 5.1

Spend a few minutes now reflecting on your own tendencies with regard to the balance between product and process. Do you tend to dive into tasks and interactions without sufficient forethought or planning? Or do you take time to ensure that an appropriate process has been established beforehand?

If you have low awareness of process in your own work, it is likely that you won't spend much time consciously thinking through how to plan your activity, organize your workload, prioritize your commitments. You will just get on and do it – and every now and again you will suffer some level of difficulty when things break down. It will be the same with your relationships and interactions. If you don't focus much on the process by which these are conducted – if you just get on with them – then there will be times when they run into problems: confusion, tension, conflict.

The drive to achieve product overrides the drive to establish effective process. But also, few people have an instinctive grasp of how to manage process well, or even an awareness of the need to do so. And process is difficult. It is hard enough on your own to think through clearly the best way of going about a task. It is even more difficult when you involve others, when a group of people have to think through how best to conduct a meeting or a team have to agree how they are going to make decisions in the future. Group process is not just about planning, it is about actively managing the issues that we have been looking at in earlier sections of the book: roles, responsibilities, relationships – and the dreadful mess and entanglements that they can generate.

In this chapter, I am going to explore process as it relates to groups and teams. I am going to break the concept down into four levels of process – a tool which I use when I observe teams in action and which I will ask you to use to reflect on the teams you manage or are a member of. In the next chapter, I will explore strategies for managing process at each of these four levels. These will hopefully provide you with steps you can take to raise awareness of and improve process in your teams.

The four levels of process

In Chapter 2, I introduced an observation tool that I use for assessing a group's available resources (the four resources: energy, control, expertise and influence). This is a macro tool that helps me to understand and identify problems a group is having as a result of the mix of people that belong to it. The four levels of process is another observation tool that I use to observe groups when they are working together, usually in a meeting.

This is a micro tool that helps me to understand and identify problems a group of people is having in working together. Even if meetings are not a big element of the team's activity, watching them work together will give me most of the information I need about how they manage their process generally, thus enabling me to identify the issues that I need to address with them.

I regard meetings as a microcosm of a team's life, and so will be using them as a context for the following section on the four levels of process. These are:

☐ Procedural.

☐ Structural.

☐ Behavioural.

☐ Social.

I will explore each of these in detail first. I will then continue the two case studies I used in Part 1 (Gavin's team and Ivana's team) to illustrate the four levels of process in action and to show how I use them to structure my observation and plan my interventions as a facilitator.

Procedural: The procedural level of process relates to the procedure the group establishes to organize its discussion of topics or agenda items during the meeting. Does it dive straight in to discussing the content of the topic, or does it spend some time first thinking through how best to discuss it? For example, does it identify the purpose of the discussion and its desired output? Is it clear about how it makes decisions?

Structural: The structural level of process relates to the roles allocated to the members of the group, both within the official and unofficial structures (see Chapter 2). How actively does the group consider people's roles during the meeting? Do different topics require changes in role, and if so does the group make these changes? Is the group making the most effective use of its people and maximizing their contribution?

Behavioural: The behavioural level of process relates to the ways in which people interact with each other during the meeting. In particular, it relates to how 'airtime' is allocated to the different members of the group and how effectively they make use of this airtime. For example, do people listen to each other, are they interested in each other's views and ideas, do they explore issues in depth or rush to solutions, are they clear about what is being discussed, do they cooperate or compete with each other?

Social: The social level of process relates to the dynamics that exist in the relationships between team members. How comfortable are people with the distribution of power and the allocation of roles? Are there tensions in particular relationships – attractions or animosities? To what extent are individuals included or excluded from the group? Is there a climate of mutual respect or disrespect?

EXERCISE 5.2

Spend a few minutes now reflecting on the four levels of process with regard to your own team, or various groups that you are a member of. How do these groups set about managing the four levels of process? How effective are they? Can you identify problems or causes of difficulty at any particular level of process?

Choices

It is important to recognize that whenever a group of people meet together, these four levels of process swing into operation automatically and are constantly active. This is easier to see when you are observing a group than when you are participating in its discussions, because the minute you start to participate, your awareness of process decreases: the more you focus on product the less you are able to focus on process.

Even if a group has little or no awareness of its process, there is still a process underpinning the meeting and the way people operate. The management of process involves a set of choices that have to be made. Not to manage it at all is one option, but this is not a conscious choice for most groups who don't actively manage their process. Even though their choice is unconscious, they should still regard it as a choice that they are making – and one they need to reflect on and evaluate clearly, because rarely, in my experience, is it an appropriate one.

Many more groups these days are making conscious choices about their process, particularly at the procedural and behavioural levels, and as a result are organizing their discussion more effectively. Having said that, the choices people make are not always effective and can lead to as much frustration as the choice to ignore process altogether. This is partly because of a lack of skill at managing procedural process and personal behaviour. But it is also because problems at the structural and social levels create a powerful undertow that can subvert attempts to improve the other levels of process. People are much less willing and able to address this undertow on their own. As I have said before, managing process, especially in groups and teams, is difficult. The first step is to raise your awareness of all levels of process and the impact that they have on the group's performance.

To illustrate how I use the four levels of process to diagnose problems and plan interventions, we are going to return to the two case studies I used in Part 1: two groups that I have been facilitating as I have been writing this book.

CASE STUDY 5.1   Gavin's team

When I first worked with Gavin's team, I spent a day with them together, having met the members briefly individually the day before. There were six people in the team, including Gavin. Alastair and Paul had both been with the team since Gavin set it up two years ago. Simon and John were relatively new members. Mary, the administrative assistant, had been with the team for about a year.

At the beginning of the day, I asked them to have a meeting, first to decide an agenda that they could usefully discuss during the day and then to start working through one or two of their agenda items. I sat quietly and observed them as they did this, taking no part in the meeting. In terms of the four levels of process, this is what I saw:

☐ **Procedural:** There was no attempt to organize the discussion at all. People immediately started proposing items that could be included on the agenda, then started discussing some of the proposed items in detail. They didn't agree an agenda for the day within the time I had allotted for the task (20 minutes).

☐ **Structural:** There seemed to be no official structure at all. Nobody took responsibility for managing the meeting. Gavin joined in the discussion along with the rest of them. Much of the energy came from Alastair. Paul was also a high contributor, but seemed to make less impact than Alastair. Mary, Simon and John were all very quiet. Mary recorded the group's decisions on a flip chart.

☐ **Behavioural:** People didn't listen much to each other. Alastair in particular interrupted a lot, in order to push forward his own point of view. He and Paul disagreed with each other frequently. The opinions and reactions of Mary, John and Simon were not sought, nor were they offered. Questions were asked, mainly by Alastair, but usually aggressively, to support his own views rather than to explore those of other people.

☐ **Social:** There were clearly some issues with group dynamics. This was being displayed overtly by the group, who seemed to be behaving very naturally, unaffected by the fact that. they were being observed by me. Three things struck me initially:

a) there were two groups working in tandem – Gavin/Alastair/Paul were the dominant group; Mary/John/Simon were the outsider group;

b) there was competition between Paul and Alastair;

c) Gavin was creating a vacuum in the official structure which provided an arena for Paul and Alastair to act out their competitive relationship.

CASE STUDY 5.2   Ivana's team

I had been asked to work with Ivana's team because it was recognized that they were in some form of crisis. The department had recently reorganized and instead of having a senior management group of five people (Ivana, Ben, Jack, Patrick, Philip), it had expanded to include another six managers (Neil, Norman, Jenny, Ann, Alice, Dick, Michael), all of whom had reported previously to one of the original five. These reporting lines had been removed to encourage a team ethos, in which all eleven people operated as equals, albeit some with more significant responsibilities than others. This new structure was proving difficult and had not surprisingly generated a number of tensions. Some of these were inherited: most members of the group represented one of two main functions, and the relationship between these two functions (one previously led by Ben, the other by Jack) was problematic – there was strong competition for resources, for example.

Having interviewed some members of the team, I had two days to work with the whole group (except for Philip and Norman, both of whom had legitimate reasons for not being there). As with the previous case study, I asked them initially to agree an agenda for the two days and then to start working through it. Again, I sat quietly and observed them as they did this, taking no part in the meeting. In terms of the four levels of process, this is what I saw:

☐ **Procedural:** Patrick made some attempts to organize the discussion on the agenda but he was not forceful enough and the meeting degenerated quickly into a free-for-all in which Ivana, Jack and Ben were dominant. Having brainstormed a long list of possible items for the agenda, an elaborate and complicated procedure was used to try to agree priorities. This did not work well and they failed to complete the task in the time allowed.

☐ **Structural:** It was assumed by the group that Ivana would chair the meetings and she was deferred to even though she never took clear control. Patrick continued to make sensible procedural suggestions, but these were usually ignored. Ben, who had high levels of energy, went to the flip chart to record decisions and tried to influence the meeting from there. Neil took on a role that I couldn't interpret fully, but which was generally counter to the direction in which the group was going. Jack tried to inject a level of calm rationality into what was often a heated and emotional discussion.

☐ **Behavioural:** There was a high level of interruption, from Ivana and Jack especially. Some people never said a word, and only Patrick made any effort to involve them. Ben was very forceful at pushing his point of view forward. Jack was more quietly assertive, but no less effective. Ivana consistently subverted the group, challenging decisions after they had been agreed, undermining the process, sending the discussion round in circles and occasionally being aggressive to people, especially the other women.

☐ **Social:** Not surprisingly, given the history of the group, there were a number of dynamics in play that impacted seriously on its performance. There was clearly a tension between Ben and Jack, although this was well hidden and managed. Neil generated a certain amount of unease. Jenny, Ann and Alice were clearly unhappy, although Ann made significant efforts to address aspects of process as the meeting went on. Patrick's potential to manage the process was being ignored. Dick and Michael seemed fed up with it all. And at the centre of the dysfunction was Ivana, who generated a phenomenal amount of confusion and hurt, and whom people clearly resented hugely. But they also seemed to be afraid of her, certainly of challenging her; she would openly attack people as well as covertly undermine them.

In both case studies, a short period of observation generated a lot of data for me to reflect on and to help me decide how best to enable each group to manage its process more effectively. I use the four levels of process first to help me organize these data, as I have shown in the way that I have presented them to you. I also use them to help me identify the starting-point for my work with the group and the helping strategies that I need to use.

EXERCISE 5.3

Spend a few minutes now revisiting your reflections in Exercise 5.2. Do the two case studies help you to understand and evaluate the four levels of process in your own team or groups?

It is unlikely that your teams will be undergoing similar degrees of distress to those experienced by those in the two case studies, but it is likely that they will be experiencing similar issues, even if not to the same extent. It may be that there is room for improvement at the procedural level only, for example; or you may recognize that there are issues with the group dynamic which, if they aren't addressed, could cause problems later, perhaps at a time when the team is under intense external pressure: workload, deadlines, organizational change, etc.

Process hierarchy

The following four levels of process form a hierarchy of complexity: each one is progressively more complex to understand and to manage:

☐ Problems at the **procedural level** are likely to be nearer the surface and can be relatively straightforward to deal with.

☐ Issues at the **structural level** are usually more hidden but can often be resolved by simple interventions.

☐ Problems at the **behavioural level**, although more self-evident than structural issues, tend to involve substantial feedback, and often skills development, in order to make significant improvements.

☐ The **social level**, the group dynamics, contains the most deep-rooted and hidden issues, and also the most entangled and intractable ones. If there are problems at this level, these are the hardest to resolve.

This 'process hierarchy' is interconnected: problems at the lower levels are usually represented in some form in the higher ones. If there are problems with the structural or behavioural levels, this will affect the group's ability to manage the procedural level well. If there are problems at the social level, these will manifest themselves at any or all of the other three, but particularly at the behavioural level. The way people interact with each other is partly dependent on their level of interactive skill. But it is also the visible expression of what is going on under the surface, in the subtext of their relationships. The group dynamic has a powerful influence on people's behaviour in ways that we are usually unaware of and therefore unable to control.

This interconnectedness means that if there are problems at lower levels, work which focuses exclusively on the levels above is unlikely to be entirely successful. This is a cardinal rule in my work as a facilitator and one that has significance for all managers and team-leaders. At some point, you have to address the problems that exist in the lower levels (e.g. social) of the process hierarchy. If you don't, they will continue to generate turbulence and this will manifest itself at the higher levels (e.g. procedural). You may resolve problems at the higher levels, but these resolutions will be subverted and undermined if the problems at the lower levels are left unresolved.

The company I used to work for went through several reorganizations in a short space of time in an attempt to sort out tensions and dissatisfactions among the workers and the managers. There was a substantial consultation process to gather analysis, ideas and commitment to change. New structures were put in place, but the old problems quickly re-emerged. Although the resentments expressed during the consultation process had focused on the structure of the organization, this had not been the real source of grievance. The old tensions simply relocated themselves, like squatters finding a new squat after they had been evicted. They emerged at different points and in different ways. Structural solutions will rarely resolve problems with group dynamics – they just move them around; they will pop up somewhere else.

I have said consistently that managing process well is difficult. This is partly because of the different levels of process that exist. And partly because, with most groups, there is a need to explore the social level at some point. People generally are not keen to do this and will resist attempts to focus on it with a determination (and often a deviousness) which is quite remarkable!

Starting-points

In both of the case studies, as my notes above suggest, there were several issues that needed to be explored at the social level, as well as issues at all the other levels. As facilitator, or team-leader, or team-member, if you want to help the group to work more effectively together, you are faced with the question: Where do you start? This is clearly a critical question to get right, because getting it wrong can make things worse instead of better. I use the four levels of process to break the question down a little: Which level of process do I address first?

This question introduces my second cardinal rule of facilitation: only address one level of a process at a time. There are three reasons for this: first, it is easier for you to manage (whether you are facilitator or team-leader); second, it is enough for the group to handle; and third, because of the interconnectedness between the levels, intervention on one level will have an effect at all the others. The knack in choosing starting-points is to identify the level which is going to 'unlock' the core issues for the group and generate the momentum for change.

ACTIVITY 5.1

Put yourself in my shoes and imagine that you are an external facilitator who has been brought in to help Gavin's and Ivana's teams to work more effectively together. Using the information I have given you, plan what interventions you might make with either team. In particular, consider which level of process you think it is appropriate to focus on initially. Bear in mind the available resources within each group.

In both case studies, there are significant problems with the group dynamic which will have to be addressed if the groups are to function effectively. There are also significant problems at all the other levels. And so it is difficult to know where best to start. The problems at the social level are entrenched, complex and well hidden (as they usually are). To start with these would be radical, probably too radical for the groups, who might resist attempts to expose the dark underbelly of their existence and the inevitable pain and conflict that this would release. They are likely to unite against such an intervention, masking their dysfunction behind a show of solidarity which denies the existence of any problems, demonstrates the healthy state of their dynamic, and repulses any challenge to the status quo.

It is necessary to find the line of least resistance and to make use of the resources that exist within the team. I will apply these principles to each team in turn to explain my initial strategy. I am not suggesting that these are 'right answers' – they are my answers, very much a result of my preferred way of working; your answers to the exercise may be equally valid.

Gavin's team: The line of least resistance with Gavin's team would be to start with the procedural level to help them organize their discussion more effectively. It is hard to say what resource exists within the team to manage procedure, but as Gavin is avoiding strong leadership, it will be best to start by seeing if he can do it. If the team's discussions are more organized this should lead to improvement at the behavioural level and make it possible to get a closer look at the structural and social issues which at this stage are not clear.

Ivana's team: Patrick's potential to manage procedure for the team and Ivana's unwillingness or inability to chair the meeting actively led me to think that my starting-point was structural: I needed to get Patrick into a position where the group gave him the authority to organize their meetings. If I could do this successfully (and it was relatively high risk), the procedural level should more or less look after itself and the behavioural level should also improve to some extent. The other benefit of starting with the structural level is that it would provide a way in to the issues at the social level. Any structural realignment tends to bring the group dynamics nearer to the surface; it also makes it more legitimate to address them directly.

Both case studies are examples of difficult situations: a complex interplay of issues at all four levels, with particularly intense dysfunction at the social level. The interventions I made were decided intuitively, having processed the data that I had gathered from my two observation tools (the four resources and the four levels of process). In both cases, the act of bringing the groups together with an outside facilitator was itself the start of a process of change. Something had to happen. I can only hope that my interventions helped to channel the energy and emotion that were unleashed towards a productive end.

ACTIVITY 5.2

Now imagine that you are an external facilitator observing your team during a typical meeting. What would your diagnosis of the group's issues be? And where would you start? What intervention do you feel might be required to help the group improve the way it works together (I don't believe there is no scope for improvement!)?

Critical awareness

In Chapter 1, I explained that part of my reservation with the team ethos is that I think it creates unrealistic expectations, and so unnecessary pressure, on groups whose working context doesn't require them to be teams. My other main reservation is that the emphasis on team identity can generate an anxiety about being a 'good team' which leads to a self-deluding need to promote the team's strengths and deny its weaknesses. I have worked with many teams who have projected a self-image of happy synergy which, at one level, is accurate, but which also serves to mask real and troublesome dynamics that lie dormant under the surface. Acknowledging these tensions is seen as threatening the self-identity and morale of the team, so they tend to get brushed under the carpet.

One of the keys to effective teamwork is a high level of critical awareness: a realistic understanding among members of the team of their strengths and weaknesses at all four levels of process. It is particularly useful to have critical awareness of the structural and social levels, as these are the ones that are less visible and so harder to identify. But critical awareness is only possible if a climate exists within the team that allows it and sees it as a necessary attribute. This climate needs to be based on the following precepts:

□ A recognition that the team will almost inevitably experience problems, tensions and conflicts within its lifetime, however unlikely that may seem in the present.

□ An acknowledgement that these problems will be the result of internal pressures to do with the team's process, even though they may be triggered by events in the external environment.

□ An acceptance of the need for internal pressures at all four levels of process to be actively managed in a way that involves all the members of the team.

□ An understanding that it is easier to acknowledge and discuss internal pressures in the team's process when things are going well than during times of tension and conflict.

□ A preparedness for individual members of the team openly and honestly to share and discuss their feelings about the team, its process and its individual members.

□ A commitment to resolving internal pressures that adversely affect the team's process as a key requirement of effective teamwork.

EXERCISE 5.4

Spend a few minutes now reflecting on the extent to which your group or team have bought into these precepts.

It is rare for me to come across a team that has consciously bought into these precepts as the underlying principles of their working together. There have been some who have openly discussed how they work together and have agreed a more or less similar set of principles. Many more claim to operate by them when they are brought to their attention, and some may in fact do so, although these precepts are easier to buy into in principle than they are in practice. In my experience, unless groups are actively engaged in managing their process – i.e. talking about it and doing something about improving it if necessary – then any commitment to the precepts is simply notional, a recognition that they are necessary rather than a desire to use them.

Summary

In this chapter, we have looked at the central tension in group work: the balance between product and process. The natural tendency is to focus on product; but the likelihood is that difficulties will be encountered if there is not enough focus on process. Finding the right balance, resolving the tension, is essential if groups are to work effectively together.

Process is a complex concept. I have broken it down into four distinct levels: procedural, structural, behavioural and social. The levels are arranged in a hierarchy of complexity, the most difficult to observe and resolve being the social level of process, often referred to as the group dynamic.

The four levels of process are a tool I use when I am observing groups in action to help me diagnose problems and identify ways in which I can intervene to help them work more effectively, or at least to start the process of improvement. It is almost always the case that problems at the social level of process will have to be addressed at some point if significant progress is to be made.

Having explored the nature of process in groups and teams, and the ways in which this underpins the operation and activity of the team, the next chapter will look at practical steps that you can take as a manager or team-leader actively to manage and improve process.

ACTIVITY 5.3

Before moving on, spend a few minutes reflecting on Chapter 5. Remember the thoughts, insights or ideas that have occurred to you about you or your group as you have read this chapter. Note down in the space below (or on a separate sheet of paper if you prefer) any of these that you feel it would be useful to record so that you can refer back to them in the future. Some may have helped you to identify things you could do to manage your group more effectively, and a space has been provided to record these separately.

Thoughts and insights   **Actions arising**

6

Managing process

In this chapter, we are going to look at some of the strategies you can use actively to manage and improve the process of your groups or teams, taking each level of process in turn, as follows:

☐ Procedure and effective meetings.

☐ Structure and the maximization of resource.

☐ Behaviour and effective communication.

☐ Social dynamics and a climate of openness.

Procedure and effective meetings

The other day I drove down to Worcester to meet a colleague. We were driving on into Somerset to meet another colleague whose house I had never been to before. I assumed that the colleague I met in Worcester knew the way. He acted as if he knew the way. My confidence in him was only slightly dented when he mistook Bristol for Wells, commenting on the wonder of such a big cathedral in such a small town! We are so different. He would never think of looking at a map before starting a journey. I would never think of starting a journey without first looking at a map. He is a born improviser. He enjoys the process of heading off in the right direction and sorting things out on the way. I prefer to know where I am going and how I am going to get there.

The procedural level of process is this same process of planning a journey before you start. The journey might be a task you do on your own – I plan the main headings for each section of the book before starting to write, for example. It might be an activity you do in a group – I am as keen to plan the process for a meeting as I am the route of a journey. I don't like getting lost. I don't like arriving late. I don't like driving longer than I have to. My friend is more cavalier – an attractive if sometimes infuriating characteristic!

In this section, we are going to apply the simple principle of thinking through what you are going to do before you start doing it to meetings: the microcosm of the group/team existence, often a source of much frustration and alienation in themselves, and often, as we have seen with the case studies in the previous chapter, the arena in which dysfunction in the other levels of process is acted out.

EXERCISE 6.1

Spend a few minutes now reflecting on the meetings (however informal) that you have with your team, or that you attend with other groups at work. How do you feel about these meetings? Are they effective or not? Are some better than others, and if so, why? To what extent is the procedural level of process actively and well managed in these meetings?

It is rare to come across people who haven't attended a 'bad' meeting at some point in their life: a meeting which bored them or frustrated them, from which they came away muttering if not seething with discontent. Some people have only ever experienced such meetings. This is less common than it used to be: most people now have some good experiences to set against the bad. But nevertheless meetings are difficult to get right because they bring a group of people together into a focused arena in which they can act out issues on all four levels of process simultaneously. Although I think there has been a general improvement in the management of the procedural level of process, the other three levels still provide massive scope for disruption.

Generating critical awareness

I will be giving you some practical tools for managing the procedural level of process shortly. Before I do so, however, I want to establish a principle about process management generally: the need to generate critical awareness within the group. This is particularly relevant to meetings. I am struck by how clearly people can articulate the causes of their frustration and dissatisfaction – what is wrong with the meeting – but how rarely they share this analysis with the other people *at* the meeting. They may talk about their feelings afterwards, complaining bitterly to some of the other participants or gossiping about the inadequacies of the chairperson or someone else's arrogance and insensitivity. But they will rarely take the initiative of telling the whole group that they are frustrated with its process.

This is because, in many cases, the tradition and format of the meetings do not allow for any expression of feelings or critique about the meeting itself. This is literally not on the agenda. I am often struck by the extent to which a group of people seem to feel bound by the formality of the proceedings to suffer in silence. They don't feel that they have any right, to criticize the process. They may fear that such criticism would be seen as disrespectful of the chairperson or as a betrayal of their affiliation to the group. Instead, their mounting frustration distorts their behaviour during the meeting, thus making it even less effective, even more frustrating: a cycle of deterioration.

All meetings need feedback from their participants – regular feedback. Even good meetings will benefit, but it is especially important if the meeting is not good. If there is to be any improvement, people's complaints and frustrations need to be voiced and heard and their suggestions need to be considered. Participants in the meeting need to know how their colleagues feel about what is happening, so that they can compare other perceptions with their own. And yet, because the format of the meeting makes it hard for people to give this feedback on their own initiative, and because we are not good at seeking the feedback, valuable information is withheld.

Groups need to find a way of safely and constructively generating critical awareness by legitimizing the giving of feedback about their meetings. We are often unwilling to take the risk of speaking out because it sets us apart from the rest of the group and brings too much focus to bear on us personally. The fact that no one else is voicing any criticism makes us wonder (a) whether we are the only person who is critical and (b) whether anyone else would support us if we expressed it. It is easier to keep quiet, look at your watch and hope that this meeting doesn't go on as long as the last one!

The solution is to reduce the level of focus on any one person, and thus the level of risk, by spreading it equally around the whole group: by giving each person an equal opportunity to say how they feel. This can happen at the end of a meeting: going round the table briefly to hear how people felt about what happened. Or at the beginning: going round the table briefly to hear any concerns that people have about the meeting or any suggestions they want to make about how it is conducted.

This mechanism of gathering feedback on process is so simple and so productive that it is astonishing how few groups actually do it. It is a direct way of raising critical awareness, not just about the procedural level of process, but possibly about the other three levels as well. It seems such an obvious thing to do, but none the less powerful for that. I am frequently surprised by the extent to which it has helped a group I am facilitating to take significant steps forward simply through giving people the opportunity to voice complaints and concerns they have often been holding onto for months.

I encourage groups to add a feedback session onto the agenda of each of their meetings. I call them **process reviews**: five to ten minutes at the end of a meeting when each person in turn is given an opportunity to say how they feel about the meeting that has just taken place and whether they would like the next meeting to be any different.

ACTIVITY 6.1

If you don't already have process reviews (or their equivalent) in your meetings, I strongly recommend that you have one at the end of your next regular meeting with your team. Explain that you want feedback from them about how they feel about the meeting as a way of seeing whether it could be improved in the future. Encourage people to express any dissatisfactions. And be prepared to listen to their feedback without getting too defensive.

Common problems with meetings

It may be that everybody is happy with your meetings and that, if you did do a process review, it would generate an embarrassing round of plaudits to your skills as chairperson and as a manager generally! I hope so. But it is likely that there will be some complaints, reflecting problems commonly experienced in most meetings. These problems can generally be divided into three main groupings, which are:

☐ **Purpose and function:** Either people feel that they didn't need to be at the meeting, or the meeting wasn't necessary in the first place, or it was unclear why there was a meeting or they didn't know what was expected of them beforehand.

☐ **Organization and control:** The meeting was badly organized and poorly controlled: it overran, or there wasn't time to cover all the agenda items; decisions weren't made or were rushed; people digressed, people weren't clear what was happening.

☐ **Behaviour and interaction:** The way that people behaved at the meeting was poor: people didn't listen to each other, interrupted each other, argued unnecessarily; or some people didn't contribute at all, just sat there, or couldn't get a word in.

In Part 3, I will be looking at effective chairing skills specifically and interactive skills generally, which will address the problems not covered here. I am now going to suggest solutions to some of the problems in the first two of these categories, by exploring the following:

☐ The need for meetings.

☐ Functions and agendas.

☐ Managing discussions.

☐ Tools and techniques.

☐ Decision-making.

☐ Recording the output.

The need for meetings

Because so many meetings are deemed to be a waste of time by the people attending them, it is advisable, before setting one up, to ask yourself three sets of questions:

☐ What is the purpose of this meeting? What do I want to happen as a result of it?

☐ Is a meeting the most efficient way of achieving that purpose (are there other options which would be more efficient)?

☐ Are the necessary people going to be there (and are people going to be there who aren't necessary)?

EXERCISE 6.2

Spend a few minutes now reflecting on a meeting that you organized recently. Use the three questions above to assess whether the meeting was necessary and whether the right people were there to achieve its purpose.

We often assume that meetings are the only way to achieve our desired outcome, or that regular meetings that have been going on for some time are still necessary. In many cases, these assumptions are accurate, but sometimes they will be false, especially with the options available through new technology. It is worth assessing carefully whether meetings are necessary and whether there are alternative ways of achieving the intended purpose. Given that meetings are time-consuming, we need to be absolutely sure that the people coming need to be there, both from your point of view and from theirs.

ACTIVITY 6.2

Make a list of all the meetings you have attended at work over the past two to four weeks. Then assess:

☐ How much of your time was spent in these meetings.

☐ How many of them were absolutely necessary.

☐ What the consequences would have been if any of these meetings had not taken place.

☐ If any of them could have achieved their purpose in less time-consuming ways.

Functions and agendas

Meetings are generally called to fulfil one or more of the following three functions:

☐ **Information exchange:** To get information to a group of people who need to know it.

☐ **Issue resolution:** To enable a group of people to come together to discuss, analyze and resolve problems and issues.

☐ **Decision-making:** To enable a group of people to review data, evaluate options and make decisions.

Some meetings have only one of these functions. Team briefings, for example, usually only have the function of information exchange meetings, which is why (unless the information is riveting stuff) they can be so unpopular with the people who have to attend. But most meetings will have a combination of all three functions: there may be some necessary information exchange – progress reports, status checks, etc. – there will be some issues that need to be discussed if not fully resolved, and there will be some decisions that need to be made.

Each of these three different functions requires particular contributions and behaviour from participants. Information exchange requires the concise presentation of information for people to listen to and understand. Issue resolution requires disciplined analysis and creativity; decision-making requires careful evaluation, clear reaction, initiative and decisiveness.

One of the problems with meetings is that they don't always make a clear distinction between these three types of function, so that people are unsure what contribution they should be making and how they should be behaving. For example, a structured information exchange can be disrupted because an issue emerges which people start trying to resolve (this is generally more interesting and engaging). The meeting can lose shape and discipline as a result: it becomes increasingly difficult to return to the original structure and complete the information exchange; and because the switch in mode has not been clearly signalled, no effective process has been established for how best to resolve the issue.

This is partly a problem with discipline: people controlling their contribution. It is also partly an issue for the chairperson, who should be making sure that such digressions do not disrupt the meeting. But it is also sometimes caused by the fact that people are not clear what is expected of them with each agenda item. And this is because most agendas are under-written and do not contain the information that people need to prepare for and contribute to meetings effectively.

In most cases, agendas just list the items that are to be discussed at the meeting in the order in which this will happen. They sometimes include the anticipated length of time that each item is intended to take. Here is a typical agenda from one of my team meetings when I was working with my previous company:

Agenda

1	Matters arising	15'
2	Account review	20'
3	Sales activity	15'
4	Forecasts	15'
5	Resourcing issues	20'
6	Marketing strategy	30'
7	Materials development	30'
8	Associates	20'
9	Any other business	15'

Like most agendas, this is written in a shorthand most of which will be unintelligible to most people. But its main shortcoming is that it doesn't make clear what the function of each item is, and so we don't know what is expected of us. All we know is that it is going to last three hours, except that, if previous experience is anything to go by, it will be more like four and we still won't have covered everything!

Here is an alternative way of preparing an agenda which contains two additional pieces of information which may be useful to the people attending the meeting. These are:

☐ **Outputs:** The *output* that you want to achieve from discussing a particular agenda item. This could be described simply in terms of its function (e.g. information exchange), or could be a more specific description.

Agenda	Output	Input	Time
1 Matters arising	Information only	Last meeting's minutes	15'
2 Account review	Information only	Account status report	20'
3 Sales activity	Information only	Next two months' calls	15'
4 Forecasts	Information only	Forecast sheets	15'
5 Resourcing issues	Problem-solving	Diaries!!	20'
6 Marketing strategy	Decide next year's priorities	Views on last year/ Ideas for next	30'
7 Materials development	Decide strategy, roles timings for TWS	Think through your own preferences	30'
8 Associates	Discuss problems with development	Discuss with associates if possible	20'
9 Any other business	??	Let me know before-hand if possible	15'

Figure 6.1 Full agenda showing outputs and inputs.

☐ **Inputs:** The *input* you want people to make to the discussion of each agenda item. This might be things that you want them to bring to the meeting or preparatory work that they need to do beforehand.

Figure 6.1 illustrates the same agenda again, this time describing the intended outputs and the required inputs.

An agenda like this is far more dynamic and functional, providing useful information in a format that helps people to prepare for the meeting and hopefully avoid those embarrassing situations when (as happened frequently to me) you forget to bring the forecast sheets and have to go back to the office to find them. There is no guarantee that people will prepare in the way you suggest – there is no guarantee that they'll even look at the agenda before the meeting – but it does increase the likelihood of people coming with clearer expectations and the necessary paperwork.

ACTIVITY 6.3

Write an agenda for the next meeting that you are organizing, including the outputs and inputs for each agenda item.

You may feel that your meetings don't require such formal or extensive agendas as the format I am suggesting. Or it may be that you don't establish an agenda before the meeting, either because it is determined by a pre-established format or because the group generate the agenda together at the beginning. I accept that the output/input format will not work for every meeting. I do feel, however, that the principle of clarifying the output for each agenda item is important (as you will see in the next section). If agendas are generated at the beginning of a meeting, I recommend that groups write this up on a flip chart, clearly indicating at least the function for each agenda item. This is likely to save time later on.

Managing discussions

Organizing the agenda proactively will help meetings to run more efficiently and for the discussion of items to be more disciplined. But these discussions will still need to be structured and managed effectively if they are to achieve the intended output within the intended time. And structuring discussions is something that, in my experience, people find extraordinarily difficult to do. This is partly because people don't like spending time on process, as we have seen; but it is also because, for some reason, most people don't naturally discuss issues in structured and rational ways.

Agendas again are part of the problem. Agendas like the one in Figure 6.1 provide people with a trigger word for each item: marketing strategy, for example. This provides a starting-point for a discussion but no more – the trigger is pulled, the starting pistol fires, and we're off! People jump in with their own interpretation of what a discussion on marketing strategy should involve, their own thoughts and feelings about the issues – with little thought for where they are going and how they are going to get there. One person says marketing is a waste of time, someone else says what they want to happen next year, someone else slams what happened this year – all at the same time.

EXERCISE 6.3

Spend a few minutes now reflecting on the last meeting you attended. How structured was the discussion of each agenda item? Was there an attempt to plan the discussion before it started, or did people tend to jump in in the way I have described above?

If discussion of an issue is going to deliver the intended output, it is likely that some kind of plan or structure needs to be established before people become too heavily involved in the content. The following three steps will help you to structure any discussion more effectively:

☐ **Define the end point:** Define a specific end point for the discussion: the exact output that you want to have achieved by the end of it. The more

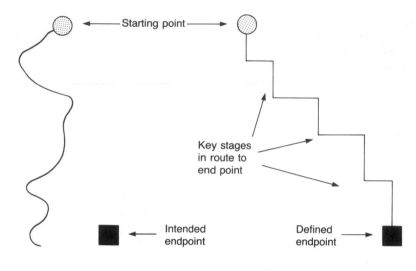

Figure 6.2 Structuring a discussion.

precise the target you establish from the beginning, the more likely you are to reach it efficiently.

☐ **Map the route:** Once you have identified the end point, you will be able to identify the steps the discussion needs to go through in order to reach the end point in the most effective way. There may be several steps which together provide a structured process, so that each agenda item has its own sub-agenda.

☐ **Manage the time:** Once you have mapped the route, you can decide how you are going to manage the time to ensure that you reach your end point in the time you have available. This might involve allocating time to each leg of the route, or appointing someone to manage the time on the group's behalf.

Figure 6.2 illustrates how a defined end point provides an anchor for a discussion and makes possible the planning of an effective route. Without a defined end point, the discussion is likely to wander at random, and will often fail to achieve the intended end point. For example, if we apply the marketing strategy item from the agenda used earlier, the structure for the discussion could look like this:

☐ **End point:** 'A list of priorities and recommended actions to present to the management team which we are all committed to.'

☐ **Route:**

(a) review last year's strategies to identify strengths and weaknesses;

    (b) review two-year business picture to explore needs;
    (c) brainstorm possible priorities;
    (d) select three priorities;
    (e) discuss possible strategies/approaches;
    (f) agree preferred strategies.

☐ **Time mgt:**

    ☐ Must start brainstorm in fifteen minutes latest;
    ☐ Sally to keep eye on time and cut discussion on (a) if it goes on too long.

Spending a few minutes at the beginning of an agenda item to structure the discussion in this way is likely to make it more focused, more disciplined and more productive. And it should only take a few minutes, especially when you are used to doing it. Defining the end point can sometimes be surprisingly difficult, the group may not agree easily on the best route – but generally, time spent structuring the discussion saves time. If there is disagreement about the end point, it is better that this is resolved at the beginning of the discussion than realized at the end of it. I always feel that if a group cannot agree on process, they are not likely to agree on the product either!

ACTIVITY 6.4

Take one item from the agenda that you wrote in Activity 6.3 and plan a structure for the discussion of that agenda item, first defining your end point and then identifying the steps you need to go through to achieve this end point.

Tools and techniques

I once had the privilege of observing a group of Total Quality facilitators from a large British corporation having a discussion about problems they were experiencing in their work. They decided to use some of the problem-solving techniques they had learnt on their facilitator training and were now teaching to the Quality Teams they facilitated. To my unconcealed and unashamed glee, they spent thirty minutes following a red herring (well, they were using the fishbone technique!), a fact that they realized in the twenty-eighth minute. They had not spent enough time deciding what they needed to 'fishbone', and so their analysis was unfocused and largely irrelevant. Not only that, one member of the group – a woman who had been particularly difficult earlier in the day – tried to point this out to them at the beginning of the discussion, but because she had generated such hostility through her earlier behaviour, they wouldn't listen to her.

I love this story. It beautifully illustrates two key learning-points:

☐ Tools and techniques like brainstorming and fishboning are not a substitute for a good structure. They may have a place in such a structure, but they are not a structure in their own right.

☐ Tension at the social level of process (the group's hostility to the woman) will have a disastrous effect on the procedural level of process if it is not resolved.

Personally, I mistrust the various tools and techniques that came to prominence with the Total Quality movement as a way of helping teams to manage the numerous meetings and discussions that it generated. This is partly because these tools are used as a substitute for structure and so get in the way of good structuring; partly because they often overcomplicate the quite simple requirements of a discussion; and partly because so often they are used badly, as in my example of the group of facilitators.

The most popular tool, and one that people often latch onto recklessly, is brainstorming. I have seen countless groups waste precious time by using brainstorming inappropriately. They know the rules – they carry them out diligently. What they don't know is how to locate the tool appropriately within a structured discussion. They tend to use it too early, before they have explored the issues sufficiently in order to give the brainstorm the right focus and to be clear about what they are going to do with the results. If you are to use brainstorming, you must make sure that the steps before and after it in the structure are in place and provide focus and purpose.

Decision-making

If the function of the meeting, or of some of its agenda items, is to make decisions, then the group needs to be clear about how it is going to make these decisions. It is surprising how often this is not discussed until serious disagreement occurs. But it is a key part of the procedural level of process and one that can have a serious impact on the group dynamic, especially in teams, because a decision-making procedure is one of the ways in which the group manages the levels of influence and the distribution of power among its members.

There are three main ways in which decisions get made in meetings:

☐ The senior manager/team-leader is the decision-maker. The function of the meeting is to help them make the right decision, but the ultimate authority and accountability rest with them. They may use a strong consultative style in reaching their decision, but it is still their decision.

☐ A majority of the group is the decision-maker. This may be managed through a formal voting system (show of hands) or through a more informal checking out or sensing of the mood of the group. The function of the meeting is for different perspectives to be aired and debated sufficiently for each member of the group to be clear about what the choices are and what their preference is.

☐ The whole group is the decision-maker. Decisions are made through consensus, so that every member of the group agrees with the outcome. The function of the meeting is to arrive at a formula which meets at least some of the criteria of everyone, negotiating concessions if necessary until a compromise solution is reached.

EXERCISE 6.5

Spend a few minutes now, using the questions below, to reflect on the ways in which the group you manage makes decisions:

☐ Has the decision-making process ever been discussed and agreed by you and the group?

☐ Which of the three methods outlined above best describes your team's decision-making process?

☐ How happy do you think people are with this process?

☐ How effective is it in making quality decisions to which the whole group are committed?

In most teams, the decision-making process emerges without open discussion or agreement. People assume that the team-leader makes the decisions or else drift into an uneasy mix of consensus or majority rule. Sometimes the need to clarify the process is forced on the group because of a failure to resolve an issue which provokes strong disagreement. Few teams, in my experience, make conscious choices about decision-making, and those that do often find that what they have agreed rationally is not upheld when the chips are down.

All three ways of making decisions have their strengths and weaknesses. Their appropriateness and effectiveness will depend on circumstances, especially the composition of the group or team and the number of people in it with high levels of influence. There are two key principles to bear in mind:

☐ It is best to agree a decision-making procedure before you have to start making decisions (although, as this is a decision in itself, you will already have started). It will be easier to reach agreement when discussing the issue in abstract, rather than under pressure. Such a discussion will inevitably raise issues concerning the unwritten constitution of the group, and may take some time, but it is better for this to happen in a calm and focused way rather than as a result of possibly heated disagreement over a work issue.

☐ No decision-making procedure is more powerful than the group dynamic in the same way that no official structure is more powerful than the unofficial structure (see Chapter 2). The people with power and influence will find ways of subverting the agreed procedure if they need to (that is one of the attributes of a high level of influence). So agreeing how to make decisions is not a solution to tensions in the group dynamic. The agreement is valid, but the tensions will still need to be resolved if it is to be sustained under pressure.

Recording the output

Very few people like taking the minutes in a meeting. They don't want the responsibility of keeping an accurate record. They certainly don't appreciate the work involved during and after the meeting. And most importantly, they don't like the effect it has on their involvement in the meeting: it is hard to participate fully when you are taking the minutes as well. On top of this, few people know how to take minutes well. They either write too much or too little, they are often inaccurate and the finished record frequently doesn't tally with other people's memory of what was agreed or discussed at the meeting.

So it is important to establish the procedure for recording the output of your meetings. Three factors need to be taken into consideration. They are:

☐ **The kind of record that is needed:** For example, do you just need a list of actions agreed or do you need a record of the discussion of agenda items?

☐ **The level of detail required:** For example, how much information about a decision or discussion is it useful to record – it is usually more important for minutes to be readable than fully comprehensive.

☐ **The existing material that could be used:** For example, photocopies of the slides used in a presentation, the notes made as preparation for a status report, etc.

EXERCISE 6.6

Spend a few minutes now reflecting on how records are kept of your meetings at work. Do they provide the kind of information that people want and will refer to? Who does them and are they happy with their role? Has there been any attempt to define the requirement and to discuss how best to meet it?

I may be unusual, but I don't think I've ever read carefully and thoroughly the detailed minutes of a meeting that I've attended. I skim read them, I check the action points, I look guiltily for the actions against my name in the sure knowledge that I probably haven't done them yet. But anything over two pages long and I've decided by the time I have lifted it from my in-tray that it is not a high priority. The record of the output of a meeting has to be functional, i.e. the content must meet the needs of the people who are going to read it and the format must make it easy for them to read it. Pages of dense text providing a detailed account of a meeting rarely meet either of these two criteria.

One option for taking the minutes is to build it into the meeting's procedure in such a way that it helps to ensure that people are clear about what has been said and agreed. This can be done by summarizing on a flip chart the key decisions or discussion points at the end of each agenda item. The flip charts can then be typed up or photocopied easily after the meeting. This method has a number of benefits, as it:

☐ Slows down the pace of the meeting by building in 'breathing spaces' which clearly mark the end of one agenda item and the beginning of the next.

☐ Ensures that there is a shared understanding of the output of the discussion of each agenda item.

☐ Means that the minute-taker can take part in the discussions because there is dedicated time for recording output.

☐ Ensures that the group, because they have been involved in generating the summary, have bought in to the accuracy and value of the minutes.

Even if the specifics of this option do not fit your requirements, the principle of incorporating the minute-taking as a dynamic part of the procedure of the meeting is one that is worth considering.

Structure and the maximization of resource

So far in this chapter, I have focused on the procedural level of process, looking specifically at four aspects of the management of meetings: setting the agenda; structuring the discussion; making decisions and recording the output. I have taken it for granted that you, as team-leader or manager, are the person responsible for managing your team meetings. We are now going to turn to the structural level of process, which concerns the roles people adopt within the group.

In Chapter 2, I explained the difference between two parallel structures:

☐ The **official** structure which designates the formal responsibilities that people have within the group.

☐ The **unofficial** structure formed by the roles people assume within the group, based on their personal resources (a mix of expertise, energy, control and influence).

When the difference between these two parallel structures is significant, a tension is generated which makes it difficult for the group to make best use of the resources at its disposal and which will contribute to problems at the social level of process. In this section, I am going to look at ways of managing the group structure in order to maximize the resource: i.e. make best use of the people in the team to ensure that they contribute to their full potential. I am going to focus on two key resources, as follows:

☐ Control and the management of process.

☐ Expertise and the contribution to product.

EXERCISE 6.7

Spend a few minutes now reflecting on the extent to which your team allocates responsibilities appropriately, i.e. in accordance with the resources people bring to the group. Specifically:

☐ Is the person who manages the process the most skilled process manager in the group?

☐ Are the people with most expertise most influential in achieving the group's product?

Generating critical awareness

As with all the four levels of process, the key to effective management is a critical awareness within the group of the issues that exist and that might need to be resolved. It can be difficult, however, to raise critical awareness of the structural issues. People are often unwilling to reflect on the distribution of power within a group (and structural issues are usually about power in one form or another). Exposing the inevitable inequalities in the distribution of power can be uncomfortable, especially for those who are less powerful. To avoid this reality, some teams invest considerable energy in convincing themselves that their members all have equal power, but this is rarely actually the case. The energy spent denying inequality would be better spent in understanding its impact on the team process in order to manage it more effectively.

The other reason why critical awareness of structural issues tends to be low is that the issues generally revolve around the leadership of the team. This is clearly central to the issue of power. But also, if the team-leader is responsible in the official structure for controlling the group process, they may not be eager to invite exploration of the effectiveness of their leadership, their use of the power that comes with their position and their ability to manage process. I have known managers to invite feedback from their teams, and this is a good step. But it is different from engaging with the team in a review of the tension between official and unofficial structures, and the extent to which people's personal resources match the responsibilities they have within the team.

If the team-leader, or senior manager, or chairperson is not aware of process issues, and is not good at managing process, it is unlikely that they will perceive the need to raise critical awareness and, if they do, it is unlikely that they will know how to do it. So unless there are other members of the group or team who have the awareness, the skills, the confidence and the influence, the leader's shortcomings will act as a block to any review of process. However, if the leader is willing and able, or if there are other people in the group who can take the initiative, the following exercise will help to raise the group's critical awareness of the structural issues at work:

□ Ask each member of the group to rank everybody under the headings of the four key resources (expertise, energy, control, influence). The person at the top of the list should have the highest level of that resource, the person at the bottom the lowest.

□ Use these lists as the basis for discussion among the group, first exploring the differences between them, then comparing official and unofficial structures and discussing the possible tensions that emerge between them.

CASE STUDY Gavin's team

When I did this exercise with Gavin's team (see earlier case studies), the following pattern was quickly agreed:

Expertise	Energy	Control	Influence
Paul	Alastair	Paul	Gavin
Gavin	John	Simon	Alastair
Alastair	Paul	Gavin	Paul
John	Simon	Mary	John
Simon	Mary	John	Simon
Mary	Gavin	Alastair	Mary

This is a picture of the group's unofficial structure. It would be difficult to tell, just from looking at the table, what the *official* structure was – and this of course was one of the problems. We know that Gavin was the leader, but the table indicates how uncomfortable he was with some of the responsibilities of the position. The table also shows that he has a healthy distribution of resources within the group as a whole if he could harness them effectively: particularly Paul's control resource and Alastair's energy. (In fact, Gavin was delegating responsibility for control to Alastair, seduced by his high level of energy – and so ignoring his low level of control, which made him inappropriate for the responsibilities being delegated to him.)

ACTIVITY 6.5

Do the exercise suggested above on your own group or team (i.e. list people under each of the four resources, arranged with the most resourceful at the top of the list and the least at the bottom). Consider the issues this raises for you about the extent to which the available resources are deployed and the match between official and unofficial structures.

If you feel it is appropriate, ask all the members of your team to do the exercise as a way of raising critical awareness about structural issues and dynamics within the group.

Control and the management of process

As I did in the previous section on managing the procedural level of process, I am again going to use the meeting as a microcosm for group process and explore the control of meetings as a metaphor for control within the team as a whole. It is here that the issues of control are most overt and also most difficult to resolve. For invariably the person controlling the process of a meeting is the senior manager or team-leader, the person who probably called the meeting and has most investment in it achieving a successful product. In other words, the meeting is an arena when the official structure is operating explicitly, regardless of the patterns of resource within the unofficial structure. And it is an arena where the person with most investment in product is also the one controlling the process.

As we saw earlier, in Chapter 3, controlling both product and process during a meeting often results in the leader dominating proceedings to such an extent that people feel either frustrated with the process or with their ability to influence product. And yet in most meetings, this is exactly what happens: the chairperson, the official 'process manager', is also the person with the highest investment in the content being discussed and in the decisions being made. Apart from the risk of dominating the meeting, it is also almost impossible to manage process effectively when you are heavily involved in the content of the discussion. This presents most managers and team-leaders with a serious problem: How can they avoid dominating the meeting? If they focus on managing process, how can they guarantee the outcome they want? And if they focus on the content, how can they guarantee that the process of the meeting is managed efficiently?

How can I avoid dominating the meeting? The answer to this, as I described in general terms in Chapter 3, is to separate process from product (the content of the discussion), and to decide before each meeting – or if necessary, before each agenda item – which of the two most needs your involvement. The advantages of managing the process to ensure group commitment to a decision, for example, may outweigh your need to determine what that decision should be.

If you feel you have to get involved in the content, either because you have information or opinions that the group need to hear, or because you want to influence the group to make a certain decision and you can't be sure that they will make that decision without your involvement – then get involved. It will be best, though, if you relinquish control of the process (see question 3).

If, on the other hand, you feel that your direct involvement in content is not needed by the group, then you can afford to disengage from it and focus on managing the process of the meeting to enable people to discuss the issues in the most productive way. It will be best, though, if you keep any involvement in the content to an absolute minimum, for the reasons already discussed.

If I focus on managing process, how can I guarantee the outcome I want? If you are like most managers, you won't like relinquishing your influence over the outcome of a meeting in order to focus on managing the process. You will be concerned that the group might make a decision you fundamentally disagree with, or that people might not have the expertise required, or just that they might not be able to get by without you! These concerns actually represent two areas of mistrust:

☐ You don't trust the group to work effectively together without your contribution to the content of the discussion.

☐ You don't trust your own ability to manage the process in order to help the group to work effectively together.

Control and influence are both forms of power: what we are talking about here is what form of power you need to be exercising. They can be of equal force – but they have different impacts. They are options. You can control the outcome of a discussion through the way you manage process. This won't be the same as exercising your influence over the content – but it can be just as effective and, in certain situations, even more effective.

I have seen maybe three or four really excellent chairpeople in my time: all of them focused on managing the process, disengaging from the content except when absolutely necessary, and ensuring that the outcomes arrived at were ones that they were comfortable with. And the group felt the opposite of dominated: they felt empowered to debate issues and make decisions, and their commitment to them was all the greater as a result.

So it is possible to focus on process without losing power, because the way you control process can itself have a major influence over the way issues are debated and decisions made. But this requires a high level of process management skill, as well as an ability to resist the temptation to dive into content when things get sticky. We will be looking closely at these skills in Part 3.

If I focus on the content, how can I guarantee that the process of the meeting is managed efficiently? There will be times when you have to get involved in the content. The question then arises: Who manages the process? If you do it, it is unlikely that you will be able to do it well because your focus will inevitably be mainly on the content. So you need to ask yourself: Is there anybody else in the group who can manage the process for me, freeing me to get involved in the content as much as I like?

There are three factors to consider here:

☐ Does anybody have the skills to manage process effectively (people with a high level of control resource)?

☐ Can they also afford not to be directly involved in the content of the discussion?

☐ Will the rest of the group respect their authority if they chair the discussion?

If the answer to these three questions is yes, then it should be possible to ask that person to chair that meeting, or that agenda item, on your behalf. If there isn't anybody, then the solution is more complex and difficult to execute. You will unfortunately both have to manage process and get involved in the content, an awkward double-act. It is likely that there will be times during the meeting when you can stand back and just manage the process, and others where your involvement is essential. The knack is to let the group know which mode you are in, clearly signalling, for example, that you are just going to manage the process for a while, or that you can't contain yourself any longer and are going to join in the discussion. Signalling in this way helps the group to recognize and adapt to your change in role, thus allowing you to move in and out of the content without causing confusion or misunderstanding.

ACTIVITY 6.6

Identify a meeting or discussion that you will be 'chairing' in the near future. Decide how you can best manage your involvement in both product and process. Should you focus on managing the process, thus enabling the group to achieve the product? Do you need to get involved in the content and, if so, is there anyone else in the group who could manage the process for you?

The last team-meeting I attended before I left to go freelance was due to be chaired by my replacement as team-leader, a woman who had been part of the team up to that point. There were several difficult issues which needed to be discussed, issues that she wanted to have a direct and powerful influence over. She asked me to chair the meeting for her. This was a brave move in the circumstances, as she was passing up an opportunity to symbolize the change in leadership; but it was also a smart move for I had very little investment in the issues being discussed – the decisions the group had to make weren't going to affect me. Therefore I was the person best placed to manage the process.

Once you realize that it is possible to separate the two forms of power – control and influence – and are comfortable with influencing the outcome through controlling the process, you have options to exercise as a chairperson/team-leader. You are able to ask yourself: What role do I need to play at this meeting? Do I need to focus on process or product or both? And you are able to adapt your style and set the expectations of the group accordingly.

Expertise and the contribution to product

On some of our teamwork programmes, we use a generic exercise to raise several issues about how groups use their internal resources, focusing especially on the use of expertise and influence. Common themes have emerged from the countless times that I have observed this exercise being carried out:

☐ There are people who have the necessary expertise but who either withhold it from the group or are unable to use it to influence the group effectively.

- People who have a high level of influence and a low level of expertise can go to extraordinary lengths to exert influence – fabricating arguments based on completely bogus rationality. And they often get their own way.

- There are people who are given authority by the group because of their expertise – which seems valid – but who then lead the group in the wrong direction. And the group allows this, suppressing any misgivings, because they are in awe of the person's expertise.

EXERCISE 6.8

Spend a few minutes now reflecting on the extent to which these three observations tally with your experiences at work. Have there been times when either you or other people have behaved in the ways described above?

I can think of situations at work when I have done all of those: failed to influence when I had expertise; influencing when I had none; influencing when I was wrong, because people believed I knew what I was talking about. I am sure that it happens all the time: people with a high need for admiration are probably the worst offenders! Just as it is important to maximize the use of the control resource within the group, it is essential to use the expertise resource effectively in relation to the influence resource. For this to happen, the group needs to acknowledge and understand:

- The extent to which each member has relevant and necessary expertise.

- The relationship between their expertise and their influence within the group.

Although reviewing expertise is usually straightforward, discussions about influence are more difficult as they touch on the distribution of power within the group. In the case of Gavin's team, for example, Paul's expertise, although greater than Alastair's, was far less influential because of Alastair's high level of energy and Paul's disinclination to take Alastair on. There were times when this was OK, but also times when it wasn't: when Paul needed to have more influence over the group's decisions. One of the ways the group dynamic worked was that Alastair, in order to retain power, found ways to devalue Paul's expertise in the eyes of the group, thus making it less influential.

The relationship between expertise, energy and influence is a complex one that frequently requires somebody with a high level of control to manage it effectively. It is usually necessary to address the issues when the group is having to make a decision or debate an agenda item at a meeting. In these instances, the group will have to face and answer three questions:

□ Who has the most expertise to help the group to make a good-quality decision?

□ Do they have an appropriate level of influence within the group at this moment?

□ If not, how can we assure that they do have the influence to match their expertise?

ACTIVITY 6.7

Using the meeting or discussion that you identified in Activity 6.6, answer these three questions, focusing on one or two of the agenda items that will be addressed.

The three questions are straightforward in themselves, but they can be difficult for a group to answer successfully. They are vital to ensuring the maximization of the expertise resource in order to achieve a good-quality product. But as with many structural issues, the questions reach into the murky depths of the social level of process – the group dynamic – and either people will resist the move into that arena or, once in it, will resist rational attempts to resolve tensions in the dynamic. We will look at both of these barriers later in this chapter.

Behaviour and effective communication

The behavioural level of process, more than any of the other levels, determines how effectively people communicate with each other. The procedural level will give a discussion structure and direction, but the discussion still has to happen, and poor behavioural skills will disrupt or undermine any procedure, however well established. Similarly, a group may have no problems at the structural level but still have problems communicating with each other, because the way people behave, or the way the group interacts when together, is not effective. With some of the groups I facilitate, the level of dysfunctionality at the behavioural level is so extreme that it has to be resolved before work at the other levels becomes possible.

Part 3 of this book examines behavioural skills in the group context in detail. This section therefore will focus on the raising of awareness at the behavioural level. There are two causes of behavioural dysfunction in groups: one is turbulence at the social level of process which generates a pressure that distorts people's normal behaviour; the other is a general lack of interactive skills which means that people aren't able to interact in groups effectively. In either case, the first step is to raise awareness, at both an individual and group level, of how behaviour is impacting on communication. If the problem is solely group dynamics, then this raising of awareness will probably lead to an immediate improvement at the behavioural level as well as providing a basis for intervention at the social level. If the problem is lack of skills, then raising of awareness is the first step in a process of skill development.

Generating critical awareness

Few people have a high level of awareness of how they are behaving when they are interacting with others. When you are focusing on the 'what', it is hard to focus on the 'how'. And because in most interactions we are more concerned with what we are saying than how we are saying it, we tend to be unaware of our behaviour most of the time. This is the same problem that a chairperson has when they become involved in product: their awareness of process is instantly reduced.

When we are interacting in groups, there are two factors: one is our own behavioural style – the way we tend to interact in most situations – the other is the way that the different behavioural styles of the people involved generate a behavioural norm for the group which affects our natural behaviour. We both influence and are influenced by the group norm – some members of the team will exert their influence actively (people with high influence and/or energy); others will exert their influence passively, by accepting (or at least not rejecting) the norm as it emerges and develops.

Groundrules

The group norm can be described as a set of *groundrules* which dictate what is and what is not acceptable behaviour in a group. For example:

It is OK to turn up late for meetings.
It is OK to interrupt each other all the time.
It is OK to gossip about people behind their backs.

It is not OK to tease people.

It is not OK to say what you think.

Groundrules like these are not usually openly acknowledged among the group, but they are nonetheless there and powerfully underpin the ways in which people interact with each other. They start to form the minute that a group of people come together for the first time. People check out the levels of the key resources and the extent to which their natural behavioural style is going to be acceptable in this new environment. They adjust, deciding whether to compete or not, exploring the ways in which they are going to get their needs for recognition met by the group. In this period of exploration and adjustment, the groundrules are formed. By the time this initial period in the group's life is over, these 'unwritten' groundrules have taken on an authority over the group behaviour which is all the more surprising given that in most cases it has never been openly discussed and reviewed.

EXERCISE 6.9

Spend a few minutes now reflecting on the groundrules that exist within your group or team. These may be 'unwritten' groundrules which have never been openly discussed and agreed, but which have emerged naturally during the life of the group.

All groups have a set of groundrules and there is an endless variety of groundrules that they could have. Of the ones that I have come across with the groups that I work with, my favourite is: 'Never accept responsibility if something goes wrong' (next on the list was: 'it is essential to blame somebody else'!). So if you found the exercise difficult, it is not because your group doesn't have them, it is because they are difficult to spot. It is worth trying again: this time think of another group that you belong to (outside work if necessary) and ask yourself the question: Do I behave differently in this second group to the way I behave in the first? And if so, how and why?

You may have found that your group's groundrules were mainly positive and that the exercise helped you to clarify why the group worked well together. However, it is likely that some of the groundrules you identified were more negative. Most groups are a mix of the two: some groundrules which help the group to work effectively, others which are counter-productive or even destructive. The problem with groundrules, especially when they are unwritten (i.e. unacknowledged by the group) is that people tend to regard them as inevitable: this is the way the group is; this is the way we behave; this is the way things are. Because they become firmly established as the group settles down in the initial forming period, the unwritten groundrules can take on considerable authority, to the extent that people assume that this is how everybody wants the team to operate. Even if they find a particular groundrule uncomfortable or oppressive, they assume that it is not OK to challenge it. (This often becomes one of the groundrules: it is not OK to challenge the unwritten groundrules.) When people talk about the power of the group norm, this is what they mean: the power of a group's unwritten groundrules to dictate behaviour and override the feelings and judgement of the group's individual members.

So a key aspect of managing process in groups and teams is to bring these unwritten groundrules to the surface so that they can be identified, reviewed and, if necessary, changed. To write them, literally, as opposed to leaving them unwritten.

ACTIVITY 6.8

Involve your group in a **groundrules review**, as follows:

- ☐ Together generate a list of the groundrules that people feel underpin group behaviour at the moment (you could ask people to draw up their own list or brainstorm in full group or a combination of the two).
- ☐ Ask people to assess which of these groundrules they feel are positive and which are negative.
- ☐ Discuss any changes that people would like to make to the existing groundrules.
- ☐ Explore whether there are any additional groundrules that people would like.
- ☐ Plan how the group could make the changes and additions that have been suggested.
- ☐ Get people's commitment to trying to work to the new groundrules.

The main function of this activity is to raise the group's awareness of its groundrules and to sensitize people both to the impact of their behaviour and to the needs of other members of the group. This can be a transforming experience: there are times when it is all I've needed to do. It is astonishing how the assumed inevitability of unwritten groundrules can cause people to accept conditions at work which they actually find insufferable. When I have done this exercise with dysfunctional groups and they have written up on a flip chart a list of negative and hurtful groundrules, it has been embarrassing sometimes for people to acknowledge that this is how they've been working together for some time. In the case of the group (two teams who had to collaborate with each other) with the groundrules 'Never accept responsibility if something goes wrong' and 'It is essential to blame somebody else' (the other one I remember from this group was 'If there's a problem, pass it to the other team'), this had been going on for years, literally twenty years of unsupportiveness, mistrust, competitiveness and blame. They reeled off these groundrules as if to say: What else do you expect? What other way of working is there? I couldn't believe it. I asked them: Is that the kind of relationship you want between the two departments? Is that the way you want to work together? Of course, they said no. But the groundrule of not accepting responsibility was so deeply engrained by now that they didn't see it as their fault and assumed that there was nothing they could do about it. This is the clearest example I have had yet of the unwritten groundrules being assumed to be inevitable.

The action of writing the groundrules initiates a process of change within the group. There is no turning back from the open, full-group acknowledgement of the unconscious choices that have been made. Even if all you do is expose the unwritten groundrules – have no discussion afterwards, just leave them on the flip chart – things will start to change. The people who were oppressed by them will feel more able to challenge them. The people who were oppressive will moderate their behaviour. And this shift, however small, however subtle, generates a momentum which can transform the climate of the team, the way people relate to each other and the effectiveness of their communication.

The exercise can be taken further by asking the group to generate the kind of groundrules that they would like to have underpinning the way people behave. This encourages groups to generate positive statements and images for how they would like things to be. It can be a very powerful device, especially if there are individuals who need support to assert themselves within the group, for such an exercise provides a low-risk, low-focus way for them to do so. A wish list of ideal groundrules is only ever going to be notional – there are no sanctions if people don't abide by it. But it does provide the group with a reference point and will hopefully give people the confidence to assert themselves against the group norm or challenge individuals when necessary.

Social dynamics and a climate of openness

The social level of process is the most difficult one to address. It involves aspects of self and of relationships between selves which people usually prefer not to bring out into the open: the needs and motivations that shape our contribution, our behaviour and our perceptions of and attitudes towards other people. It is hard to get a clear picture of a group's dynamics, because the picture is always a complex and entangled web of feelings and connections. A group, like a family, produces strong emotional reactions and intense relationships, frustrations and resentments, attractions and alliances. Sometimes, the social dynamic is healthy and provides a sound basis for teamwork and collaboration; sometimes it isn't, and can provide a recipe for disaster. Either way, it needs attention, it needs to be nurtured, because the nature of a group's dynamic is constantly shifting. There is no room for complacency.

The key to managing the social level of process is a climate of openness within the group. People need to feel able to discuss the issues that arise in their relationships with each other, to confront and resolve problems, to help each other learn how to relate and work better together, to learn how to accept and respect the ways in which people differ from them. And to do this, they need to feel that it is safe to express their feelings, to take risks in challenging other people and that they can do this without transgressing the group's groundrules, and without fear of ostracization or retaliation. Such a climate is difficult to create – and once created, is easy to destroy. In this section, we are going to look at how to create an open climate in order to manage the social level of process.

Generating openness

Critical awareness of what is going on at the social level of process depends on people being open. The group dynamic is formed by the interconnection of people's feelings about each other, and feelings are invisible. You might think you know how someone feels about you, or about other members of the team, but this is only your fantasy – you may be convinced that you are right, that you *know*. But this is only your fantasy, influenced as much by your feelings about yourself and your feelings about the other person as by whatever they have done to lead you to think that way. Unless people tell you what they are feeling, you will never know for sure. In order to generate critical awareness of the social dynamic, people have to be open about the way they feel about the group and about each other.

Openness is a word that often crops up when I do work on groundrules with groups. It has an almost talismanic quality, as if just saying it will create an open climate by itself. People know that openness is a good thing, a necessary prerequisite to effective teamwork, but rarely do they specify what they mean by it. Open about what? How open? Totally open? What does totally open mean to you? Openness comes in layers: as trust grows in your relationship with someone, you feel safe to peel away another layer, to take the risk of exposing a bit more of yourself, you become more open with them, sharing more of your thoughts and feelings – about them, about yourself, about other people, about events that have happened to you. The opportunity to do this, to unburden yourself of your secrets, is what makes relationships so exciting and rewarding, and also so dangerous, because the more you expose, the more vulnerable you become.

Groups and teams need to find the right level of openness in order to manage their social dynamic, and it is identifying and achieving this that is so difficult. In Chapter 1, I said that one of the differences between groups and teams is that teams require a higher level of openness than groups, because people are more dependent on each other to meet their objectives and to carry out their daily activity. The greater the dependency, the greater the likelihood for intense relationships and the greater the intensity, the greater the likelihood for friction in those relationships. I have been astonished by the strength of my feelings about some of the people in the team I used to lead: seething with anger in the car on the way home; raging with frustration. Whenever feelings such as these start to affect people, distorting their perceptions, their judgement and their action, then the only way to address the situation is to create an arena in which people can discuss the issues in question openly and safely. I am not saying that this will always resolve the problems, but that it is the only way that they can be resolved.

The knack is to generate the right level of openness. The device that I use to do this is called 'the round'. It is very straightforward. The principle of the round is that everyone is given a safe space to talk in which they have the opportunity to be open with the group, sharing their feelings in general or on specific issues. The 'space' is a period of time, which can be as long as you like. I usually suggest two minutes – which can be an awesomely long time if it is just yours to fill – but I vary it according to need and to people's comfort level. In order to make the space safe, the following rules apply:

☐ Each person has the same amount of time. Even if they finish speaking within the two minutes, for example, the space is still theirs until the time is up.

☐ No one can interrupt someone else's space with any verbal or non-verbal reaction.

☐ No one can say anything about what somebody has said when their time is up. You just move on to the next person in the round (you can either go round the group as they are seated or let people have their turn when they are ready).

☐ No one can refer back in their own round to what someone has said in theirs.

☐ Everyone must talk for themselves only, not on behalf of the group as a whole or a subgrouping. To do this, they should use the first person singular pronoun, 'I', as opposed to 'we' or 'you'. For example, instead of saying: 'We don't listen to each other', people should say: 'I don't listen to other people' or 'I don't feel that I am listened to'; instead of saying: 'You always find that people irritate each other', people should say: 'I tend to irritate/be irritated by other people'.

☐ When people are listening, they should listen 'passively', i.e. focus on what the other person is saying without letting their thoughts and feelings interrupt their attention. We often interpret and evaluate what people are saying as they speak which stops us from truly hearing what they have to say.

The focus of what people talk about in the round can be as broad or as specific as you want – it depends on the group and the kind of issues it is facing in its social dynamic. Often I will use a broad focus, with the instruction: 'Tell people how you feel about the group and the way it works together', or 'Tell people how you feel about being a member of the group'. This gives people more freedom to select what they talk about and how open they are in talking about it (I am as interested in what people choose not to say as I am in what they actually say). A more specific focus might be, for example: 'Use the space to talk about any difficulties you experience as a member of the group', or 'Use the space to talk about any frustrations you have with other members of the group'. These give people less room for manoeuvre and put them under greater pressure, but because they are more challenging they can get more directly to the root of an issue. I would not usually give such specific instructions until I had prepared the ground with the group, and will almost certainly have done a gentler round with them first.

ACTIVITY 6.9

Use the round as a way of reviewing the social level of process with your group. You could do this as part of a normal team meeting or as part of a separate team-building exercise. Follow the rules listed above. You will need also to decide:

☐ How long the space should last.
☐ What you want people to talk about in their space.
☐ What you will do after the round has finished.

The round is a more structured and in-depth version of the *process reviews* that I suggested earlier in this chapter. The principle is the same, but whereas process reviews focused on the procedural level of process, the round focuses on the social level, and because this is potentially more risky, the rules are more elaborate and need to be enforced.

You may feel that doing the round with your group is too dangerous and might blow the lid off a can of worms, or that it is too alien and that people would resist doing it. Nevertheless, I would encourage you to consider using it: it provides a relatively safe way in to facing difficult issues and dynamics and a relatively gentle way of encouraging people to be more open with each other. I have used the round countless times now to enable groups to find a new level of openness. It always works. The new level may not be significantly deeper than the old level, but the exercise will have made some impact and the group will remember it as a tool that they can use when their need for openness is greater.

When the tension at the social level of process is great, the round can move a group into significantly more open channels of communication. Not only does it give people the opportunity to speak openly, but it also puts some pressure on them to do so, especially if there are things they need to say. In spite of this pressure, people will select the level of risk they are prepared to take; for some people, this is very little risk at all, for others the risk is enormous and they take the opportunity to share much of what they think and feel about the group, and this has a radical effect. There is no right and wrong here. If people don't want to share, that is their choice and it must be respected, as with people who are open to a level that the rest of the group are uncomfortable with. No pressure should be put on anyone to be more open than they have been – except for the pressure inherent in the exercise itself. Apart from anything else, it is useful to know how open people are prepared to be.

The round has a number of benefits. Not only is it a simple way of generating a more open climate within groups and teams and of giving people the opportunity to get things off their chest, it also models a way of managing open communication. People tend to listen to each other during a round in ways that they haven't done before and this is a useful precedent which can have a positive impact on the group's basic communication. People are more sensitized to each other: during a round you see aspects of a person that you haven't seen before (either because they haven't shown it or because you have not been aware of it) and this can on its own shift a relationship out of the rut of preconceptions and assumptions into which it had fallen. Sometimes, telling the group how you feel can of itself unburden you of a weight of emotional turbulence that has got heavier the longer you have been carrying it around. Having unburdened yourself, you are free to move on – aware of the extent to which your own feelings have coloured your perception of the behaviour of others.

There are times when the round can be electric, unleashing such a torrent of suppressed feelings that I wonder how people have been able to carry on any kind of normal existence with all this bubbling away inside! I used the round at the beginning of my workshop with Ivana's team (see earlier case studies) and the level of openness that people moved to instantly was extraordinary given that this was right at the beginning of the first of my two days with them. Some people were so open about the level of distress they felt they were suffering, and so forceful with their openness, that there was no going back. Once that level of openness is set, it is difficult not to be that open yourself, and so by the end of the round (and there were a dozen or so people in it), the group had been transformed, in that it could never be the same again. There was still a lot of work to do, and there was no guarantee of success, but the group could not go back to how it had operated before: too much had been shared with too many people.

Even if there are no apparent or actual tensions in the group dynamic, periodically doing the round provides an opportunity to check that everything is OK and that there are no problems looming. It also maintains a climate of openness which will be essential if problems do occur. It may feel unnecessary, artificial, even dangerous to dabble in the social level of process when there are no burning issues to address – but most of the groups I work with need help precisely because the appropriate level of openness had not existed when the burning issues came to the surface. Raising critical awareness of the social level of process, in my opinion, is a maintenance activity which should be carried out by all teams and most groups.

Quick guide to managing the social level of process

I have tried to give a flavour of the complexity of managing process at this level without making it seem like a forbidden zone where only facilitators dare to tread! Most managers and team-leaders will experience problems with their groups at the social level of process at some point. I would say it is inevitable that, sooner or later, there will be tensions within relationships that interfere with the group's ability to operate effectively. Resolving these tensions can be one of the hardest aspects of a manager's job and can consume much time and emotional energy. In this section I have provided an approach which will both help you to prevent and to manage crisis. Let me summarize it for you now:

1. The group as a whole needs to have a critical awareness of the group dynamic if it is to manage it effectively.
2. You need to create an open climate in the group in order to generate critical awareness – people need to feel safe to share their feelings about each other with each other.
3. The round is a tool which creates a safe environment for sharing feelings and so for developing an open climate.

4. The round should be used regularly to review the group dynamic and to give people an opportunity to face problems early.

5. Raising critical awareness through the round generates a positive momentum which is the key to resolving problems (and is sometimes all that is required).

Summary

In this chapter, we have looked at the management of the four levels of process. I have focused in detail on the management of meetings at the procedural level of process, looking specifically at:

☐ Writing agendas.

☐ Structuring discussions.

☐ Making decisions.

☐ Recording output.

The main focus of this chapter, however, has been the need to generate critical awareness within the group or team about all four levels of process. I have suggested tools or activities you can use with your group which will help to raise their awareness of its process and create an arena in which people can discuss this openly and constructively. These are:

☐ **Process reviews** at the end of a meeting to review the procedural level of process: how people feel about a specific meeting and to explore ways in which future meetings could be improved.

☐ **Resource analysis** to review the structural level of process. This helps the group to identify its available resources and compare the official and unofficial structures. It can help the group to allocate responsibilities more effectively and maximize its resources.

☐ **Groundrules reviews** to review the behavioural level of process. This helps the group to reflect on the group norms and the way these affect their own and other people's behaviour. It provides a framework for reviewing and changing the groundrules that underpin group behaviour.

☐ **The round** to review the social level of process. This is a technique which generates new levels of openness in groups, providing a safe arena for people to share their feelings about themselves and other members of the group. It can generate a positive momentum which can ease frictions and tensions in relationships.

ACTIVITY 6.10

Before moving on, spend a few minutes reflecting on Chapter 6. Remember the thoughts, insights or ideas that have occurred to you about you or your group as you have read this chapter. Note down in the space below (or on a separate sheet of paper if you prefer) any of these that you feel it would be useful to record so that you can refer back to them in the future. Some may have helped you to identify things you could do to manage your group more effectively and a space has been provided to record these separately.

Thoughts and insights   **Actions arising**

7

Process and the individual

In the previous chapter I talked about the management of group process, which I regard as the key requirement of the effective leadership of groups and teams. As we move down the process hierarchy, however, and examine the social level of process more closely, it becomes clear that group process is the expression of the cumulation of the attitudes, needs and responses of the individuals who make up the team. Group dynamics are formed by the level of satisfaction and fulfilment of the people involved. If the people in your group enjoy the work they do and get the recognition they need from doing it, then it is likely that the dynamic in the group will be positive and that there will be few problems at the social level of process. It doesn't guarantee that people will like and get on well with each other, but it makes it less likely that any interpersonal tensions that exist will be too disruptive.

When people are not fulfilled by the work they do, the nature of their relationships becomes an alternative source of satisfaction and stimulation. This greater focus puts pressure on interpersonal relationships and magnifies any tensions and frustrations, giving them a significance and potency that they otherwise might not have. When we are dissatisfied or unhappy, we tend to externalize our negative feelings, attributing them to the presence or behaviour of the people around us. Put simply, we blame other people for how we feel. This naturally creates problems at the social level of process.

As team-leader, it is usually necessary for you to intervene in process with the whole group, to enable them to manage their responses to each other. It may also be necessary to intervene with each individual, to help them achieve satisfaction and fulfilment through membership of the team and to manage their dissatisfactions and frustrations so that they don't generate negative dynamics.

In Chapter 4, we explored four sources of personal fulfilment:

☐ Feelings of accomplishment.
☐ Recognition.
☐ Authority.
☐ Purpose.

In this chapter, we are going to revisit these concepts, developed by the Pellin Institute, to explore briefly ways in which you can manage process through intervention with individual team members. We are also going to look at another Pellin concept: the pendulum, a tool which helps us to manage our emotional swings. Given the tendency for emotions to swing violently when we encounter problems in group dynamics, awareness of the pendulum will help you to manage the social level of process more effectively.

Feelings of accomplishment

Feelings of accomplishment are the feelings of gratification derived from our daily activity. The emphasis is on the feeling rather than the accomplishment. It is possible to accomplish a great deal in our daily work and yet not derive any feelings of accomplishment from doing so. You might think that the work you are asking somebody to do is intrinsically gratifying. This does not mean that they will derive feelings of accomplishment from doing it. Each member of your team is likely to have different sources of feelings of accomplishment. This will determine what they like doing and how they like doing it.

EXERCISE 7.1

Spend a few minutes now reflecting on the people in your group or team. To what extent does their activity at work provide them with feelings of accomplishment? If you feel it doesn't give them enough feelings of accomplishment, can you see ways in which this affects their performance and behaviour?

As we saw in Chapter 4, when we are deprived of feelings of accomplishment, we are in trouble. Our energy and motivation suffer. We become dissatisfied and listless. We blame our work, our colleagues, our environment for the boredom and frustration that we feel. When we are not getting feelings of accomplishment, we put our energy into problems rather than solutions. The problems become our source of stimulation and satisfaction. In groups and teams, these problems often manifest themselves at the social level of process. You may become the problem, branded as an inadequate leader, or it may be other members of the group, resented and blamed for crimes that are often quite intangible. The excitement of the negative feelings becomes a substitute for feelings of accomplishment.

It is important then, as team-leader, to recognize that problems with the group dynamic are sometimes caused by one or more people not getting enough feelings of accomplishment. Rather than address the symptoms in such cases, it will be more helpful to address the cause: to see if you can help someone to get the feelings of accomplishment that they need. First, you have to understand why they are not getting enough feelings of accomplishment at the moment. This may be for one of two reasons:

☐ They find the work itself ungratifying.
☐ The way they do the work is denying them feelings of accomplishment.

It is important to accept that work you consider gratifying won't necessarily provide feelings of accomplishment to someone else (and vice versa). It may be that they have ceased to find the work satisfying because they have been doing it for so long. It may be that they find it inherently unsatisfying. Sometimes the solution is radical: the person needs to get out, get another job, find new areas of activity. To continue in a job that affords so few feelings of accomplishment can be as dangerous as the risk of leaving to find new employment.

Sometimes it is possible to identify areas of work which will be more gratifying and which can compensate for the areas which aren't. This will depend on the extent to which you are able to create opportunities and be flexible with their current workload. I managed a secretary once who was so frustrated with the work we were asking her to do that, in spite of my efforts to find more challenging responsibilities for her, she left the company. The fact was that she didn't want to be a secretary any more: she had long since ceased to find secretarial work a source of feelings of accomplishment.

Sometimes it is not the activity itself but the ways in which people organize and manage their workload that deny them feelings of accomplishment. This might be because someone is essentially disorganized, or because they are unable to prioritize effectively, or because their work is constantly changing in response to new demands and priorities. In such chaos, activity is not completed or not done well enough for people to derive feelings of accomplishment and they can quickly become demoralized. They will need help to learn how to manage their workload to ensure that it gives them sufficient feelings of accomplishment. Effective time management partly revolves around the rational processes of prioritizing and planning. But it also hinges on the emotional need for feelings of accomplishment, and if you can help people to organize their work in ways that gives them these feelings – often quite small steps which will enable them to feel that they are in some control of their activity and making visible progress – then you can transform their experience at work.

ACTIVITY 7.1

If there are people in your group whom you feel are lacking feelings of accomplishment, plan ways in which you could intervene to help them. This might involve:

☐ Reviewing and modifying their activity to ensure that it is more gratifying for them.

☐ Helping them to manage their workload in order to gain more feelings of accomplishment from it.

Recognition

Pellin regards our need for recognition as a motivating force which shapes the contribution we make in the world, both at work and outside. If we can make contributions that get us the recognition we need, this will generate energy and motivation. If our work doesn't provide the arena for us to get the recognition we need we are likely to lack motivation and commitment. We will often seek recognition in inappropriate ways, thus reducing our effectiveness and having a negative impact on the social level of process.

The three kinds of recognition that I described in Chapter 4 are:

☐ **Admiration:** When we are motivated by our vanity, our need to be admired by others.

☐ **Respect:** When we are motivated by our need for control of our material world.

☐ **Acceptance:** When we are motivated by our need to be liked and accepted by others, our need for closeness and intimacy.

EXERCISE 7.2

Spend a few minutes now reflecting on recognition as a motivating force. First, think about the people you manage: What kinds of recognition do they need (e.g.

are they particularly motivated by the need for admiration, respect or affection, or by a combination of all of these)? Second, think about the work that they do: Does it provide them with enough of the recognition they need?

If any members of your team are demotivated, it is likely that at least part of the problem is that they are not getting enough of the right kind of recognition. This may be because their work is not the right arena to provide the kind of recognition they need. This is a serious problem, which we will look at later. It may be that work is the appropriate arena but that the recognition is not forthcoming. In this case, it is your job as team-leader to help the person get the recognition they need. The following questions will help you to assess how you could do this.

If someone is not receiving the amount of **admiration** that they need, it is worth considering the following:

□ Do you give them enough positive feedback when they do things well?

□ Do you ensure that other people are aware of their good performance?

□ Do you provide them with sufficient opportunities to exercise their talents?

□ Do you help them achieve a high profile in the organization?

□ Do you encourage them to be innovative and take risks?

□ Do you give them opportunities to perform in front of others (make presentations, etc.)?

If someone is not receiving the amount of **respect** that they need, it is worth considering the following:

□ Do you show them that you respect their contribution to the team when it is appropriate?

□ Do you encourage others to show them respect when it is appropriate?

□ Do you provide them with sufficient opportunities to exercise control in the   various ways in which this might be possible in your team's work?

□ Do you entrust them with sufficient responsibility in their work?

□ Do you support them to receive the appropriate level of status and reward for their efforts?

If someone is not receiving the amount of **acceptance** that they need, it is worth considering the following:

□ Do you show them that you like them (if you do)?

□ Do you encourage a friendly climate within the team generally?

□ Do you provide them with sufficient opportunities to work closely with others?

□ Do you provide them with opportunities to be supportive and caring of others?

ACTIVITY 7.2

Focus on each of the people you manage in turn and identify ways in which you can help them to get more of the recognition they need at work. Use the questions listed above as a starting-point for this activity, but do not be constrained by them.

It is not always easy to identify specific ways in which you can help people get more recognition, and even if you can, it is not always in your power to make them happen. You might not be able to provide somebody with the kind of responsibility they want – you may not think they are capable of handling such a responsibility anyway; opportunities for people with a high need for admiration may be few and far between. But there are often small ways in which you can help: it is important, for example, not to underestimate the importance of your own feedback as a valuable source of recognition. Shaping your feedback so that it meets their needs can have a significant impact on people's motivation.

It is more difficult if a person's work is not the right arena for them to get the recognition they need: someone with a high need for acceptance, for example, working in a cut-throat and calloused business environment; or someone with a high need for respect working in a job that they feel is far below their proper station in life. Such situations often lead to feelings of bitter resentment and unhappiness which can be expressed indirectly and destructively. The fact of the matter is that the person is in the wrong job, and attempts to make the job more acceptable are usually doomed to failure. In such cases, the best course of action may be to help the person find a job that better suits them or to support them to develop the skills and gain the qualifications required to do such a job. This might be more than you are prepared to offer: I have come up against the limits of my generosity with someone who in the end was going to have to sort things out for herself.

Authority

In Chapter 4, I explained the Pellin approach to the development of authority: that it builds through a combination of gaining feelings of accomplishment and recognition. In other words, we develop our authority in any area of activity through making the right kind of contribution, one which both brings us the kind of recognition we need and also an internal sense of satisfaction.

Authority is intangible: it is hard to describe but easy to recognize. Its opposite is similar: lack of confidence, low self-esteem, self-doubt. We tend to know which of our people lack authority and can sometimes be exasperated by their slowness in developing it.

EXERCISE 7.3

Spend a few minutes now reflecting on the people you manage in terms of their authority. Which of them do you regard as having authority, and why do you think this? Which of them do you regard as lacking authority, and why do you think this?

If people are to develop their authority in a given area, they must have the opportunity to practise. Only through *doing* will they experience feelings of accomplishment and receive recognition. They need to be encouraged to take the risk of doing, and also to be supported by someone who can give them feedback. If you want someone to develop authority in making presentations, for example, they are going to have to make a presentation. If they receive support beforehand to ensure that the presentation is successful, they should receive the buzz of feelings of accomplishment. If they are supported afterwards to review the experience, they will receive the feedback and recognition that they need.

If you want your people to develop their authority, you have to delegate and you have to coach (*The Essence of Managing People* covers these topics in greater detail). There is a common double-bind which goes: 'They don't have enough authority for me to trust them to take the risks they need to take in order to develop their authority.' The responsibility for breaking out of this double-bind is partly theirs and partly yours. But it is likely that the initiative will have to come from you, not just in creating the opportunities but in providing the support and feedback to ensure that the opportunities provide a positive experience.

ACTIVITY 7.3

If you would like to help a member of your team to develop their authority in an aspect of their work, plan now how you could create the opportunities for them to do the activity. Make sure that you also provide them with the support they will need to be successful and the feedback they will need to know that they have been successful.

Purpose

I was working in a factory in Belfast recently and talking to a woman who had worked her way up from the shop-floor to become a team-leader. She was expressing her frustration that the women she managed didn't share her ambition. She was keen to give them opportunities to develop and to support them. She believed absolutely in their potential and gave them feedback to this effect. They didn't want to know. They were happy with what they were doing; they didn't want the added responsibility of being a team-leader, nor all the hassle that went with it. I felt for this woman: for her passion and her frustration. I didn't have to say to her that she needed to accept the level of aspiration of her team-members – she knew that. It was just that it felt like such a failure to do so.

I too have invested in the development of others in my time, passionately committed to lifting them out of the troughs in which I found them and single-handedly elevating them to new peaks of fulfilled potential. Even more than the team-leader in Belfast, it is my deep and sustaining purpose. Like her, I have been flummoxed when the other person doesn't want to play ball, doesn't perceive the trough as a trough and is not interested in the peak I have identified for them. Their sustaining purpose is elsewhere. Work provides an underlying purpose and no more (see Chapter 4 for definitions of these two types of purpose). My passion has made me blind to their need, just as the team-leader struggled to accept that the needs of the women on the shop-floor in Belfast might be different to hers.

EXERCISE 7.4

Spend a few minutes now reflecting on the sustaining purpose of the individuals who work for you. Do you know if they have one? Do you know what it is? Is it connected to their work? If not, how does it impact on their work?

For many people, their sustaining purpose lies outside their work: through their involvement in a community, through voluntary work, through a leisure pursuit, through a political campaign or a religious belief. In such cases, work may be a relatively low priority, and their commitment and motivation will be in proportion to this. When managers and leaders talk about the problem of motivating people, they are often describing the difficulty of influencing people's purpose. And this is almost impossible to do: you can't make someone's work their sustaining purpose. The Belfast team-leader knew that she couldn't make people want what she wanted for them.

Much effort can be wasted in trying to motivate people who are not going to feel motivated by the work because it doesn't tie in with their purpose. This may mean that they are not suitable members of the team, passengers whom the team can't afford to carry for very long before the work is impaired and morale suffers. If it is possible, it may be best to replace them with people whose purpose is more congruent. But if there is no scope to change the composition of the team, it will be more helpful for the manager to try to negotiate rather than motivate: i.e. to strike a balance between the requirements of the team and the needs of the individual. There are many people who do their job because it pays them the wherewithal to fulfil a purpose which is not connected to the work they do. Trying to force the connection is unlikely to be successful.

The pendulum

When there are problems at the social level of process, it is usually the case that strong emotions are generated. People can get very angry, very frustrated, very upset, very depressed by the dynamics in the group. When I have facilitated groups in crisis, I have witnessed extreme expressions of the emotional distress that can be caused by problems at the social level of process.

These violent swings of emotion need to be taken into account when we are intervening to improve the group dynamic. We need to be aware of the emotional state of the people involved and we also need to understand our own emotional state, and the ways in which this affects our judgement and behaviour. I am going to introduce a tool that I use to help me manage my emotional swings, another of the tools developed by the Pellin Institute, which is called 'the pendulum'.

The theory behind the pendulum is that our emotions are in constant movement: a swing one way produces an equal swing in the opposite direction. If we take the inevitability of this movement into account, we are better able to manage the size of the swings so that they do not become too extreme or compulsive. There are three key positions on the pendulum, as illustrated in Figure 7.1.

The calm

The calm is the area of the pendulum where we have most awareness, where we can keep a sense of perspective, where we can evaluate effectively. It is where we need to be when we make decisions. The calm is where we find our true strength, our ability to cope with change, our ability to manage well. As we move further away from our calm, towards

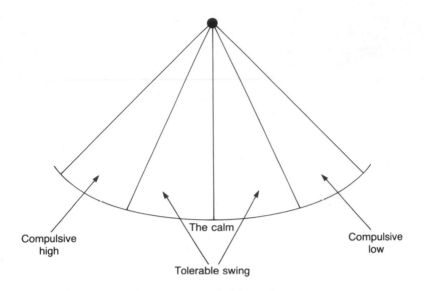

Figure 7.1 The pendulum.

either end of the pendulum, we become more likely to act irrationally in ways that are damaging to ourselves and hurtful to other people.

The low

We swing to the low end of the pendulum when we feel depleted, either physically or emotionally. If the swing away from the calm is not too great, and stays within the tolerable area of the pendulum, we can experience a pleasant low: the feeling of flatness that comes after a period of intense but satisfying work, for example, can sometimes be a pleasurable relief. Lows can be useful places where our doubt and misgivings cause us to take stock, re-evaluate, challenge some of the assumptions that have been underpinning our lives. Pleasant lows can provide periods of essential reassessment. But if the pendulum swings further away from our calm, and our low becomes compulsive, it is more likely to become unpleasant – a place where we are likely to be hurtful, either to ourselves or others.

In our extreme lows, we tend to focus only on the negative aspects of our lives, our dissatisfactions and grievances with the outside world, our own faults and shortcomings. We blot out the positives, we ignore any evidence which may contradict our misgivings and self-doubt. We get caught up in our negativity in a compulsive way, so that it becomes hard to extricate ourselves, and we can then spiral downwards into a miasmal void where life itself becomes meaningless.

When we become stuck in unpleasant, compulsive lows, we lose perspective on issues and people and therefore cannot evaluate effectively. Our emotions turn inwards on themselves and become convoluted. We become convinced that we are a failure, or a victim, undervalued, passed over, misunderstood. We manufacture problems to feed our low, we make poor decisions, act inappropriately, judge people negatively, distance ourselves from others, reject their attempts to help us, hurt people with our remoteness and rejection. The quicksand of our depression sucks at our ankles, and although part of us wants to escape, another part of us wants to surrender to the intractable pull.

The high

We swing to the high end of the pendulum when we experience surges of energy and excitement: before we make a presentation, for example, we often need to be high in order to take the risk of stepping out in front of the audience; and if the presentation goes well the swing towards the high end of the pendulum increases. If the presentation goes badly, it is likely that we will swing into a corresponding low, in which our self-belief crumbles and we feel inept and worthless.

When we become compulsively high, we lose awareness of ourselves and other people. We are not aware of what we are doing or its impact on the people around us. We need to control our high so that it gives us energy and courage without taking away our awareness. When we are high, we are in touch with our power, but the power we feel when we are high is different from the true strength we feel when we are calm. When we are high, we confuse power for strength: we feel that anything is possible, we focus on the positives and ignore the negatives, and can make poor decisions and rush into inadvisable action as a result.

When we lose awareness in a compulsive high, we become hurtful: we can ignore people, misinterpret their behaviour or misjudge their needs. Our emotional responses become exaggerated, often out of proportion: we are more likely to get angry or upset, to lash out at others or hurt them through our insensitivity.

The swings of the pendulum

One way that we can use the pendulum as a tool to manage our emotions is to recognize the interrelationship of our emotional swings: our emotions are never still, we are in constant movement through the calm into highs and back into lows. An extreme swing in one direction will be followed by an extreme swing in the opposite direction – as sure as night follows day. The high we feel after a successful presentation will be followed at some point by an equivalent low, and it is useful to anticipate this and to recognize the low as a natural reaction to the high. Similarly, if we have been feeling low or depressed for a period of time, it is useful to know that the pendulum will swing back into the high and to understand that the extreme low is likely to be followed by an extreme high, which if not managed well, will be followed by another extreme low.

The pendulum also helps us to see that our true strength lies in the calm and to understand that if our emotional swings are extreme, moving from compulsive low to compulsive high and back again, then it is likely that we will not be spending enough time in the calm and therefore not drawing enough on the strength that we can find there: the perspective that we need about ourselves, our strengths and weaknesses, our potential and limitations. We are more effective when we are in the calm. This is not to say that we should spend all our time there – the movement of the pendulum would not allow this – but we need to make sure that we spend *enough* time there.

EXERCISE 7.5

Spend a few minutes now reflecting on your own emotional pendulum. Do you feel you spend most of your time in the calm, swinging gently between tolerable lows and tolerable highs? Or do you feel that your swings are more extreme, moving from compulsive highs to compulsive lows and back again?

For most people, their pendulum swings between tolerable limits, with occasional movement into extreme highs and lows triggered by events in their lives. Some people are compulsive swingers, living an emotional roller-coaster in which extreme highs are followed by extreme lows in endless succession. In either case, problems at the social level of process tend to generate movement, swinging people into compulsive highs. This tends to exacerbate the problems for the reasons stated above: we lose awareness, we lose perspective, we are more insensitive, our reactions are more extreme, we are more hurtful. When we are trying to manage problems in the social level of process, it is helpful if the people involved can be brought into the calm area of their emotional pendulum.

Managing the swings of the pendulum

The pendulum teaches us that we do have choices and that we can take steps to manage our emotional swings to minimize the hurt we can cause to ourselves and others. These steps help us to limit the swings of the pendulum so that we break the compulsive pattern to ensure that our highs and lows are tolerable rather than compulsive.

When we are **compulsively low**, we need to:

☐ Accept the fact that we are low and make allowance for the extent to which this is colouring our view of people, events and the world in general. We should avoid making important decisions, however tempting this may be, for when we are compulsively low we have lost perspective and it seems that only extreme solutions are possible. Whatever dark thoughts we have, we should wait until we have swung back into the calm before making a final decision. (When we are compulsively low, it can be hard to believe that we will ever be anything else. The pendulum shows that the swing back to the calm is inevitable, but that we must work to stay long enough in the calm before swinging into the high.)

☐ Avoid focusing on the *content* of the low and focus instead on managing the low to make it tolerable. When we focus on the content – on the fact that we are not the person we want to be or that the world doesn't appreciate who we are – we feed the low and get sucked into a negative spiral that increases the swing of the pendulum. The content of a low can be valuable and worthy of reflection: the point is that we will not reflect usefully on the content *when* we are low.

☐ Find ways of getting small feelings of accomplishment. When you are low, activity that would normally be straightforward can seem impossible – there are times, for example, when I put off phoning a client because the thought of having to manage the conversation is paralyzing! But if I can find small, low-risk tasks to carry out which will give me small feelings of accomplishment, this often helps me to build a positive momentum which literally swings me back into a more tolerable low. I can believe that I am not a total incompetent!

☐ Make contact with people whom you can trust to be understanding and supportive. There is a tendency to turn in on ourselves when we are low, to retreat from the world, either because we don't want anyone to see us in our sorry state, or because we don't want to burden them with our troubles or because we feel let down by them, by the fact that they haven't already recognized that we are in need. But when we retreat from people our pendulum tends to swing further into the compulsive low because we shut ourselves off from other people's calm, more rational perspectives. Reaching out for small forms of support – letting someone know how you are feeling, asking them to make you a cup of tea, to give you a hug – and so making contact, will help you to swing back towards the calm.

When we are **compulsively high**, it is almost impossible to manage ourselves to bring ourselves back into the calm. One feature of the compulsive high is that we cannot bear to be interrupted. If we get high in a meeting, for example, we can find it intolerable if someone tries to cut across what we are saying. If a group involved in creative endeavour become excited by their ideas, they can fiercely resent anyone who tries to question the validity of these ideas. So rather than manage the compulsive high when we are in it, we need to manage the pendulum to ensure that we only get compulsively high when it is useful for us to do so. To do this, we need to:

☐ Recognize what triggers our highs so that we are aware of the risk of swinging uncontrollably. We all have our own patterns. I recently ran a training programme with another consultant for the first time and, in our pleasure at finding how compatible we were, I became high, losing control of my behaviour, joking with and teasing my colleague, often to the confusion of the group. I know I tend to get high when I meet new friends. Other people get high on ideas, on working in groups, on overworking, responding to pressure or tight deadlines. If we are aware that we are likely to swing into a compulsive high in such circumstances, we are better able to manage the pendulum to stay in the tolerable zone.

☐ Recognize the point at which we are about to move from a tolerable into a compulsive high, i.e. the point at which we are about to lose control, when we still have some choice over our behaviour, so that we can evaluate whether it is useful and appropriate to allow ourselves to swing further. It is the emotional equivalent of being able to decide whether to stop drinking alcohol or not – one more drink and you will be too drunk to stop yourself from drinking compulsively.

☐ Make a change in our physical environment. This is the most effective way of preventing the swing from a tolerable to a compulsive high, as it breaks the momentum of the swing. It might be as small a move as sitting down if you are standing up, or moving to sit in another chair, or leaving the room briefly during a meeting, or going for a short walk. Sometimes when I am training and I feel myself getting high in relation to the group, I will move away from the flip chart and sit down closer to the group. By breaking momentum and gaining a new perspective, I am able to manage my pendulum and swing back into a tolerable high. The movement calms me down.

You can use these steps yourself to manage your own emotional pendulum. You can also use them to help the members of your group to manage theirs. If they naturally tend to swing compulsively, this will help them generally in their work. If they are embroiled in issues at the social level of process, when their pendulum will typically swing into compulsive highs, there is an even greater need to try to bring them into the calm. This can be extremely difficult, but it is worth remembering the following:

☐ When people come to us in an emotional high to air grievances, there are times when engaging with them on the content of their issues will feed their highs and lows, swinging their pendulum further into the compulsive zones. It might be better to postpone a full discussion until later, giving them a chance to regain the calm.

☐ Small changes in environment have a positive impact on the pendulum. When people came to me worked up about an issue with another member of the team, I would suggest that we went for a walk, preferably outside. This got us out of the office environment and the action of walking itself had a calming effect.

☐ When people are compulsively high or low, they find it difficult to make contact. They can find it difficult, for example, to look you in the eye. Asking them to make eye contact has a grounding effect on them, bringing them into contact with you and so steadying their emotional swing. You will hear that people talk differently when they are in contact with you in this way.

ACTIVITY 7.4

If there are members of your team who tend to swing compulsively or who are in a compulsive high currently because of issues at work, consider ways in which you could help them to move into the calm, using some of the steps listed above if appropriate.

Summary

In this chapter, we have looked at the ways in which issues faced by individual members of your group can affect the social level of process and have explored interventions you could make to help individuals address these issues. We have revisited briefly the four concepts that were used to help you reflect on your own needs in Chapter 4, applying them to your people as follows:

☐ How **feelings of accomplishment** can be used as a tool to understand people's dissatisfaction with their work and to help them gain greater satisfaction.

☐ How the **sources of recognition** can be used as a tool to understand people's lack of motivation at work and to help them get the kind of recognition they need.

☐ How the **development of authority** can be used as a tool to understand people's lack of confidence and self-esteem and to help them to develop their authority.

☐ How **purpose** can be used as a tool to understand people's commitment to their work and to help you accept the limits and maximize the potential of their engagement.

We also looked at a fifth tool, **the pendulum**, which can be used to understand the movement of our emotions and to help people to manage their emotional swings so that they spend enough time in the calm.

ACTIVITY 7.5

Before moving on, spend a few minutes reflecting on Chapter 7. Remember the thoughts, insights or ideas that have occurred to you about you or your group as you have read this chapter. Note down in the space below (or on a separate sheet of paper if you prefer) any of these you feel it would be useful to record so that you can refer back to them in the future. Some may have helped you to identify things you could do to manage your group more effectively and a space has been provided to record these separately.

Thoughts and insights   **Actions arising**

Part 3

Skills

Part 3 helps you to improve the way you interact with other people. It focuses on the behavioural skills required to participate in and manage formal and informal group discussions effectively. The exercises and activities in Part 3 give you the opportunity to reflect on how you manage interactions at the moment and to identify how to develop your skills further.

8

Interactive skills

So far we have explored the management of process by focusing on interventions you can make to raise awareness of process issues in your group or team and to enable them to discuss and resolve these issues. In Part 3, we are going to focus on the behavioural level of process in detail in order to help you to:

☐ Understand individual and group behaviour.
☐ Be more aware of your own behaviour.
☐ Identify the causes of problems at the behavioural level of process.
☐ Manage key interactions effectively.

The behavioural level of process reflects the ability of a group of people to communicate well with each other. This depends partly on the group's ability to manage the procedural level of process; but it also depends on the interactive skills of each individual and on their ability to manage interaction effectively.

EXERCISE 8.1

Spend a few minutes now reflecting on your effectiveness at communicating with people. Use the space below to note down what you think your strengths and weaknesses are:

Strengths   **Weaknesses**

There has been much discussion and exploration about why some people are better at communicating than others and there are many ways of addressing this issue. I am going to focus mainly on the behavioural aspects of communication: what people say and how they say it. There are other aspects which are equally important: the kind of person you are, your attitude to other people, body language. I am concentrating on verbal behaviour because that is the field I have been working in extensively for the last eight years, and because I believe that it can provide you with clear structures for assessing your effectiveness and with practical steps for developing your skills.

In behavioural terms, effective communicators share the following attributes:

☐ **Self-awareness:** They tend to be aware of what they are doing as they are doing it. For example, they are aware of the degree to which they interrupt other people.

☐ **A range of options:** They have a wide range of options for how to behave. For example, if chairing a meeting, they will be able either to control the process or to influence the content.

☐ **Flexibility:** They have the flexibility to adapt their behaviour according to circumstances. They can assess the situation, select the right option and behave accordingly.

In Part 3, we will be focusing on the first two of these attributes. By reflecting on the way that you tend to interact with people, you will develop greater self-awareness. This will be limited, however, by the accuracy of your self-perception – we all have more or less distorted pictures of how we behave. We need feedback from others if we are to get a more rounded picture, and some of the activities will be asking you to get that feedback.

The main function of Part 3 will be to present you with ways of effectively managing certain types of interaction. Some of these will be part of your existing range of options. Others, hopefully, will be new, alternative approaches which you can build into your repertoire. Many of the activities will be asking you to consider whether applying these options will be appropriate for you given your situation at work.

What Part 3 can't do is help you to become more flexible. This will only happen if you practise using those options that you think will be of benefit. There are many people who know how to communicate effectively yet who don't seem able actually to do it. Some of the activities will provide you with structures for practising the skills that have been explored.

Part 3 is divided into three chapters, each focusing on a particular area of interactive skill. Between them, these three chapters will cover the key interactive skills involved in managing groups and teams. The three areas are:

☐ **Groupworking skills,** i.e. the core interactive skills involved in communicating effectively in groups. These help you better to understand and control your own behaviour and also the behaviour of others.

☐ **Process management skills,** i.e. the skills involved in managing two of the four levels of process: the procedural level and the management of meetings and group discussions; the social level and the management of group dynamics.

☐ **Influencing skills,** i.e. the skills involved in persuading people to do what you want them to do, overcoming their resistance and developing their need to change.

The chapters in Part 3 focus on the 'group interaction' – when some or all of a group or team are working together in formal or informal meetings. It therefore only focuses on some of the interactions people will have within their working groups. I have covered the skills involved in managing one-to-one interactions extensively in *The Essence of Managing People*.

The chapters build on each other incrementally, and the skills become more complex and sophisticated as you work through Part 3. We will be looking at interactions through a microscope, and there may be times when you find the level of detail unsettling: when interactions are dissected in this way, they can become unrecognizable from the conversations you have quite naturally at work. There are three general principles that will help you to make good use of this part of the book: choices, feedback and practice.

Choices

We make choices about how we interact all the time. They are usually unconscious, instinctive responses to people and situations, but what you may regard as your natural interactive style is in fact a set of sophisticated choices that you have learnt as you have grown and developed. Most of them will have become second nature to you by now, so that your level of awareness of them is low. And this means that you tend to be unaware of the alternatives that exist: because our choices are so entrenched, we believe they are the only way to behave. As interactions are put under the microscope in the coming chapters, we will be exposing and dissecting the kind of choices you make all the time – it is just that they are not visible to the naked eye!

Feedback

The exercises that you will be offered in Part 3 will sometimes ask you to reflect on the choices you make instinctively in order to heighten your awareness of them. It is only then that you will be able to evaluate their effectiveness and take more control over them. The trouble is that they are often so entrenched that reflection alone will not be enough. There will be times when it is suggested that you get feedback from other people about how they perceive your behaviour.

Asking people for feedback is potentially risky. To minimize that risk, here are some guidelines for you to refer to if you decide to get feedback about your interactive skills:

□ Ask people who you can trust to give you honest feedback. These will be people who want to help you and who are prepared to challenge you if necessary.

□ Explain why you are asking for feedback and what precisely you want feedback on. You should not be getting feedback about the kind of person you are, but on specific aspects of your behaviour.

□ Hear the feedback people give you as their perception of you. This is not the 'truth' – it is just their perception, and says as much about them as it does about you. Try not to react defensively – you don't have to take it on board.

□ Give yourself time to reflect on the feedback: don't reject it or agree with it too quickly. Think about it for a while to see if it is of any value to you before deciding what you want to do with it.

Practice

Some of the activities in Part 3 suggest ways that you could practise the skills being explored. Practice is vital if skill development is to take place, but you may feel that the activities suggested are not appropriate for you. Here are some guidelines to help you identify alternatives:

- Pick specific meetings or discussions in which you are going to practise doing something. You will only really practise a skill if you make a conscious decision to do it at a specific time.
- Pick low-risk practice opportunities, so that you can focus on your skill development without worrying too much about the outcome of the meeting or discussion.
- Set yourself achievable goals, so that you don't try consciously to practise too much at once. Focus on one or two skills or behaviours at a time – any more and you are likely to overload yourself.

9

Groupworking skills

In Chapter 9, I am going to cover the five main aspects of interaction that occur in any meeting or group discussion and to provide you with a way of observing and understanding behaviour which will provide you with the basis for reflecting on and developing your own groupworking skills. The five aspects are:

☐ **Airtime:** The ways in which the available airtime is distributed among group members and the ways in which this distribution is managed by the group. (Airtime refers to the opportunity people have to speak during the meeting.)

☐ **Information:** The ways in which information is exchanged between group members during the meeting.

☐ **Ideas:** The ways in which ideas are generated by the group and in which the group relate to each other's ideas.

☐ **Reactions:** The ways in which group members express their reaction to the ideas and information of others and the impact this has on their contribution to the meeting.

☐ **Clarity:** The ways in which individuals ensure that they understand what is being discussed and proposed during the meeting, that others understand them, and that there is a shared understanding throughout the group.

EXERCISE 9.1

Spend a few minutes now reflecting on the strengths and weaknesses you identified in Exercise 8.1. How do these relate to the five aspects of effective interaction outlined above?

These five aspects of communication provide me with my third structure for observing groups in action. (The first is the four resources, described in Chapter 2; the second is the four levels of process, described in Chapter 5.) I will now explore this structure in detail, taking each aspect in turn.

Airtime

When I am observing a group in action, I am keen to understand how the group manages the available airtime. I look for the answers to three groups of questions:

☐ Who has done the most talking? Who has said virtually nothing? Who has tried to speak but has been shut out by other people? Who has been shutting them out?

☐ Was this distribution of airtime appropriate and effective? Who should have been doing the most talking? Was it the person who was dominating the discussion or not? Would the group have benefited from a higher level of contribution from the quieter people, or were they right to keep quiet?

☐ Were people aware of how the airtime was being distributed? Were they consciously choosing to share it out in that way? Was anybody trying to manage the distribution of airtime? And if so, how effective were they at doing it?

EXERCISE 9.2

Spend a few minutes now reflecting on a meeting or group discussion you have attended recently. Use the questions above to assess the management of airtime in this meeting.

The distribution of airtime tells me so much about all four levels of process. High levels of interruption, for example, indicate usually not just low behavioural awareness but low awareness of others and of group process generally, which tends to have a negative effect on the procedural level of process. The patterns of inclusion and exclusion which are generated by the distribution of airtime can also indicate issues at the structural and social levels caused by tensions within roles or relationships.

Appropriate distribution

When I give feedback to groups about how they have distributed their airtime, they will often ask: So what is the right distribution then? Are we all supposed to be equal? The answer to the first question is: 'There isn't one'. The answer to the second question is simply: 'No'. Airtime needs to be distributed according to the demands of the situation and the potential for individuals to contribute to the meeting of those demands.

There is no one right answer. The issue, as ever, is about awareness. The group as a whole needs to ensure that the people who have got something valuable to say are given the opportunity and time to say it; and that the people who have little of value to add do not take up too much of the airtime. Unfortunately this is not always as easy as it sounds. Awareness is required at several levels. For any given topic within a meeting, the group needs to be aware of:

- □ Who can contribute usefully – who needs to be involved in the discussion and who needs *not* to be involved in the discussion.
- □ How easy people find it to speak up during the meeting, whether they need encouragement, whether they need help to create the space to contribute.
- □ How people are behaving during the meeting and the extent to which they are interfering with the appropriate distribution of airtime.
- □ What behaviour is required to counteract inappropriate contributions in order to involve the necessary people at the right time.

For the distribution of airtime to be managed effectively, the group needs to have at least some of the awareness detailed above. The problem is, as we have seen in earlier chapters and will see repeatedly in Part 3, that the more involved we are in the content of a discussion, the harder it becomes for us to retain awareness of our behaviour. The minute we decide, rightly or wrongly, that we have something valuable to say on a topic, our capacity to retain any awareness of other people and what is happening around us reduces instantly. And the more involved we become in the content of the discussion, the less able we are to assess whether our contribution is valuable, whether we should be contributing at all, whether it would be more useful for other people to be having the airtime, and indeed, whether we are preventing them from having it through our own behaviour.

It is because of this difficulty of retaining awareness when involved in discussion that people often say that it is the chairperson's role to manage the distribution of airtime in a meeting. This is true: if the meeting has a chairperson, or at least someone responsible for managing process, and if they are skilled in doing this, then it is certainly more likely that the airtime will be allocated to people in a coordinated and constructive way. However, this does not mean that it is *only* the responsibility of the chairperson – the corollary being that no one else has to take any responsibility at all!

Although, as we will see in Chapter 10, one of the functions of the chairperson is to manage involvement in meetings and discussions, it is also and at the same time the responsibility of each member of the group to help in this process, both through an awareness of their own needs and behaviour and that of the other members of the group. I stress each member: this does not just mean the noisy, dominant ones who find it easy to speak out in groups, who have low self-awareness and who can hog the airtime for long periods without even knowing they are doing it and who wouldn't care even if they did know. They need to take responsibility for their impact on the meeting, but so too do the quiet ones, who sit waiting for opportunities to be created for them, who don't speak unless invited, or until they have got something to say by which time somebody has said it anyway so what's the point. They too have a significant impact on the meeting, one that is easy to overlook or underestimate and which, in its own way, can be no less dominating.

So although airtime is the responsibility of the chairperson, it is also everyone's responsibility. And one of the ways we can exercise this responsibility is to increase our awareness of two key behaviours which underpin our individual relationship to the distribution of airtime. These behaviours are **interruptions** and **invitations**.

Interruptions

There are three common forms of interruption. They are:

☐ Cutting across someone as they are speaking, thus taking the airtime away from them and using it yourself.

☐ Talking at the same time as one or more people so that none of you can be clearly heard, thus denying airtime to all of you.

☐ Answering a question asked of somebody else, thus denying them the opportunity to respond themselves.

We see these behaviours constantly in group and one-to-one discussions and, in fact, we use them constantly ourselves – to a degree we would probably find shocking if we were made aware of it. Most people have a low awareness of the extent to which they interrupt. This is because we are usually so absorbed by what we want to say ourselves that we have stopped listening to what is going on around us: who is speaking, what they are saying and whether they are near to finishing. We tend to speak when we are ready rather than when anybody else is!

I want to establish here a principle that runs throughout this chapter especially, and throughout the whole of Part 3. *No behaviour is in itself good or bad*. This is particularly relevant to interrupting because people, when they become aware of the extent to which they do it, tend to feel embarrassed and ashamed. They assume that it is wrong to interrupt and that they have been demonstrating crass insensitivity by doing so much of it. Far be it from me to argue with this new perception: they may well have been crassly insensitive, and it can be useful for them to realize this. But this does not mean that interrupting is of itself a bad thing. As with all the behaviours that I will be discussing in this chapter, I am not attaching any moral value to interruption. It is more useful to think in terms of appropriate and effective rather than right or wrong, good or bad. There are times when you need to interrupt and your contribution to a discussion or meeting will depend on your ability to do so effectively. And there will be times when this is not the case, when it will be more appropriate for you to listen carefully, pushing back your own thoughts before they turn into words, stopping yourself from butting in, waiting for the right time to make your contribution.

ACTIVITY 9.1

It is hard to know how much we interrupt during a meeting or discussion. If you feel it would be useful, get feedback from people about your interrupting behaviour. Ask them if they think you interrupt:

☐ Too much and if so what impact this has on them.

☐ Effectively, claiming airtime when you need it.

☐ Enough, or whether you should interrupt more often to increase your involvement in meetings.

(NB Read the guidelines on asking for feedback on page 140 before doing this activity.)

Airtime issues

I am now going to explore some of the typical issues that I come across in groups that are generated by the extent to which people do or do not interrupt. This is not an exclusive list, and you may want to add scenarios from your own experience.

The dominant individual: In most of the groups I have observed over the years, some people talk more than others, and one or two people talk most, taking up huge chunks of the available airtime and as a result dominate the meeting – often to the frustration of other people and to the detriment of the discussion. Their dominance is based on two factors: they tend to be very effective at interrupting other people; and they are very hard to interrupt themselves. This means that once they start talking they can carry on talking for a long time – often without realizing how long and to what effect. And because these people are usually forceful characters, the effect on the rest of the group can be significant: people give up trying to speak themselves, but also stop listening to the dominant individual, building up a level of resentment which will seek expression in indirect and destructive ways. In the end, the quality of the dominant individual's contribution is immaterial – an example of process (behaviour) overriding content.

The competitive relationship: If there are two or more dominant individuals in the group, a more complex pattern emerges where they compete with each other for airtime and increasingly interrupt each other in the process. Other members of the group tend to fall by the wayside as the meeting becomes an arena for two verbal gladiators to slug it out – the need to come out on top having long ago superseded the official purpose and content of the meeting. The level of interruption in the group tends to rise in this scenario, partly because the level of the protagonists' interrupting behaviour is high and partly because the only way other people can get a word in is if they interrupt too. This is an example of social process subverting a meeting through its effect on people's behaviour.

The chaotic group: There are times when the level of interrupting within the group as a whole is high. There may be several reasons for this: the subject of the meeting might be engaging and exciting, for example. At the beginning of the meeting, the level of interruption may have been acceptable, but when everybody is doing it, especially in smaller groups of five to eight people, the behaviour tends to feed on itself, spiralling upwards until it becomes dysfunctional. In their excitement, people stop listening, tumble over each other in their eagerness to speak, have to say the same thing two or three times before it gets heard, if it ever does. The group becomes chaotic, no longer able to manage its own energy effectively because there is insufficient control available.

These scenarios show examples of problems caused by high levels of interruption and these are the ones I come across most frequently. However, problems can be caused when not enough interrupting is being done, either by an individual or group, as follows:

☐ There are many people who are not good at interrupting and who consequently find it difficult to get involved in meetings. There are several reasons why they may not be good at it: some people have been brought up to believe it is rude to interrupt and as a result find it almost impossible to do so; others have soft, quiet voices and find it difficult to make themselves heard; some people lack confidence in groups and are unassertive and shy; others like to keep their own counsel, only speaking when they have something to say and if someone else hasn't said it first. Whatever the reason, people who tend not to interrupt much will often find themselves being excluded in meetings. This is not being done deliberately: it is just that if you don't claim much of the airtime, people will start to forget about you; they will become used to your low level of contribution and will stop expecting you to speak. The longer you stay quiet in a meeting, the harder it becomes to break in – once the pattern of airtime distribution has formed, it becomes self-reinforcing and increasingly difficult to change.

□ I sometimes come across groups where the level of interruption generally is very low. You might think that this would be a positive sign: an indication of self-awareness and consideration of others. It sometimes is, but the lack of interruption is more often a cause for concern because it indicates a lack of energy within the group, or a lack of engagement. If people aren't interrupting each other much they are either being excessively polite or there is something going on: a dynamic within the group that is causing them to be careful with each other; or a negative response to the subject of the discussion – confusion, boredom, cynicism.

EXERCISE 9.3

Spend a few minutes now reflecting on the above scenarios. Do any of them remind you of meetings you have attended in the past or groups that you have worked with? Are any of them problems that you are experiencing currently with your own group or team? Are there other scenarios, not mentioned here, that you have come across where the nature of the interrupting behaviour has caused problems for the group?

Managing interrupting behaviour

The scenarios we have looked at above, where the level of interruption has been unusually high or low, enable us to look at interrupting in three ways:

□ As a **strategy** – consciously or unconsciously, people are using it as a way of achieving their objective in a meeting, either by dominating (or trying to dominate) the discussion; or by withdrawing from the discussion and letting other people do the work.

□ As an indicator of **energy** – the level of interruption is like a barometer which can be used to measure the energy level in a group, and to evaluate its appropriateness. If a high level of energy is required – in order to generate new ideas, for example, or to get to the end of a difficult task – high levels of interruption will be appropriate. However, if the discussion involves quiet reflection or careful evaluation, then lower levels of energy, and of interruption, will be more effective.

□ As a **skill** – above all, interrupting is something that can be done well or badly. Some people are good at it: they break in, stop someone in their tracks and take the airtime from them cleanly so that they claim and receive the attention of the group. Others are less skilful in their attempts to interrupt: they fail to break in cleanly, don't stop the other person and either back off, thus not getting the airtime they want, or carry on 'overtalking', so that neither they nor the other person can be clearly heard by the rest of the group.

I am going to focus on this last aspect now: the skill of interrupting effectively. This is a key interactive skill and one that is often undervalued. It is often assumed to be a skill that need only be taught to quiet people, and it is certainly useful in this context. But in my experience it is a skill that needs to be learnt by many people, regardless of their level of self-confidence. I have come across some individuals who are blessed with an innate sense of timing and who can therefore involve themselves in meetings without interrupting much. They have the knack of finding the gaps between one person finishing and another starting to speak and moving into that gap before anyone else. But these people are few and far between. I come across many more people who interrupt a lot but who don't do it very well and who cause themselves and the groups they belong to problems as a result. Because when you fail to interrupt effectively, you fail to get heard clearly, and so either the point is lost or you have to make it again – and again – interrupting more frequently to do so, not listening to others, fragmenting the discussion, adding to the confusion, causing repetition and duplication. When I am facilitating groups, I am often amazed at the positive effect that is achieved on the quality of their discussion (content *and* process) when the group reduce their level of interrupting.

So how do you interrupt well? Here are some steps that you may find helpful:

1. **Know that you are doing it.** As with most behaviour, we are more likely to do it effectively if we are aware of what we are doing, if we have consciously chosen to do it. This is difficult, especially with interrupting: we shut out when we have something to say, and by the time we have sorted out what we want to say we have usually stopped listening to other people. The knack is to interrupt yourself before you interrupt

someone else. Practise waiting before starting to speak in order to become aware of what is happening around you. It may be then that you will find a gap which you can slip into. If not, you will interrupt more effectively simply through knowing that it is what you need to do to claim airtime.

2. **Look at the person who is speaking,** preferably making eye contact with them. This lets them know both that you are aware they are speaking and that you have something to say. They are more likely to allow you into the conversation as a result. They may stop you in order to finish what they are saying, but they are likely to finish more quickly and you are more likely to get in when they have finished.

3. If eye contact is not enough, **make some kind of gesture** that indicates you want to stop the person speaking – I usually hold my hand out, palm facing the speaker in a classic 'stop' signal. This is more emphatic, and also is more visible to the rest of the group, who are likely to back off and let you in as a result.

4. **Tell people what you are going to do before doing it.** If you are going to ask a question, for example, say that this is what you are going to do: 'Can I just ask you something . . .', or if you want to give your opinion, 'I'd like to tell you what I think about this . . .'. Labelling your behaviour in this way helps because it tends to catch people's attention and sets their expectation so that they listen to you in the right mode (e.g. question-receiving mode). Labelling also has the advantage, in noisy groups, of giving people time to quieten down so that they don't miss the main body of what you are saying.

ACTIVITY 9.2

If you feel you need to improve your interrupting skills, identify a specific meeting or discussion which will be appropriate for you to do so. Practise the steps outlined above, perhaps arranging to get feedback from a colleague afterwards to help you assess how successful you have been.

Invitations

Our interrupting behaviour influences the extent to which we get involved in discussions and meetings. If the level is low, the risk is that we will be sidelined, unable to make the contribution we want to. Invitation, on the other hand, is the behaviour we use to influence the involvement of *other* people and is therefore the second key behaviour in managing the distribution of airtime. It is a direct attempt to invite someone to speak, clearing a space for them in the discussion and drawing the group's attention to them. For example:

'What do you think about this, Frank?'

'Why don't you tell us what you know of this from your previous experience, Sally?'

'You've been quiet for a while, John, do you need to say anything or are you happy to listen?'

'I want to hear how Carol feels about this before we go any further.'

We invite people to contribute in this way usually either because we are aware that they have been silent for a while, or because we want to hear what they have to say about a specific issue. By inviting their participation, and so hopefully making it easier for them to speak and to be heard, we are directly influencing the way airtime is allocated. But we are also exerting a more subtle influence, because we are raising awareness within the group as a whole of the way airtime is being distributed: partly because we are creating a hiatus, cutting through the pattern of interrupting that has been established; and partly because we are highlighting the fact that someone hasn't been able to 'get in', someone, perhaps, whom the group needs to be paying more attention to. Invitation is a tool that can be used to educate the group about their airtime management and to facilitate group process generally.

Having said that, it is dangerous to assume that invitation is of itself a good behaviour to use, just as it is misguided to think that interruptions are of themselves bad. I remember once participating in a meeting several years ago which was attended by the client's secretary – a young woman who was unused to such meetings and nervous about being at this one. She was quiet for most of the meeting, and I kept asking her if she had anything to say, any comments or feedback that she could give us. Nobody else was making an effort to involve her and I felt sorry for her, and wanted to be seen to be sensitive to her predicament, to be the one who noticed and who was prepared to do something about it. She hated me for it: she was more than happy to sit quietly, had nothing to say and wanted to listen and absorb as much as possible. In the end, the secretary turned to me, almost in tears, and asked me to leave her alone.

So invitation is a behaviour that needs to be used with care, because it puts a degree of focus on the other person that they may not be ready for or feel comfortable with. Here are some situations when invitations will be appropriate:

☐ **Protection:** When people are trying to get involved in a discussion but are unable to because of the level of interrupting that is going on. People with quiet voices, for example, or who lack self-confidence, will find it difficult to break in and may need help. Inviting them to contribute can provide them with the protection they need and once they have got involved once, it is generally easier for them to get involved again later.

☐ **Climate:** Inviting someone to participate is a strong signal about the kind of climate you feel is appropriate for the discussion or meeting. It sensitizes people to the needs of others and makes them more aware of the way airtime is being distributed among the group. It also raises their awareness of the extent to which they are interrupting and encourages people to listen to each other more.

☐ **Pressure:** There are times when people are quiet in meetings, not because they are shy or unassertive, but because they are refusing to commit themselves to the group or to the issues being discussed. They are withholding their participation deliberately and can create doubt, anxiety or resentment as a result. Directly inviting them to participate puts pressure on them to become involved or to explain why they don't want to.

☐ **Persuasion:** There are times in meetings when persuasive arguments can become focused on two or three people, who are in effect 'acting out' the issue for the rest of the group. It is usually helpful to break this dynamic at some point and to invite other people's views so that the argument doesn't become personalized. It is especially useful, of course, to invite participation from people whom you know support your views – but we will look at this in more detail in the next chapter.

EXERCISE 9.4

Spend a few minutes now reflecting on a meeting or group discussion you have attended recently. To what extent was invitation behaviour being used to involve people deliberately in the meeting? If the level was low, would the meeting have benefited from more? If it was being used, was it being used for any of the four reasons listed above?

When I am observing groups, I listen out for invitations, and am particularly interested to see who, if anyone, is using this behaviour. This is one of the ways I assess the control resource within the group (see Chapter 2). People who invite the participation of others are demonstrating both an awareness of process issues and also a desire to influence or help manage the group's process. Hopefully the person doing it will be the chairperson, which will indicate some congruence between official and unofficial structures (see Chapter 2). But I have long since given up expecting that the chairperson will necessarily be skilled in that role. It is just as likely that another member of the group will be the one inviting contribution from others. Once I have identified who it is, I need to understand why they are using this behaviour – which of the four reasons listed above (protection, climate, pressure or persuasion) – as this will indicate the extent to which they are using invitations to serve their own or the group's ends. And if they are not the chairperson, I also need to assess whether they are compensating for or competing with the chair, and the extent to which this reflects and affects the structural level of process.

Managing invitation behaviour

As with every behaviour, involving people through invitation is a skill, although in this case the skill lies primarily in awareness. If you want to influence the distribution of airtime in a meeting by involving people, the following steps will be of help:

☐ 'Step out' of the discussion for a period of time in order to observe the group to identify who is contributing and who isn't.

☐ Try to assess why people aren't saying much: are they happy with their level of contribution or not?

☐ Evaluate whether the group will benefit if they are more involved: Will they add value to the discussion? Will they feel more committed to the outcome? Is their commitment important?

☐ Decide whether to invite them to contribute by:
   (a) **creating opportunity**, e.g. 'Do you have anything you want to say at this stage, Sarah?', thus giving them the option to decline the opportunity;
   (b) **creating pressure**, e.g. 'What do you think about this, Sarah?', thus forcing them to respond, or to explain why they don't want to.

The option you choose will depend on how you think they will feel in response to your invitation, and the extent to which you want to take their feelings into account.

ACTIVITY 9.3

If you feel you need to improve your invitation skills, identify a specific meeting or discussion which will be appropriate for you to do so. Practise the steps outlined above, perhaps arranging to get feedback from a colleague afterwards to help you assess how successful you have been.

Summary

Invitations and interruptions are two ways in which we directly influence the distribution of airtime in a discussion. Interruption is far more common and far more frequently used. We are usually unaware of and surprised by the extent to which we have interrupted others. Although a meeting needs a certain level of interrupting if it is not to feel slow, overpolite or unenergetic, it is more often the case that there is too much of it going on and that this has the effect of excluding some people or generating confusion or competition.

Invitations are rarer, mainly because they are often not needed. We are usually aware of our behaviour when we invite people to participate in a way that we are not when we interrupt. And because this demonstrates an awareness of others and of group process, our invitations can have an impact on the climate of the meeting as a whole.

Interruptions and invitations are the first two of a list of behaviours that I will be introducing to you in this chapter. In fact, interrupting and invitation are almost always used in conjunction with one of these other behaviours. When we interrupt, for example, we might do so by making a statement of some kind. When we invite someone's participation, we are likely to do so by asking them a question. The behaviours happen simultaneously: we interrupt *by* making a statement; we invite *by* asking a question.

The next section looks at the key behavioural choice that I have just alluded to: the choice between making statements and using questions, the two behaviours which most influence the way we exchange information. We will see that this choice also has a profound influence on the way airtime is distributed among the group during a meeting as well as on the quality of the discussion that takes place.

Information

Once I have got a sense of how a group is managing the distribution of airtime in a meeting or discussion, the next thing I listen for is how they manage the exchange of information, and in particular the extent to which they ask questions as opposed to giving information to each other. This is a key indicator for me, both of the level of awareness that exists within the group, but more importantly, of the level of interactive skills. This may sound terribly crude and simplistic, but the extent to which people ask questions is a quick and accurate indicator of their likely effectiveness as a communicator.

So when I observe the way groups manage the exchange of information, I am looking for two things:

☐ How well is the necessary exchange of information organized at the procedural level? Is the meeting organized so that people who have information to convey are given the opportunity to do this effectively? If decisions are to be made, is the information required to make that decision gathered at the right time and to the appropriate level of detail? Is too much time spent exchanging information which is not directly relevant or of interest to people at the meeting?

☐ How well is the exchange of information managed at the behavioural level? Are people given the space to speak? Are they listened to? Are people interested in what others have got to say? Or are they just interested in expressing their own views and opinions? Do people ask questions of each other in order to understand better, to explore, to probe or to challenge?

EXERCISE 9.5

Spend a few minutes now reflecting on a meeting or group discussion you have attended recently. Use the questions above to assess the management of information in this meeting.

We will be looking at the issues involved with the first set of questions in the next chapter, which focuses on the skills of effective chairing. In this chapter, I want to look in detail at the fundamental behavioural choice that we make each time we speak: the choice between telling and asking.

Telling v asking

Telling and asking are the two basic blocks of behaviour. All other verbal behaviour will fall into one or other of these two categories – as we will see with the behaviours that we will explore later in this chapter. So focusing on the telling/asking ratio is a crude measure, but it is one that is worth exploring because it reveals so much about the ways in which individuals are choosing to contribute to the group and about how the group as a whole is choosing to work together. For, above all, it is useful to regard telling and asking as *strategic* choices which have a considerable impact on both individual and group effectiveness.

Put simply, in most of the meetings I observe, people don't ask enough questions. They are far more concerned to get their own point of view across, to demonstrate what they know, to refer to their own experiences and so on. Their chosen strategy is to tell – even though this choice is often made instinctively – and they perceive their role and influence within the group to be based on *what* they tell. This is not necessarily wrong, but it is often not appropriate and can interfere with the successful achievement of the group's purpose in a meeting.

EXERCISE 9.6

Spend a few minutes now reflecting on how you would describe yourself. Are you someone who generally in meetings:

☐ Does a lot of telling and not much asking?

☐ Does mainly telling with some asking?

☐ Asks a lot of questions?

This is a difficult exercise to answer accurately: very few of us are aware of how much time we spend telling – although it is almost always much more than we think. This is because, when we are telling, our mind is taken up with what we are saying and what we are going to say. Because we are focusing on content, we are less aware of how we are behaving and how our behaviour is impacting on other people. When we ask questions, on the other hand, we tend to be more aware of our behaviour because asking a question is more difficult: you are not just thinking about what *you* are saying, you are thinking about what you want the other person to say and how best to get them to say it. We tend to know when we have asked a question because we have concentrated on putting the right form of words together. When we are telling, the words can tumble out automatically.

ACTIVITY 9.4

Here are two activities which will help you get a more accurate picture of the balance of your telling and asking:

☐ Listen to yourself: choose an interaction where your contribution is not vital and monitor your instinctive behaviour. See how many times your instinctive response was to tell; keep a check of how many times you asked questions.

☐ Get feedback: ask someone who knows you well and whom you trust to give you feedback about your behaviour generally. Ask them if they think you:

  (a) tell too much and if so what impact this has on them;
  (b) are mainly interested in your own thoughts and opinions;
  (c) would benefit from asking more questions and if so, how you would benefit.

(NB Read the guidelines on asking for feedback on page 140 before doing this activity.)

Being aware of the amount of telling you do is one of the first steps towards becoming an effective communicator. Most people tend to do more telling than asking: the exact balance will vary according to circumstances, but the pattern is fairly constant. Some people do a lot of telling and hardly any asking at all, whatever the demands of the specific interaction. And there are others who ask a lot of questions and do relatively little telling in most situations. The key is the extent to which you can use both styles: I have come across some people who are literally unable to ask questions – they try, but it comes out as a statement. They are rare, but many people are not used to asking questions and do not find it easy to adopt that style. They are far more comfortable telling. At the other extreme, I have come across people who can switch easily from telling to asking and are comfortable using both styles.

The impact of the tell/ask balance

The balance of telling and asking affects a meeting in several ways. Here are five areas which illustrate the extensive impact of this basic behavioural choice:

☐ **Involvement:** We have seen how participation in meetings can be directly influenced through invitations. But the extent to which people are involved in a discussion depends to a large extent on the number of questions being asked. The fewer the questions, the less likely it is that everyone will be participating, because it is more likely that there will be high levels of telling and that this will be dominated by some members of the group to the exclusion of others. A high level of questions is no guarantee of shared participation, because the questions could all be being asked by or directed at one person. But asking questions is a way of managing the involvement of a group and one of the ways that as a participant in a meeting, you can increase your own contribution or the contribution of others.

☐ **Climate:** The level of questioning often has a direct impact on the climate of a meeting, as it indicates the extent to which people are interested in and respect each other's views on the one hand, or are being egocentric and competitive on the other. Questions are not always asked out of genuine interest, as we will see later, but they do always give people the opportunity to speak and thus express their views and opinions. The fact that these opportunities are being created affects how people feel about the meeting and how they participate in it. Just as, if there is a low level of questioning, so that people are having to create their own opportunities or even fight for airtime, this too will affect how they feel about the meeting and the way they participate.

☐ **Use of resource:** Questions are a way of ensuring that the group is making full use of its resources – in terms of the knowledge and experience of its members. I am often struck by how little effort is made in meetings to find out what people know and whether they have relevant experience and then to maximize the value of this knowledge and experience. Just as I am struck by the extent to which people can use up large amounts of the available time speaking from what I have to come to call a 'zero knowledge base'!

☐ **Commitment:** Most people tend to think they are only being persuasive or influential if they are telling – and they choose this behavioural strategy in order to get their own way: to force their views and opinions on to the group. And in order to be successful when using a tell style to influence, you do need to be forceful, either through the power of your position within the group or through the power of your personality. Fewer people are aware that you can be persuasive through the questions that you ask – and even fewer are any good at it. We will look at the skills involved in more detail in Chapter 11. It is worth noting here, however, that the different persuasion styles (telling and asking) can have a significant impact on the level of commitment that is felt to the final outcome. A questioning style is more likely to generate commitment. A telling style might, but runs the risk of not doing so – and thus fails to achieve the longer-term objectives of the meeting.

☐ **Quality:** Mainly as a result of the aspects covered above, the balance of telling and asking can have a profound influence over the quality of decision-making. I have been in too many meetings myself where we have got high (see Chapter 7 on the pendulum) because of an exciting or creative discussion and made decisions which have not looked quite so impressive in the cold light of day! And this is mainly because we didn't ask enough questions at the time, thus not gathering all the information we needed, did not evaluate the options sufficiently or test out the true merits of our preferred solution.

EXERCISE 9.7

Spend a few minutes now reflecting on your own group or team. Referring to the five points listed above, do you feel that the balance of telling and asking is effective in your team meetings? Is there too much telling generally? Would the meetings be more effective if there was more questioning? If so, why?

It may look as if questions are the answer to all your problems and this is not the case, although I often feel that it is not a bad start. There aren't many meetings I come away from, either as participant or observer, which would not have been more effective if there had been more questioning and less telling. But this is too simplistic: some discussions do require high levels of telling; some meetings are called in order for people to present large amounts of information that others need to receive; there are times when it is appropriate for members of the group to use a high telling style to put across their point of view and for others to listen silently for long periods; just as there are times when high levels of questioning are going to lead to confusion or slow down the decision-making process in ways that aren't practical.

There are times when we need to be predominantly telling and times when it would help if we were asking more questions. We will be more effective in group discussions if we consciously choose which strategy we need to adopt at a given time, according to the requirements of the discussion. This should be based on the answers to the following three questions:

1. What do I know and what do I need to know?
2. What do others know and what do they need to know?
3. What are we trying to achieve and what is the best way of achieving it?

It is worth asking yourself these questions prior to a meeting, as they will help you to think about the information exchange that is required and how you need to behave in order to achieve it successfully.

ACTIVITY 9.5

Before the next meeting you are attending or chairing, ask yourself the three questions above to help you plan how to behave during the meeting to achieve your desired outcomes. You may need first to clarify what your desired outcomes are – this too is good practice.

The value of questions

Because most people find it relatively easy to tell, I want to spend some time now focusing in more detail on asking, and in particular exploring the function and value of questions in interaction. There are two main areas of value. The first concerns the impact on others; the second concerns the direct benefit to you.

Impact

When you ask questions, you are sending signals to other people which affect the way they perceive you and therefore respond to you. You are signalling that you:

☐ Want to involve them in the discussion.

☐ Are interested in them and what they have to say.

☐ Respect their opinions and ideas.

☐ Are open-minded and prepared to move your position.

☐ Are willing to learn from them and their experience.

None of this may in fact be true. You might have already made up your mind about an issue and not be in the slightest bit interested in what anybody else has got to say. (In which case, you will sooner or later be sending at the same time a set of counter-signals which will lead people to mistrust you and regard your questioning as a manipulative strategy.) But if the above signals are genuine, people will tend to respond positively, are more likely to open up, to collaborate with you and to work cooperatively with the group as a whole.

Benefit

Apart from the favourable responses of others, there are several direct benefits that you will gain from using questions. They are the behavioural tool which enables you in particular to do three things effectively. These are to:

☐ Gather and process information in order to make decisions.

☐ Challenge people to think, to think harder and to re-think what they have said.

☐ Control interactions.

Whereas the first two of these benefits are straightforward, the last one requires further explanation. It is often assumed that we are in control of a discussion when we have the airtime, when we are talking and when we are telling, because it is in those circumstances that we are in control of what we say. Although this is true, it does not necessarily follow that we are in control of what the other people are thinking and so we are not in control of the interaction as a whole. When we ask questions, we are deliberately attempting to shape what other people are thinking about, and through this, we are controlling what is being discussed and to a large extent how it is being discussed.

The fact that questions control interaction is a basic premise of interactive skills development. When I observe groups, I look for the people who ask questions because this will indicate a level of behavioural awareness and skill. People who ask questions are potential control resources within a group. But because questions can also be used in order to influence, I need to understand why someone is asking questions: it may be that they are using a questioning style to exert influence rather than control – either of which may be or may not be in the best interests of the group.

Managing the tell/ask ratio

In every interaction, we strike a balance between telling and asking. Sometimes we don't ask any questions at all, but usually there is a mix of both behaviours. The exact balance – the tell/ask ratio – will vary depending on the specific demands of each interaction, although we are likely to have recurring patterns of behaviour which reflect our dominant style.

There are two specific behaviours which heavily influence our balance of telling and asking. These relate to the way we manage the exchange of information during interactions. Because a large proportion of almost every interaction is given over to information exchange of one form or another, these two behaviours are the ones we tend to use most frequently. They are:

☐ **Giving information:** When you give information, facts or opinions to other people.

☐ **Seeking information:** When you ask for information, facts or opinions from one or more other people.

Figure 9.1 uses these behaviours to illustrate the tell/ask ratio.

As I have said, a hefty proportion of the people who go through my programmes talk too much. But their behaviour is not just characterized by high telling; they also don't seek much information (position 1 in Figure 9.1). It is this combination of behaviours that is significant in determining the impact of people's behaviour and the way they are perceived and responded to by others. Somebody who gives a lot of information and who also asks a lot of questions (position 2), will impact very differently, as will someone who seeks information without doing much telling at all (position 3). So when we are attempting to control our information behaviours, we need to be actively managing the balance between the two rather than focusing on one behaviour in isolation.

When high tellers receive feedback which shows them the extent of their telling behaviour, their initial response is often to give less information. They end up overcompensating by not contributing to the discussion at all.

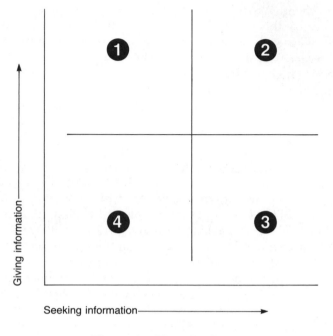

Figure 9.1 The tell/ask ratio.

This is indicative of their problem, because it suggests that they think that the only way they can contribute to a discussion is to tell; they do not consider asking as a viable option. This is also sometimes true of low contributors (position 4), who don't give or seek much information and who may justify their lack of contribution by claiming that other people had already said what they wanted to say. Many people think that the only legitimate way to contribute to a meeting or discussion is to tell.

The tell/ask ratio shows that it is not just the level of giving information that is significant but the balance between telling and asking, and this creates two options for affecting the balance: one is to reduce the amount of giving information; the other is to increase the amount of seeking information. Of these two options for changing the tell/ask ratio, I favour the latter for two reasons:

☐ It is easier to do more of a behaviour than it is to do less of one.

☐ If you increase your level of seeking information, this tends to reduce your level of telling – by asking others to speak you are cutting down the opportunities for you to tell.

So if you want to address your tell/ask ratio, the issue usually is: how can you ask more questions?

Asking more questions

As we move through this chapter and through Part 3, we will be looking at different kinds of questions which have specific functions and which require skill if they are to be used effectively. At this stage, I want to focus on the basic behaviour of seeking information. Because almost everyone knows how to ask questions and asks questions every day of their lives, the issue at this level is not one of skill, but of awareness.

If you want to ask more questions, you need to be aware of:

☐ Your tell/ask ratio during a discussion or meeting (i.e. How much of your airtime is taken up by you giving information? How many questions are you asking?).
☐ Opportunities when asking questions that would be useful for you or for the rest of the group.

The opportunities might be varied:

☐ There may be quiet people who you could involve through asking them questions ('Have you got anything you want to say, John?').
☐ There might be information, opinions or reactions that you would like from certain individuals ('What do you know about this, John?').
☐ There might be data that you want to gather from the group as a whole ('How many of you have read my memo?').

The questions in the above examples are not in themselves difficult to ask. They are basic questions which seek information, facts and opinions from other people. The key is to be aware of the need and opportunities to ask them. The best way to develop awareness is to spend a period of time observing the group and listening to the discussion.

ACTIVITY 9.6

This activity will help you to increase your level of questioning. Select a meeting that you will be attending in the near future in which you will not be playing a pivotal role. During this meeting:

☐ Stop participating at some point for five minutes so that you can just observe and listen.
☐ Study the behaviour of the other people at the meeting, in particular listening for their balance of telling and asking.
☐ Become aware of opportunities for seeking information: times when it would be helpful to you or the group if you asked questions.

Observing and listening won't of itself lead you to ask more questions. But it will sensitize you to what is going on around you and in particular to the needs and behaviour of the other people in the group. This should help you to identify how you could help them, and the meeting as a whole, through questions. These may be questions which you ask because you don't know the answer, and only by stopping and listening sometimes can we realize what we don't know. Or they may be questions which you know the answer to, but which you ask in order to make things clearer for others, or to get other people to think things through more carefully.

Even if you don't ask more questions during the meeting as a result of the activity, you will be able afterwards to reflect on the questions that you could have asked.

Summary

Telling and asking are the two key behavioural choices that we make each time we open our mouths to speak. They have a profound impact on our effectiveness as a communicator and therefore on the quality of our interactions. People develop dominant styles of communicating: some people tend to be high 'tellers', asking relatively few questions; others are balanced, able to tell or ask with equal facility; some people tend to ask a lot of questions and are relatively low 'tellers'.

Most people will be more effective communicators if they ask more questions. This is because by asking questions, we are usually focusing on the other person and are thus more aware of their needs; and also because we are more likely to be aware of the process of the interaction and thus better able to manage it. If we ask more questions we also tend to do less telling, shifting the ask/tell ratio from both directions. The perceptions other people have of us shifts accordingly: they see us as being more interested in and respectful of them and more keen to work cooperatively as part of the group.

Ideas

I have talked about the exchange of information in terms of two core behaviours: telling and asking. We can learn a lot about how a group or individual communicates just by observing their use of these two behaviours. They are only a starting-point, however, and I am now going to look at them in more detail, exploring different kinds of telling and asking, behaviours which have specific functions and specific impacts on the effectiveness of the way groups and teams work together. In this section, we are going to look at the behaviours involved in the generation and development of ideas. These are behaviours which can indicate the extent to which a group of people are collaborating well with each other or not.

Collaboration is most clearly expressed in the extent to which people are interested in each other's ideas. When I observe groups, I watch out for two indicators of this:

☐ To what extent are people seeking ideas from each other? Are they primarily just putting forward their own ideas? Or are they asking questions in order to find out what ideas other people have – questions which directly encourage other people to propose their own solutions?

☐ To what extent are people only interested in their own ideas? Do they listen to and take into account the ideas that other people introduce into the meeting, or do they ignore or dismiss them? Do they try to build on other people's ideas in order to develop a solution, or do they try to make sure that their idea is the one that is accepted by the group?

EXERCISE 9.8

Spend a few minutes now reflecting on a meeting or group discussion you have attended recently. Use the questions above to assess the generation and development of ideas in this meeting.

The two sets of questions sound as if they are addressing the same issue, but they involve the relationships between three distinct types of initiating behaviour. The first relationship concerns the source of ideas; the second concerns the development of ideas. I will look at each of these in turn.

The source of ideas

In any discussion that requires ideas to be generated (whether it is deciding what to eat for dinner or a strategy for organizational change), there are two possible sources of ideas: you or the other person/people. This must seem obvious. You might think I am being facile even to point it out. But it amazes me how many people do not consider that it is an option to ask other people for their ideas. I am sure this is not because they don't realize that the option exists. They just never think of doing it. Or to put it another way: they assume that the ideas should come from them. Managers are particularly prone to this assumption because many of them think that one of the responsibilities of being a manager is to come up with the ideas, and that asking other people to do so – especially the people you manage – is a sign of weakness, an indication that you don't know the answers yourself.

For managers and team-leaders, their attitude to the generation of ideas revolves around two issues: one is about interpretation – the way you interpret the meaning of the role of leader – the second is the way in which you enact this interpretation through the behavioural choice of **proposing** or **seeking ideas**. We have looked at the meaning of leadership in earlier sections of this book, but it is worth spending a few minutes here on this specific issue of interpretation, as it is one that crops up quite frequently in different areas of my work.

Interpretation

I have been working with managers from one of my clients recently on conducting career planning discussions effectively. The greatest concern that the managers have is that they won't know the answers to the questions they are likely to get asked by their people. They are right: in these days of change and uncertainty, it is increasingly difficult to be able to predict the future with any degree of accuracy – thinking further than two years ahead can feel like an absurd self-indulgence. But what interests me is that they think they should be the ones providing the answers. This is a particular and instinctive interpretation of role that goes to the heart of their self-perception of management and of the price to be paid in return for the power gained. It is hard for me to persuade them not only that there are no answers any more, but that there are other ways of conducting such discussions. They could, for example, enable their people to reflect on their aspirations, capabilities, potential, motivation, to identify directions worth pursuing and to explore ways in which these directions could be best pursued. In other words, to use a consultative rather than directive style of leadership (see Chapter 3).

I thought that they would be relieved – here is a clear example where the consultative style has benefits for the manager. Some are relieved, but many more are uncomfortable. Even though this is a solution to their problem, it is in conflict with a deeply engrained self-image as leader: 'I should know the answers and it is my job to provide them'. It is this mindset that encourages a directive leadership style which needs to be addressed if managers are to commit themselves to developing a consultative style. For it is a limited and rigid interpretation that is becoming increasingly redundant. The career development discussion is a good example of the new environment, in which managers are unlikely to know the answers, in which right answers might not exist, in which people need to be helped to manage uncertainty and complexity rather than given a clarity which is short-lived or illusory.

Choice
Leadership style is most overtly revealed in the choices managers make about how they generate ideas. There are two behaviours that I have referred to:

☐ **Proposing ideas:** When you put forward your own ideas, suggestions and proposals.
☐ **Seeking proposals:** When you ask other people for their ideas, suggestions and proposals.

As with the 'parent' behaviours, telling and asking, it is the balance of use of these behaviours that is significant. This balance will partly be determined by the nature of the discussion and the relationship with the other people involved. But it is also largely influenced by the behaviour patterns that you have developed. Many people have a strong tendency towards high-proposing and low-seeking proposals. They will be preoccupied with putting their ideas into the meeting, either because they want to be regarded as positive and creative or because they want to get their own way. Others have a preference for finding out what other people think, either because they don't like to commit themselves or because they want to involve others in the decision-making process.

EXERCISE 9.9

Spend a few minutes now reflecting on your own behaviour when it comes to the generation of ideas. Do you actively seek ideas from other people? Or do you usually prefer to come up with the ideas yourself?

Impact
Effective communicators are able to operate at either extreme, choosing which style is appropriate according to circumstances. We will look at what these circumstances might be in a moment, but first I want to explore the impact of this behavioural choice, so that we have an understanding of what is at stake.

Participation and energy
The generation of ideas requires people to be constructive and creative and therefore usually generates energy and excitement. The meeting or discussion becomes more dynamic when it is time to develop solutions. If everybody involved is happily contributing ideas, the meeting can get out of hand because there is too much energy and not enough control. But if some people are not contributing, then they will feel excluded and

uninvolved. Managers often ask me how they can get their teams to participate more in meetings. The problem is often that the manager is proposing ideas and this tends to depress proposing behaviour in other members of the group. Why bother when it is clear that the boss has already made up her mind? Seeking proposals when generating ideas is often a way of encouraging participation and generating energy.

Climate and respect
The way in which we generate ideas sends a clear signal about how we regard the potential contribution of others at the meeting. As with our telling and asking behaviours generally, the choice we make about the balance of proposing and seeking proposals will indicate the extent to which we are interested in what people have to say. When we are dealing with ideas, it also indicates the extent to which we respect the ideas of others, as opposed to believing that only we will be able to come up with the required solution. This might seem a bit harsh, but I know for myself times when my drive to come up with the 'best answer' has demonstrated both my competitiveness with others in the group and my disrespect for them. I am saying in effect: 'Your ideas are not as good as mine.' Such an attitude has a major impact on the climate of an interaction and often gets in the way of the group being able to work together effectively to develop a solution.

Ownership and commitment
It is unavoidably true that people tend to be more committed to their own ideas than they are to anybody else's. After years of trying to persuade my son to live his life the way I want him to, I am left in no doubt of this. Any grudging agreement that I may be able to exact pales against the enthusiasm with which he carries out his own preferred solutions! Commitment is stronger if it is based on a sense of ownership and one way in which you can encourage ownership is to ask people to put their own ideas forward. They may come up with the same idea that you would have done, but they will be more committed to it precisely because they came up with it. The risk is that they come up with ideas that differ from your preferred option. At various points in this chapter we will look at ways of handling this. But although it is a risk, it is not of itself reason enough not to seek ideas from others.

Options and flexibility
Once we latch on to an idea or solution, it is surprising how difficult most people find it to conceive that other possible solutions might exist. Our admiration for our own idea blinds us both to its limitations and to the existence, let alone virtues, of other options. We get 'locked in' to our preferred option and believe that it is the only possible solution. One

advantage of seeking proposals is that, through asking other people for their ideas, we are generating options which gives us a wider range to choose from. This can 'unlock' us from our preferred route and makes us more flexible in our pursuit of the best possible solution. And given that one of the criteria for 'best possible' is likely to be that the idea has the commitment of the people who have to implement it, inviting them to propose their preferred solutions might be essential anyway.

EXERCISE 9.10

Spend a few minutes now reflecting on your own group or team. Referring to the four points listed above, do you feel that the balance of proposing as opposed to seeking proposals is effective in your team meetings? Are people generally too interested in their own ideas? Would the meetings be more effective if people were encouraged to propose ideas themselves? If so, why?

Appropriateness

The previous section might seem to suggest that seeking proposals is the right thing to do and that you should do it all the time. This is not the case. I do think that seeking proposals is an extremely useful behaviour which many managers should use much more often. But I don't think it is always appropriate, in every situation. There will be many meetings you attend when you are expected to be proposing ideas, and many situations when it is appropriate for you to be doing so. This is particularly true when you are a participant in the meeting or discussion rather than the chairperson or manager. But when you are the leader, the choice becomes more significant, and it is important that you get it right.

Its appropriateness as a behavioural choice will depend partly on your position and partly on the position of the other people, as Figure 9.2 illustrates.

EXERCISE 9.11

Spend a few minutes now reflecting on these conditions. Refer back to an occasion recently when you either sought proposals from one or more of your team, or when you could have done so? Which of the above conditions applied? How did this, or how should this, have affected your decision about which behavioural option to use?

Generating options

You will find that there are situations which fall between the two stools illustrated by Figure 9.2: times when, despite the other person or people's inability or unwillingness to respond, you still need to seek ideas from

Your position	Their position
Need for commitment If your need to gain commitment is high, it is likely that seeking proposals will be the best bet. But if the need for commitment is low, proposing your ideas may be more appropriate.	**Ability to respond** Seeking proposals will only be appropriate if the people you are asking will be able to respond to your questions. If they won't be able to come up with ideas, for whatever reason, then proposing is likely to be more appropriate.
Room for manoeuvre It may be that you have little room for manoeuvre in that your preferred option is the only acceptable option (it may be an order from above, for example). If this is the case, seeking proposals becomes high risk if people are liable to come up with alternatives which, whatever their merits, will not be acceptable.	**Willingness to respond** There may be times when the other people may be unwilling to respond to your attempts to seek their ideas. There could be several reasons for this: they don't trust your motives; they don't want to expose themselves in front of others; they know their preferences will be unacceptable. If these reasons are valid, it may be best to to propose rather than be met with a stubborn silence.

Figure 9.2 Conditions for proposing/seeking proposals.

them. This might be because it is the only way to gain their commitment, or because you know they will be resistant to your ideas. In such circumstances, you need to find a behavioural mid-point between proposing and seeking proposals. There are two other behaviours you can use to generate ideas which perform this function. These are:

☐ **Making suggestions:** When you put forward your own ideas in the form of a question, thus inviting the other person or people to evaluate its suitability. For example: 'Do you think it would work if you suggested the idea to her rather than proposed it?' This is a subset of proposing ideas, in that you are still putting your idea forward. The difference is that, by inviting them to evaluate your proposal, you are allowing them to reject it if they have grounds for doing so. Although it is still your idea, it is their decision and they will feel some ownership as a result. If they reject your suggestion, they are more likely to be willing or able to come up with an alternative suggestion of their own.

☐ **Seeking options:** When you ask the other person or people to come up with the various options which could be considered in order to identify the best solution. This is a subset of seeking proposals and is particularly useful if you want people to think creatively or if you want to unlock them from their own preferred solutions. By generating a list of options together, you can ensure that your ideas are included and that each idea is evaluated on its merits.

ACTIVITY 9.7

Identify a situation in which you can practise generating solutions, ideally one in which you need the commitment of the other person/people involved. Use the conditions illustrated in Figure 9.2 to analyze the requirements of the situation and then decide whether to seek proposals, seek options or make suggestions. Then do it.

Managing the proposing ideas/seeking ideas ratio

Although there are situations when proposing is more appropriate than seeking ideas, and at times when seeking options or making suggestions might be more effective, the key change that most managers have to make in my experience is to seek more ideas from others. There are exceptions, but in most cases the ratio is tipped heavily towards proposing, the clearest behavioural indicator of the directing style.

Happily however, in my experience, and for reasons I don't fully understand, most people find it relatively easy to achieve this change. Once they have become aware of their habitual choice and recognized the value of seeking ideas, the skill development involved in doing so is not great. The questions: 'What do you think?' or 'What ideas have you got?' are not difficult ones to ask. The difficulty lies in suppressing our natural tendency to leap in with our own ideas. For some people, this natural tendency is very immediate and they are concerned that they will never be able to interrupt it in time, to remember not to do it and to seek ideas instead. Some people's concerns are justified. But more often, people are able to do it, not all the time, but more often than they would think. I was delivering a course on one of my client's sites recently and bumped into a manager who had attended a previous course. I remembered him as a highly directive manager, yet when I asked him how things were going he beamed at me: 'It works a treat', he said, 'I ask them for their ideas and they tell me. What a difference. Brilliant.' I beamed back.

The addition of seeking ideas to your repertoire, if it is not already there, is simple to achieve but can be profound in its effect, both on the quality of the solutions you generate and on your relationship with other people. As before, when we looked at asking more questions, the key is to raise your awareness. The following steps will help you to do this:

□ Be aware of the times in a discussion or meeting when you proposed an idea and of your tendency to put your own ideas forward.

□ Consider whether proposing was the only option. Could you have sought ideas from others? Would that have been more effective?

□ Become aware of opportunities to seek ideas from others. There might be points when a meeting would have benefited by hearing ideas from more people; or there might be particular people at the meeting whose ideas you would like to hear or who are finding it difficult to get their ideas heard.

ACTIVITY 9.8

This activity will help you to increase your level of seeking proposals. Select a meeting that you will be attending in the near future in which you will not be playing a pivotal role. During this meeting, take some 'time out' to reflect on your behaviour, following the three steps suggested above.

Sensitizing yourself to the sources of ideas in a meeting or discussion is good practice in developing your awareness of group process and can teach you a lot about the dynamics of the group. It won't of itself give you the discipline to resist your natural tendency to propose (I'm afraid that has to come from within), but it will teach you to recognize the opportunities for seeking ideas, and once you start to do this, the habit becomes self-reinforcing because the benefits are so immediate.

The development of ideas

Once an idea is introduced into a discussion, one or more of several things may happen:

□ It may be completely ignored by other people.
□ It may be rejected by them, more or less scornfully.
□ It may be supported, more or less enthusiastically.
□ It may be discussed, explored and evaluated.
□ It may be further developed.

Some of the items on this list will be looked at in detail in the next section of this chapter, which focuses on reacting behaviours. Here I am going to look at the last item: the development of ideas.

When I am observing groups in action, I am interested in how they manage ideas because this tells me so much about the social level of process, in particular the competitive dynamic within the group and the extent to which this gets in the way of them collaborating effectively. One indicator of the competitive dynamic is the proposing/seeking ideas balance that we have just explored. The development of ideas is another initiating behaviour.

Ideas are developed when you enlarge on or progress the idea of another person, adding to or modifying the original proposal whilst retaining its essential identity. Developing ideas (or 'building' as it is sometimes called) is a behaviour which reveals how people are relating to each other's proposals. It is possible, of course, to develop your own ideas, adding to an original proposal of your own and expanding it as you see fit. But this wouldn't tell me whether you are interested in developing other people's ideas as well, and it is this that I am interested in. By defining the behaviour as only developing the ideas of others, I can gauge the extent to which you work collaboratively or not. I can do this best by comparing your levels of proposing ideas and developing ideas. If the balance is tipped in favour of proposing, with relatively little developing, then this would indicate that you were more interested in your own ideas than the ideas of others. And vice versa.

Developing ideas is both a commonplace and a rare behaviour, as we will see later when we look at how to develop it. You may suggest to a friend that you go to see a film tonight (a proposal). If the friend then suggests that you go for a drink afterwards, she has developed your idea. If you then suggest that you could arrange to meet some other friends in the pub, you have developed the idea further (building on your friend's build); if your friend then offered to phone up the cinema to see what time the film ended, then she has developed the idea again. There are times when building is a natural, effortless part of generating solutions. And there are times, especially at work, when the development of ideas does not take place, or at least, not to the extent that it needs to.

EXERCISE 9.12

Spend a few minutes now reflecting on a meeting or group discussion you have attended recently. To what extent are people interested in and prepared to develop each other's ideas? Or are they mainly interested in promoting their own ideas at the expense of other people's?

There are three main reasons why the development of ideas does not happen:

☐ **The requirement:** Certain types of meeting or discussion are focused on the generation of ideas rather than their development. Their purpose is to come up with a range of options, or to select one solution from such a range. It is not their job to develop the ideas – this will be done by another group or at another meeting. For example, a management team may make a decision, having evaluated several possibilities, and then pass their decision on to someone else to work out the details of how best to implement it. Such a meeting is likely to be legitimately high on proposing (as options are identified) and low on developing ideas.

□ **The dynamics:** The dynamic within the group may generate a climate which discourages the development of ideas. A competitive dynamic is the most obvious example of this, where people, in their eagerness to influence the group or to be seen to be better than their colleagues, will focus on their own ideas to the exclusion of anyone else's, thus raising the level of proposing and lowering the level of developing. Any dynamic, however, which generates tension and unhappiness is likely to depress the level of developing ideas, as people tend to withdraw in such an atmosphere, withholding behaviour which reveals their interest in or support of other people.

□ **Skill level:** Some people are not good at developing ideas, especially in the work context. The example above of the social arrangement may make the behaviour look straightforward, even mundane. But it involves a complex set of thought processes which we will explore in more detail later in this section. At work, in group discussions especially, the pace of the interaction makes it difficult to think quickly enough to develop ideas effectively. When the ideas are complicated and several people are speaking at once, building can be a difficult behaviour to use. By the time your thought process is complete, the discussion is likely to have moved on!

EXERCISE 9.13

Spend a few minutes now reflecting on your own team in terms of these three factors. To what extent do the requirements of your meetings, or the dynamics within the group, or people's skill levels raise or decrease the level of building behaviour?

The impact of building

In spite of the difficulty of building in group settings, the impact of the behaviour is so considerable and almost always so positive that it is one that all leaders should look to encourage in their teams and to do so primarily by modelling the behaviour themselves. Before looking at how to develop the skills of developing ideas, I will go through some of the benefits to be gained by raising the level of building generally in groups and teams.

Climate and teamwork
When there is a high level of building going on, thus balancing the proposing and developing of ideas, this has a significant impact on the climate in which the group is working in a number of ways: people are tending to listen to and show interest in each other, so that the climate is more considerate and respectful; developing ideas generates energy within the group, often drawing people in to a shared creative activity; and people are showing that they want to achieve an outcome through working with each other, which has a significant impact on the sense of team and of being part of the team.

Ownership and commitment
When an idea is developed successfully by the group, the ownership of the idea is shared by the group, but in such a way that the originator of the idea does not feel deprived. It is still their idea and the contributions of others hasn't taken that away. But these contributions have enhanced the original idea and allowed others to feel some ownership of it too, so that the whole group feel committed to its successful implementation. The energy generated by building adds to this commitment, often binding the group together in a communal feeling of accomplishment which encourages them to repeat this way of working in the future.

Quality of outcome
When ideas are developed effectively, they tend to be better. Building almost always improves an idea, adding to it in ways which ensure that it becomes a more complete solution, taking into account the requirements of the issues it is addressing and the factors that will get in the way of a successful implementation. When a group invests in developing ideas thoroughly, it indicates that they are committed to achieving a quality solution. When groups accept an idea too readily, without exploring and developing it, then it indicates that they are more interested in achieving an outcome than they are in achieving a quality outcome.

Doing more building
I have already said that developing ideas involves a complex mental process and I am now going to explain why as a preface to exploring how you can do more of it if you feel that you need to increase your use of this behaviour. There are five stages in this process:

1. **Listening** to the proposal that has been made, hearing it and understanding it clearly.

2. **Evaluating** the idea and your reaction to it: Do you like it or not? What don't you like about it?

3. **Identifying** areas for improvement: either enhancements to the original or weaknesses that need to be overcome.

4. **Formulating** specific ideas for developing the original, whether enhancements or solutions to the weaknesses identified.

5. **Articulating** the development: finding space in the discussion to express the build that you want to make.

If you want to develop your building skills, you need to focus on the first two of these steps. There are people who have a natural facility for developing ideas, but at the root of this skill is their ability to listen closely and to ask questions to explore and evaluate the original idea. This is obviously necessary as preparation for the other three stages, but it has one other crucial advantage: it buys time. Discussion in groups tends to move quickly and chaotically, as people jump in with what is uppermost in their minds, which is invariably unconnected to what has just been said by someone else. Because the process of developing ideas involves the five stages listed above, it can take time, especially if the issue is complex, or the proposal is one that is difficult to evaluate.

So if you want to improve your building, the first step is to ask questions of the person making the proposal in order to find out more about it. This will give you more information, will focus the attention of the whole group on the proposal and will give you the time to identify areas for improvement. Once you have done that, you should be able to develop the idea relatively easily. You will also have paved the way for others to build as well (they may of course beat you to it!).

Proposals are deceptive. They often sound straightforward but contain a depth of possibilities and ambiguities that go unnoticed unless explored more fully. Even the example I used earlier – to go and see a film – contains a number of component parts: Which film? Which cinema? What time? How to get there? When do we eat, before or after? We need to unpack even the most simple proposal in order to find the components that are there or that need to be there. Then we are in a position to evaluate it and to identify areas for enhancement or improvement. Sometimes this process happens almost instantly: with simple ideas or ideas that we are familiar with (like going to the cinema), the first four stages in the process can happen in our head in nano-seconds and we have articulated the build seemingly without thinking. But with complex, unfamiliar ideas this is unlikely to be possible and we will need to ask questions about the original proposal to provide the basis for the development of ideas.

Our response to other people's ideas is often instant. I have a colleague who disagrees with my ideas almost before I have finished articulating them, as a matter of policy. It is a feature of our relationship. I have to say: 'I want you to listen to this, don't disagree instantly, just hear what I have got to say and then think about it', and this will remind him to listen! To some extent we are all like that: we hear an idea and decide very quickly whether we like it or not. Often, we are reacting to one aspect of the idea rather than its entirety.

The process of using questions to 'unpack' ideas in order to identify common ground and areas of difference is the precursor to developing ideas. It is a powerful process, particularly when there are aspects of the idea that you don't like, but the situation is one in which you don't want to disagree openly. This will be the case if you are encouraging members of your team to come up with ideas, or if you are coaching individuals to improve their performance. It is a skill worth practising in its own right as well as one that will help you to increase your building behaviour.

ACTIVITY 9.9

This activity will help you to increase your level of developing proposals. Select a meeting that you will be attending in the near future in which you will not be playing a pivotal role. During this meeting, pay particular attention to proposals made by other people. Listen out for them, listen to them carefully and ask questions to explore them more fully. This should create opportunities for you to build on the idea to develop it further.

Summary

The ways in which we go about generating and developing ideas are one of the key indicators of the choices we have made about our leadership style and our interpretation of the role of leader. The choice simply is whether to put forward our own ideas or encourage and enable others to do so. The impact can be profound, both on the climate of an interaction and on the quality of the outcome.

For most people, their natural style is to propose their own ideas. This is an extension of the tendencies to tell and to dive into content (see Chapter 5). Seeking proposals is generally a strategic choice that has to be consciously made. In order to increase our use of this behaviour, we have to resist our tendency to propose and be alive to opportunities to seek proposals from others. When we have done this, we have also created the opportunity to develop proposals. Having sought the idea, we are more likely to listen to it and explore it, the necessary prerequisites to effective building.

Reaction

In the previous section, I listed the various responses we make when we hear a proposal. Two of these signalled our reaction to the idea: the extent to which we liked it or not. In this section, I am going to focus on how we react in interactions, and in particular on the ways in which we choose to express our reaction. These choices are usually deeply habitual, to the extent that most people are unaware of the behaviour patterns that they form. Our reactions are instinctive: like the colleague I referred to in the last section, I hear myself disagreeing with somebody and a part of me is thinking 'why did I do that?' It is a strong internal drive which is sometimes outside my control and barely within my awareness. Next to interrupting, in my experience, people are least aware of their reacting behaviour. And these are also the behaviours which have a major impact on how others experience you and respond to you. This combination of low awareness and high impact means that much of the deeper work I do with people revolves around the management of their reactions.

When I am observing groups, I listen carefully for reacting patterns, both within the group as a whole and within the behaviour of its individual members. In particular, I listen for:

☐ The **overall level** of reaction within the group. How much reaction is going on? Are people clearly signalling their responses to each other? Is there enough reacting? Is there too much?
☐ The **balance** of reacting behaviour. Is there a balance of positive and negative reaction? Or are people being mainly negative? Or positive?
☐ The **nature** of the reacting behaviour. Are people expressing their reaction rationally? Or emotionally? Or both?

EXERCISE 9.14

Spend a few minutes now reflecting on a meeting or group discussion you have attended recently. Use the questions above to assess people's reacting behaviour in this meeting.

People's reacting behaviour has a significant impact on meetings and group discussions, both in terms of the climate of the meeting and of the group's effectiveness in evaluating options and making decisions. I am going to look at each of the three issues outlined above in turn, starting with group behaviour and the impact of the overall reacting balance on the group's effectiveness.

Overall level

People can express their reaction to what someone has said or proposed in several ways. Many of these are non-verbal. We shrug, we sigh, we grimace, we groan, we wince, we smile. But all these non-verbal reactions are ambiguous: they are not a reliable indicator of what people are actually thinking or feeling, and it is for this reason that I am going to focus here only on verbal behaviour and on the clear and unequivocal expression of reaction. There are two key behaviours that we will be focusing on. They are:

☐ **Agreeing:** When you clearly state your agreement with a piece of information or idea that someone has put forward.

☐ **Disagreeing:** When you clearly state your disagreement with a piece of information or idea that someone has put forward, or raise objections or obstacles to block a proposal.

When I am observing groups, I am listening for the extent to which these two behaviours together are being used: the total amount of agreeing and disagreeing, and I am observing the ways in which this volume reflects and affects the dynamics within the group. I want to know if there are extremes of behaviour: whether the level of reaction seems very high or low. This is not an absolute level, it is in relation to other behaviours: how much reacting is going on relative to initiating and the exchange of information. These are clearly connected. For example, if the level of initiating is low, then the level of reaction might be low too, as proposals tend to provoke reaction. But the level of initiating may be low because the level of reaction is low, as this can create a climate in which people don't feel comfortable to take the risk of putting their ideas on the table.

I am going to look now at the two extremes of overall level of reaction, both in terms of what this might reflect of the group dynamic and how it might affect the group process. As this is a complex area, I will explore some of the possibilities rather than provide a definitive breakdown of the issues.

High reaction

The reflection of the dynamic
If the overall level of reacting is high relative to other behaviours (if I am aware that there seems to be a lot of it going on – people frequently expressing their reaction to what other people have said), this tends to suggest that the group dynamic is open and extrovert. People feel free and are willing to express their reaction. Whether this is a good thing or not depends partly on the balance of their reaction. If people are mainly

disagreeing with each other, this could signal an intensely competitive environment where people are shooting each other down. If it is mainly positive, this might indicate a desire to encourage and support each other which overrides a proper evaluation of the quality of people's contribution. Either way, I would need to look for other evidence before I could make up my mind.

The effect on process
Similarly, the effect on group process of high reacting can be positive or negative. On the plus side, it is a sign of people's personal engagement with the issues and tends to generate energy and encourage contribution. On the down side, it can lead to discussions becoming chaotic and unstructured, especially if there are high levels of disagreement. High reacting tends to accelerate the pace of meetings and can generate a more emotionally charged atmosphere, both of which can make meetings harder to control. The balance of reacting behaviours is significant here, but I also check on the amount of questioning that is going on. If the reacting level is high and the overall questioning level is low, it is likely that people are not evaluating before they react. This can often waste time and lead to poor-quality decisions.

Low reaction

The reflection of the dynamic
If the overall level of reaction is low, this tends to suggest that the group dynamic is closed and introverted. For some reason, people don't feel free to react openly: this may be because it feels too risky; it may be because they are withholding their energy and commitment from the group. Either way, people are being cautious or ungenerous. There could be several reasons for this: they may not feel engaged by the work being done; they may not get on with other members of the team; the climate of the group may be risk-averse, encouraging careful consideration and low profiles; it might be a reflection of the style of the leader – if they are impatient, or intolerant, if they generate anxiety or fear, then this will usually reduce the level of reacting within the group as a whole.

The effect on process
Low reacting can have a quite startling effect on process, in that it can generate considerable uncertainty and anxiety. When we are not sure what the other people around the table are thinking, it feels more risky to react ourselves, so we tend to hold back on our own reactions – thus generating a downward spiral. Our initiating behaviour is to a certain extent fed by reaction – we need feedback and we need encouragement. If both of those are not forthcoming, we tend to initiate less. When this happens,

discussions can go round in circles, energy and enthusiasm drain from the group and meetings can feel flat and purposeless.

EXERCISE 9.15

Spend a few minutes now reflecting on your own group or team. Referring to the four points listed above, do you feel that the overall level of reacting behaviour is effective in your team meetings? Are people reacting too much and too quickly, before properly evaluating issues and proposals? Or are people tending to withhold their reactions? If so, why do you think this might be?

The overall level of reacting has a profound influence on how effective groups are in working together in formal meetings or informal discussions. Because we tend to have a low awareness of our reacting behaviour, we are often unaware that this is the cause for some of our dissatisfactions with meetings we attend. We usually have an awareness of high levels of interrupting, for example, and can cite this as the cause of our frustration. We are less likely to recognize that our anxiety stems from a lack of reaction, or our confusion from a surfeit of it. So the first step in managing group reaction levels effectively is, as always, to raise your awareness of what is happening.

ACTIVITY 9.10

Select a meeting that you will be attending in the near future in which you will not be playing a pivotal role. During this meeting, spend five minutes observing the behaviour of the other participants. Listen in particular for the times when they clearly express their agreement or disagreement with what other people are saying. Become aware of how frequently this happens, and assess what impact this is having on the dynamics and process management of the group.

Balance of behaviours

Figure 9.3 represents the two core reacting behaviours – agreeing and disagreeing – on a graph. I have marked on this graph four extreme positions and will now explore each of these in order to address the issue of balance.

1. The high supporter
The characteristics of the high supporter are a high level of agreeing and a low level of disagreeing. It is the combination that is significant. As we

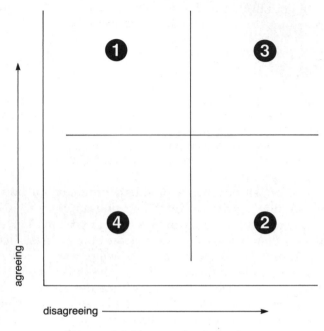

Figure 9.3 The reacting behaviours.

will see, high levels of support have different impacts depending on the level of disagreeing behaviour. Here, where there is little balance, the main impact is that the value of the support becomes devalued. Initially, the agreement will be taken at face value. If it is not balanced by disagreement, however, people soon start to question the degree to which the agreement is based on careful evaluation. Because the high supporter rarely disagrees, people start to question why s/he is agreeing so much: Does s/he mean it or is it just habit, or worse, a deliberate strategy? After a while, people have discounted the agreement to such an extent that they can literally stop hearing it.

Our reacting behaviours tend to be less dependent on the specific nature of the interaction. They are usually habitual. If I observe a high supporter in a meeting, I can safely assume that this is the way they react in most situations. There may be several reasons why they have developed such a profile: they may have been brought up as a child never to disagree; they may have a need to be positive or be afraid of conflict; they may do it in order to please people or to be sycophantic. High supporters tend to be regarded as yes-people and consequently their opinions may be discounted by the rest of the group.

2. The high 'disagreer'

At the other opposite corner of Figure 9.3 is the high 'disagreer'. Again, the relationship between behaviours is the key. High disagreeing of itself is not necessarily negative. In some circumstances, it can be invaluable – a break on the headlong rush of an excited group towards an inappropriate solution; a challenge to sloppy thinking; a stimulus for careful evaluation and debate. But if you *only* disagree – and this is not balanced by support – then it becomes wearing, people become irritated, they perceive you as being negative and destructive, they start to resent your contribution, to ignore your disagreements, to become ever more irrational in their attempts to prove you wrong. It is the combination of high disagreeing and low support that creates the negative impact.

Most high disagreers that I have come across are not aware of this aspect of their behaviour. Or rather, they know that they disagree, but they don't realize the extent to which they do; nor are they aware of the absence of support. They value their ability to disagree and they are right to. It is a valuable behaviour. They often think that they don't need to express their agreement clearly, assuming that the absence of disagreement will be a clear enough signal (they sometimes find it almost impossible to increase their expression of support). But they are all relieved when I tell them that the answer is not to disagree less but to agree more.

And when they do it, the impact can be quite astonishing. I was working with a group in the United Kingdom on which there was a technical expert from Germany who was a high disagreer. He never agreed with anything. He always looked for the problem, for the flaw in the logic, for the reason why it wouldn't work. It was his job to do this – he was an engineer. People got so fed up with him. He came to me during a break and said: 'This is what happens to me, all the time, I tell people what I think and they become defensive, they become irritated, they withdraw'. I told him that the next time he agreed with someone he must say 'I agree with you'. He practised doing this: it completely transformed his relationship with the group.

3. The high reactor

The high reactor is blessed with the fact that their behaviour is balanced: a roughly equal mix of agreeing and disagreeing. The trouble is that they do a lot of it, too frequently and usually too quickly. They often interrupt people with their reactions, so that the person speaking feels as if they haven't fully been heard: 'How can they agree with me when they didn't know how I was going to finish?' The speed and frequency of their response usually suggest that they are reacting impulsively, without careful evaluation. This is almost certainly the case if they are not asking many questions. And often, because they haven't evaluated carefully, they change their minds – they hear a counter-argument or an alternative proposal and they realize that their first reaction was wrong, so they react again. Which of course raises the level of their reacting behaviours. This impulsiveness can be attractive, but it can also be intensely frustrating and alienating.

It is difficult to know why people are impulsive: enthusiasm, anxiety, a need to be accepted, a need to be influential. The causes are deeply engrained in the person's psyche and may make them resistant to change. But the change they need to make is quite simple and relatively straightforward: they need to ask more questions and try to make sure that they ask them before they react. This is easier once they have become aware of their reacting level, because, as with the other scenarios, they tend not to know that they are doing it. But the pattern runs deep, and it is better to concentrate on doing more of something rather than less. If you are a high reactor, ask more questions (don't just agree with me – ask me why!).

4. The low reactor

The low reactor's behaviour is also balanced, but its impact is very different. Sometimes consciously, often not, the low reactor is withholding their reaction – giving little indication of their responses to what other people are saying or proposing. This can have an extremely unsettling effect. When we don't receive any feedback from someone, we tend to assume that they don't like what we are saying, and so we often confuse the low reactor with the high disagreer. Starved of direct feedback, we become anxious and eventually desperate to get some kind of response and so the low reactor, through their behaviour, is putting themselves in a powerful position.

As I have indicated, some people low react as a deliberate strategy – and it is a powerful one which needs to be used carefully, for it can affect the climate of an interaction considerably. Professional buyers and negotiators are trained to do it in order to deliberately unsettle people. Managers often develop the habit of low reacting because they have to process and evaluate so much information and so many options – they don't want to commit themselves until they are absolutely sure, and it is right of them not to do so, however disconcerting this may be when you are presenting to them. We will look later at what you can do to counter this strategy if you are confronted by it.

Some people, however, have unknowingly developed low reacting as part of their behaviour profile. They are not choosing to do it. They don't know that they are doing it. They just instinctively give nothing away and so unwittingly can accrue power or attention in discussions and meetings. It is hard to know why such patterns have developed. At some point in their childhood, I imagine, they have learnt that it is safer to keep your own counsel, and over the years it becomes a habit which governs their behaviour, and pervades almost all their interactions. And because it is so deep, it can be hard to shift. The solution is straightforward: react more! But for the low reactor, this can be extremely difficult to achieve – the deeply engrained habit overrides the intention to change.

ACTIVITY 9.11

Here are two activities you can use to help you get a more accurate picture of the balance of your reacting behaviours:

☐ Listen to yourself: choose an interaction where your contribution is not vital and monitor your reacting behaviour. See how many times you clearly express your agreement and disagreement with what other people are saying.

☐ Get feedback: ask someone who knows you well and whom you trust to give you feedback about your reacting behaviour generally. Ask them if they think you express:
  (a) your reactions often enough;
  (b) a balance of agreement and disagreement;
  (c) your reactions too frequently and impulsively.

(NB Read the guidelines on asking for feedback on page 140 before doing this activity.)

Changing behaviour

The first step in modifying your reacting behaviour is to raise your awareness of your natural tendencies and patterns. Once you have done this, if you feel you need to change, it is likely that, from one direction or another, you will need to move towards the middle of the graph illustrated in Figure 9.3. The specific solution will depend on where you are moving away from, as summarized in the table below.

Issue	Solution
High supporter	Be aware of moments when you disagree with what someone is saying and express that disagreement clearly in the discussion.
High disagreer	Be aware of moments when you agree with what someone is saying and express that agreement clearly in the discussion.
High reactor	Monitor the impulse to react and interrupt this by asking questions to clarify or further explore the issue or idea before you do so.
Low reactor	Be aware of the moments when you are reacting internally to what someone is saying and express that reaction clearly in the discussion.

ACTIVITY 9.12

Select a meeting that you will be attending in the near future in which you will not be playing a pivotal role. During this meeting:

- □ Stop participating at some point for five minutes so that you can monitor your internal reactions to what people are saying.
- □ Become aware of how you are responding: do you agree or disagree with what people are saying?
- □ Consider how you would normally convey these responses: would you express all, some or none of them?
- □ Identify opportunities to use the behaviours which you feel you need to increase.

If, through the previous exercises, you have identified people that you know who have behaviour profiles like those illustrated in Figure 9.3, you may want to try to help them towards a more balanced reacting profile. The table below suggests some things you could do during a discussion or interaction.

Issue	Solution
High supporter	Point out to them that they are agreeing a lot and check out whether there is anything that they don't like or have concerns about with regard to what is being discussed.
High disagreer	Point out to them that they are doing a lot of disagreeing and check whether that is because there is nothing they like or agree with in what is being discussed or proposed.
High reactor	Try to intervene before they react by asking questions of the speaker yourself or suggest to the high reactor or to the whole group that you adopt a groundrule of evaluating before reacting (see Chapter 6 for more on groundrules).
Low reactor	**Seek reactions** from the low reactor. This is a subset of the asking behaviours (e.g. 'What do you think?'; 'Do you like the idea?'; 'How do you feel about it?', etc.). It is necessary to use this tactic when the group's overall reacting level is low. It is essential with a low reactor. At the least you will discover whether they are low reacting deliberately or not; if they are, they will resist giving you a clear answer!

The nature of reaction

So far, I have described reacting in terms of two behaviours: agreeing and disagreeing. We use these behaviours generally to express our rational response to information or ideas, to convey what we *think* about what is being said or proposed. There is another dimension to our reactions – and this is our emotional response. In this section I am going to look briefly at the relationship between our rational and emotional responses and then at the ways in which we can convey how we *feel* about what is being said or proposed during a meeting or discussion.

The rational and the emotional

At work especially, we tend to present ourselves as rational beings, operating rationally in the way that we process information, evaluate options and make decisions. Our work processes tend to strive for objectivity. Rational values are promoted: professionalism generally describes the ability to control our emotions so that they do not cloud our judgement or impair our effectiveness. Subjectivity is frowned upon. Overt displays of emotion threaten the calm constructs, the rational processes, the professional climates that we seek to create. Emotion, on the whole, is suppressed in the workplace.

As a result, our emotions tend to be disregarded, undervalued and denied. Emotionality is more chaotic than rationality, less predictable, sometimes wildly ineffectual. This is why most people prefer to shy away from it. But it is always there. In fact, it is at the heart of our rational processes: these are only ever the surface representation of our emotions. We often contrive to make our reactions seem purely rational and objective. But they can never be *purely* rational. Such a possibility does not exist!

Sometimes our emotions break through the shield of rationality in which they are usually encased, so that they are apparent to the people we are interacting with. They see our anger or delight, they hear our frustration, they know how we feel. At other times, our emotions are not greatly exercised by the issue or people we are dealing with: we do not have strong feelings either way, we stay calm, our rational processes dominate. And there are other times when the extent to which our emotions penetrate is not revealed: when the strength of feeling is strong but we use our rationality to disguise our feelings; we hide our emotions behind a screen of discourse which is masquerading as rational but which is in fact dominated by our emotions.

EXERCISE 9.16

Spend a few minutes now reflecting on how you manage your emotional responses to people and situations at work. Do you tend to suppress them because you feel that they will disturb your effectiveness? Do you take them into account when reacting or making decisions? Do you tend to share your feelings with people, or do you keep them to yourself?

The greater our awareness and understanding of our emotional responses and the ways in which they affect our thought processes and behaviour, the greater will be our effectiveness at working in or leading groups and at managing interactions generally. This awareness does not come easily – most of us have been schooled to dissociate thought from feeling. Our emotions derive from a complex maze, built from layers of experience, which are not easy to unravel and make sense of, and which can confront us with aspects of ourselves that we would prefer to keep hidden. But awareness, however slight, is better than denial. When we pretend to ourselves that our reactions, our evaluations, our decisions are purely rational, then we are likely to be deceiving ourselves in ways which could impair our judgement and which can cause hurt either to ourselves or others.

A raised awareness of the extent to which our rationality is influenced by our emotions in a given situation helps us to control the extent of that influence. For example, a decision about who to allocate a piece of work to will be affected by our feelings about each of the people we are considering – not just the extent to which we trust them, but how much we like them, the degree to which we find them irritating, disappointing, threatening. Heightened awareness allows us to take our feelings into account, to set them alongside the other, objective factors that we need to consider and to ensure that they do not influence us unduly.

Heightened awareness also helps us to choose whether to express our emotions to others. On the one hand, we need to manage our emotions ourselves, internally. On the other, we may need to give the other people involved an understanding of the extent and ways in which our feelings are affecting our thought processes, so that they can take them into account too. This is not always wise: there will be times when revealing your emotional processes will make you vulnerable to abuse and exploitation. This will depend mainly on the other people and the extent to which you trust them and their goodwill towards you. But there will be times when sharing your feelings is a valuable contribution, helping you to manage yourself and helping others to understand and respect your position. So I am going to look now at how we express our emotions, and in particular at the key behavioural choice that we make when we choose to do so.

Expressing emotions

In broad terms, there are two ways in which we can express our emotions. We can:

☐ **Enact** the feelings. If we feel frustrated, we tear our hair out! If we feel angry, we behave angrily, shouting, thumping the table. If we feel upset, we are upset, crying, withdrawing. If we feel hurt, we may withdraw, we may lash out, attacking the person who we feel has hurt us. There are countless ways in which we can enact our feelings. When we do so, we will probably no longer be in control of our behaviour.

☐ **Describing** our feelings. If we feel frustrated, we explain that this is how we are feeling. If we are angry, we let people know, not by *being* angry, but by telling them that we are feeling angry. If we feel hurt or upset, or if we feel pleased or delighted or impressed or jealous, we describe to people how we are feeling. We can do this because the strength of our emotion has not escalated beyond our control; we are able, relatively calmly, to describe the emotions we are experiencing without acting them out. As we will see, the process of describing is one of the ways in which we can stay in control of our emotions.

Each of these modes of expression have significant impact on interactions and can make a major contribution to effective communication. However, although dealing with the same content, they each impact differently and need to be considered as options. I will now look at each of them in turn.

Effective enactment

When we use emotional behaviours, whether enacting or describing, they tend to have a significant impact on an interaction. It becomes less focused on rational processes and more open to the possibility of exploring the emotional backdrop to our reactions and opinions and positions on an issue. They therefore need to be considered as strategic options, because moving from the rational into the emotional can be a necessary step in managing difficult interactions. There is a section in the next chapter that looks at this in more detail. Here I want to give you an overview of the behavioural options, first by exploring enactment.

There are times when enacting your feelings will be appropriate and effective: you need to get things off your chest; people need to be made aware of the strength of your feelings. Sometimes a sudden explosion of anger or display of hurt can break through blocks in relationships and interactions. It can have a dramatic impact on the behaviour of the other people, causing them to focus on their own emotional responses and thus enabling them to become more open and direct. The immediate effect might be unpleasant – a blazing row, floods of tears – but this can provide a necessary catharsis, after which, feelings on all sides having been vented, people are better able to operate rationally again with their judgement less clouded by their emotions.

The risk, of course, is that rather than have a cathartic effect, the enactment of feelings can lead to crisis. Things are said that were best left unsaid. The relationship reaches a point of no return. Damage is done which can't be undone. The return to rationality becomes impossible. And because when we act out our feelings we are usually not in control of them, we are rarely able to steer the interaction towards the more positive outcome. In other words, it could go either way, and which way it goes usually depends on how the other person or people respond and their ability to manage their own move into the emotional zone.

EXERCISE 9.17

Spend a few minutes now reflecting on the enactment of emotion. Have there been times when you have, consciously or not, expressed your feelings forcefully at work? What impact has this had? Has it helped to resolve difficult issues? Or has it made them worse?

Although enactment is high-risk, it is nevertheless a viable option, precisely because of its dramatic impact, its ability to break through resistance and negative dynamics in groups. The risk derives mainly from the fact that when you enact, you lose awareness, and thus control, of your behaviour. Sometimes this risk is worth taking in its entirety: lose awareness, lose control, let it all hang out! However, it is possible to choose consciously to enact, to decide, for example: 'I am going to get angry now, I am going to show them how angry I feel!', and to shout at them, or thump the table. If you can retain awareness as you do this, you can retain enough control to pull back before you get sucked down by the quicksand of spiralling emotionality. This is a strategic intervention which won't be appropriate very often and which is difficult to execute well.

The uses of describing feelings
The outcome of describing feelings is in essence the same as enacting them: you are letting somebody know how you feel. It is the differences between the two behaviours which is significant. There are two main differences that I want to focus on now:

☐ **Self-control:** When you are enacting, you are experiencing the feelings intensely. When you are describing them, the experiencing of them is much less intense. When you tell someone that you feel angry with them, it is likely that you will be feeling some of that anger as you speak. But you won't be feeling it to such an extent that it takes away your ability to control your behaviour and manage the interaction.

☐ **Impact:** Although, like enactment, describing feeling moves people into the 'emotional zone', it does so less violently and therefore has a very different impact. It is more likely that the other people will recognize and acknowledge your feelings if you describe them. If you enact them, the risk is that they start experiencing their own feelings intensely before they have a chance to reflect on yours. Blazing rows are characterized by each protagonist's inability to acknowledge the other's feelings.

Because of these two differences, describing feelings is a far safer way of moving into the emotional zone and can therefore be an invaluable way of resolving difficult situations and interactions. We will explore this in more detail in the next chapter. Here I want to give you an overview of the value of this behaviour and then look at ways in which you can increase your facility to describe your feelings if this would be useful to you.

There are are four main reasons why you might use describing feelings. These are to:

□ Create a more **open climate**. When you describe your feelings you are being open with people, showing and sharing more of yourself and your inner world than is usual in ordinary conversation. You are therefore increasing the level of openness and by so doing, encouraging others to be more open in return. This can have a significant effect on the climate within a meeting or within a group generally. The more comfortable people feel to share and discuss their feelings, the better able they will be to handle interpersonal tensions and difficulties when they arise (see Chapter 6).

□ Shift the **level of discourse**. This is particularly valuable in meetings where it is proving difficult to reach agreement and where rational argument is becoming an obstacle to progress. People can often become entrenched in rationality, especially when it is acting as a screen for their emotions. The argument becomes more important than the outcome. Switching from the rational to the emotional zone shifts the level of discourse and can sometimes unblock the logjam. It can help people to refocus on the real issues or to talk more openly about the feelings that are at the heart of their resistance.

□ Provide an **alternative to disagreement**. There may be times when you disagree with something that has been said or proposed when open disagreement would not be appropriate. This might be because it is your boss's idea! Or because you don't want to appear negative or to discourage people from putting ideas forward. Describing your concerns with the idea, your worries about why it might not be practical is an alternative way of disagreeing. It tends to be softer, and therefore less likely to lead to defensiveness and to encourage people to develop the idea further to overcome your concerns (see the section on developing ideas earlier in this chapter).

□ Give **feedback**. If you want to give feedback to a group or an individual, describing your feelings about their performance tends to have greater impact (because it is more personal) as well as being easier for people to hear. For example, 'I am really pleased with how well we have worked together on this' is more powerful than, 'We have worked together on this really well'. These are both forms of feedback. But because you are describing your feelings with the former, you will be making greater contact with the group, and this adds to the power and impact of the feedback. This is even more the case when you are giving critical feedback. We will look at this in the next chapter.

EXERCISE 9.18

Spend a few minutes now reflecting on situations recently either when you have used describing your feelings for one of the reasons listed above, or when doing so might have been a more effective option.

Increasing your describing feelings behaviour

Some people describe their feelings readily and frequently. It is part of the way they operate in the world. Others don't. They are not used to, and don't feel comfortable, being that open. I usually encourage people to describe their feelings more because, apart from all the other reasons listed above, I believe that it is generally useful for them to be able to talk about how they feel, both for their own sake and for those of the people around them.

Like most of the behaviours discussed in this chapter, describing feelings is not in itself difficult to do. It is not difficult to say, 'I am delighted with your performance', or 'I am disappointed with the way you did that'. But to do this, you need to be aware of what you are feeling. I remember once encouraging a group of managers to use describing feelings as a way of creating a positive climate in their appraisal interviews. They wanted to do it, but were really struggling. They could tell me what they thought about someone's performance, but not how they felt about it. I got them to write down the issues they wanted to discuss with one of their appraisees – the different aspects of their performance that they wanted to review. I then got them to write one word to describe how they felt about each agenda item: pleased, delighted, impressed, relieved, disappointed, frustrated, irritated, angry. 'How do you feel about them?' I kept asking 'Not what do you think. How do you feel?' It was not that they didn't have feelings; it was just that they were not used to knowing what they were.

ACTIVITY 9.13

This activity will help you to increase your level of describing feelings, as an alternative to agreeing or disagreeing. Select a meeting that you will be attending in the near future in which you will not be playing a pivotal role. During this meeting:

☐ Stop participating at some point for five minutes so that you can monitor your internal responses to what people are saying.

☐ Become aware of how you are feeling about what is happening in the meeting.

☐ Consider how you would normally convey these responses: would you express all, some or none of them?

☐ Identify opportunities when it would be helpful for you to describe your feelings about what is happening or being said.

Summary

The ways in which we respond to people are one of the key factors that shape the way they perceive us, feel about us and relate to us. They are also behaviours which are deeply engrained. We tend to have low awareness of our habitual responding patterns. In group settings, the ways in which people respond to each other will have a significant impact on their effectiveness at working together. Reaction is feedback, and feedback is essential to communication. The more we know about how others think and feel about us, our opinions and ideas, the better able we are to work with them collaboratively.

There are three aspects of our reacting behaviours which we need to consider:

☐ The overall level: Do we react enough? Do we react too much?

☐ The balance of behaviours: Do we agree too much and disagree too little? Or vice versa?

☐ The nature of our responses: Do we primarily respond rationally, with agreeing and disagreeing behaviour? Are we able to describe our feelings?

It is possible to modify your reacting behaviour, but it is difficult because our habitual patterns are so engrained. As with all the behaviours, the starting-point is to become aware of these patterns. When you become aware that you are an instinctive disagreer, for example, then at least you can try to balance this with more support when you hear yourself instinctively disagreeing.

Clarity

The final set of behaviours that I look for when I am observing groups in action are the behaviours involved in managing clarity during the discussion. This tells me whether and how the group ensures that everyone is clear about what is being discussed and what has been agreed. I have left these behaviours until last not because they are the least important – far from it – but because they lead into the first section of the next chapter of this book, which examines the skills involved in effective chairing. So in this section, I am going to give you a brief introduction to the behaviours involved in order to finish the chapter with a complete list of the behaviours that I want you to consider when thinking about the ways you participate in group discussions and meetings.

It is hard to overestimate the scope for misunderstanding that exists when a group of people come together in discussion. It is hard to overestimate the amount of work that is required to ensure that people leave the meeting with a shared and accurate understanding of what has been discussed and agreed. Many of the groups I observe simply don't do enough and, as a result, people get confused during the meeting: unsure about what they should be discussing, where the discussion is going, what people mean exactly, what the outcome of the discussion is. And they get confused after the meeting: they find they can't remember what has been agreed or their understanding of what has been agreed does not tally with other people's.

So when I am observing groups, I pay special attention to the work they are doing to ensure clarity. In particular, I listen out for the extent to which people are clear about:

☐ The **structure** of the meeting and the discussions that take place within it. Is it clear: What is being discussed? How it is being discussed? Where the discussion is heading? What will be discussed next? How the current discussion relates to the next discussion? and so on.

☐ The **true meaning** of what people are saying: the words they use, the points they are trying to make, the ambiguities that lurk within the most innocent of statements.

☐ The **outcomes** of the discussions that have taken place during the meeting, and are sure that their understanding of these outcomes is shared by the other participants in the discussion.

EXERCISE 9.19

Spend a few minutes now reflecting on a meeting or group discussion you have attended recently. Use the questions above to assess people's clarifying behaviour in this meeting.

I am now going to look at each of these issues in turn, introducing a new behaviour which can be used as a tool to manage these different aspects of clarity in group discussion.

Structure

A discussion between two people is complex. People think differently, have different preoccupations, attitudes towards the issues being discussed, different preferences for how the issues should be resolved or the discussion should end. The more people are involved, the harder it gets. The factors just multiply. People hear what they want to hear, ignore what they don't. They wander off the point into areas that they find more conducive. They become interested in side issues, lose sight of the core issues, and after a while it is hard to know how you got where you are and even harder to remember where you are supposed to be!

The key to managing the structure of a discussion or meeting is a behaviour called **giving directions**. This is another initiating behaviour, in that it involves putting forward proposals or suggestions for how a discussion should be structured. Here are some examples:

'Let's start by reviewing the project plan.'
'I want to go round the group so that each person has a chance to say what they think the key issues are here.'
'Why don't we move on now to discuss the cost implications of the time slippage?'
'I think we should spend a few minutes brainstorming the possible ways in which we could make up the shortfall to ensure we cover all the options.'

The clarity of structure in a meeting is almost entirely dependent on the extent to which this behaviour is used. In meetings where somebody has been appointed as chairperson or process manager, it is likely that they will be using this behaviour frequently, and if they are doing so, there may be no need for anyone else to do so. Often, however, the chairperson does not do enough structuring, either through lack of skill or because they have allowed themselves to become overinvolved in the content of the discussion. The minute this happens, their ability to manage process diminishes, as will their usage of giving directions.

ACTIVITY 9.14

Select a meeting that you will be attending in the near future which is going to be chaired by someone other than you. During this meeting:

- ☐ Stop participating at some point for five minutes so that you can monitor the extent to which the chairperson is giving directions to structure the meeting.
- ☐ Evaluate the effectiveness of his/her use of giving directions, both in terms of frequency and quality.
- ☐ Imagine you are chairing the meeting: How would you use giving directions to help people understand the structure and direction of the meeting?

True meaning

A simple statement: 'I don't like employee satisfaction surveys.' On the face of it, the meaning is straightforward. But as with many seemingly simple statements, it contains a wealth of possible interpretations, variations and ambiguities. In order to fully understand the true meaning of this statement, or rather the intent behind the words, it is necessary to ask a particular kind of question, called **testing understanding**. Here are some examples:

'Is that because you don't think they are effective?'
'Are you saying you don't like our surveys in particular or the idea in general?'
'Do you mean that you disagree with the process or that you don't like the feedback the surveys are producing?'
'Is that because you don't think the data are reliable?'

Questions such as these help to expose and clarify the potential areas for confusion and ambiguity. They help people to think through what they are saying and articulate it more clearly. They can gently expose the weaknesses in a proposal, thus providing another alternative to disagreeing. They can ensure that not just you but everybody in the discussion is clearer about the issues at hand. Testing understanding is an extremely useful and versatile form of question. If there is a low level of it in a discussion or meeting, it is almost inevitable that people will become confused to some degree. Testing understanding contributes primarily to the clarity of a discussion. It has another considerable value. It can be used to force people to think harder and thus tends to improve the quality of the discussion as well as its clarity.

ACTIVITY 9.15

Select a meeting that you will be attending in the near future which is going to be chaired by someone other than you. During this meeting:

□ Stop participating at some point for five minutes so that you can monitor the extent to which you fully understand what people are saying; listen particularly for potential gaps and ambiguities.

□ Observe other people in the group: Can you tell whether they have fully understood what is being said? Do they test understanding to achieve clarity?

□ Reflect on how you would normally behave: Would you test understanding to clarify what people are saying or not?

□ Consider the questions you could ask to make sure that you and others do fully understand what is being said.

Outcomes

A meeting can generate several outcomes: these may be decisions, actions, new insights, issues and information. These are all likely to have been discussed in some detail and some of that detail is an essential part of the outcome: it needs to be clearly understood and remembered by the participants in the discussion. But because meetings go on for long periods of time, and because people have different priorities and preoccupations, they are unlikely, off their own back, to be able to retain a clear record of what has been discussed and agreed. Even if they take their own notes, it can be surprising how often these will differ from the notes taken by another participant. This can add to the confusion during a meeting, especially if it is necessary to refer back to previous agenda items. And it can be frustrating after the meeting, when people realize that their version of events is not the only version.

The key to managing a shared understanding of the outcomes of a discussion or meeting is a behaviour called **summarizing**. A summary is a compact and accurate restatement of elements of a discussion or a meeting. Here is an example:

'So you don't like employee satisfaction surveys because your experience of them in the past is that they focus too much attention on symptoms rather than causes, allow minor issues to get out of proportion, and tend to highlight negatives rather than positives.'

Summarizing is a key indicator of the level of process awareness and management that is going on in a group. I listen carefully for how much of it is happening and for who is doing it, as it helps me to identify the control resource within the group. Like giving directions, summarizing is usually the responsibility of the chairperson. But for the reasons given above, it can be unwise to assume that they will provide the level of summarizing necessary to ensure clarity. Summarizing is one of the ways in which you can contribute to the process management of a meeting when you are not the chairperson.

ACTIVITY 9.16

Select a meeting that you will be attending in the near future which is going to be chaired by someone other than you. During this meeting:

☐ Stop participating at some point for five minutes so that you can monitor the extent to which the chairperson is summarizing to ensure that people are clear about the outcomes of the discussions.

☐ Evaluate the effectiveness of his/her summarizing, both in terms of frequency and quality.

☐ Imagine you are chairing the meeting: When and how would you use summarizing to help ensure clarity in the meeting?

Summary

In this chapter, we have looked at a range of verbal behaviours which underpin effective communication. They are a way of describing what you are doing when you are interacting with other people, and so they are referred to as interactive skills. I have summarized all the behaviours referred to in the chapter in the table below. None of these will be new to you: you will have used them and heard them frequently. What might be new is the process of categorizing and defining them, and thus isolating them and examining them in detail. This can make the behaviours seem unfamiliar and can make you feel self-conscious whenever you open your mouth: 'What behaviour am I using now?'.

From an early age, we each develop our own behavioural style. This is shaped by our experiences and by the demands these experiences make on us. Our work, for example, will often require quite specific types of interaction, which, as we repeat them daily, subtly influence our patterns of communicating. We may develop the habit of asking a lot of questions or of not asking any; we may learn to low react, or we may have got into the habit of being a high disagreer; we may be obsessed with clarity, so that we are constantly testing understanding, or we may only be interested in our own thoughts and ideas and develop a high telling style accordingly.

At the beginning of Part 3, I described effective communicators as having three attributes: awareness, choice and flexibility. They are able to use all the behaviours covered here, to choose when to use them and to use them well. Most of us don't have this facility. Our behavioural habits often limit our options and make us inflexible. In this chapter, I have asked you to consider three connected processes: awareness of your own behaviour and the behaviour of others; assessment of what is appropriate behaviour given the conditions; effective use of the behaviour to achieve the desired outcome. Most of the activities have been designed to develop your awareness of your own behaviour patterns and of the options that exist. If you feel that it would be useful to extend your repertoire or increase your flexibility, I encourage you to experiment. Only through practice and experimentation can we develop our interactive skills.

Summary of behaviours covered in this chapter	
Telling behaviours	Asking behaviours
Giving information	Seeking information
Proposing	Seeking proposals
Suggesting	Seeking options
Building	
Supporting	
Disagreeing	Seeking reaction
Enacting feelings	
Describing feelings	
Giving directions	
Summarizing	Testing understanding

ACTIVITY 9.17

Before moving on to the next chapter, consider whether there are particular behaviours that have been covered in this chapter that you feel it would be useful for you to practise. If so, plan how you intend to practise them. It is best to identify specific meetings or discussions where it would be appropriate for you to practise.

10

Process management skills

Throughout this book we have been exploring the issue of leadership in terms of the effective management of process. In Chapter 6, I looked at strategies you can use to generate critical awareness at all four levels of process: procedural, structural, behavioural and social. In Chapter 9, I looked at the core interactive skills which underpin the behavioural level of process. In this chapter, I am going to expand on the usage of these behavioural skills by exploring the ways that they can be applied to managing two other levels of process, first, by looking at the skills involved in managing meetings (procedural); and second, by looking at the skills involved in managing group dynamics (social).

Managing meetings

In Part 2 of the book, I explored the difference between product and process and looked in detail at strategies for managing process in meetings. In this section, I am going to focus on the interactive skills involved in managing the procedural level of process in the ways I described in Chapter 6. These skills will be applicable when you are formally chairing a meeting and when you are leading informal discussions. During this section, I will refer to chairperson, 'process manager' and 'meetings manager' interchangeably to describe these roles. The skills will also be useful when you are simply participating in a discussion, if the control required is not forthcoming from other sources.

If you are responsible for managing the process of a meeting, either as team-leader or formal chairperson, there are three functions that people will be hoping you will carry out effectively. They want you to manage:

☐ The **direction and structure** of the meeting.
☐ The levels of **participation and involvement** in the meeting.
☐ The **clarity of understanding** about the content of the meeting.

EXERCISE 10.1

Spend a few minutes now reflecting on your effectiveness at managing meetings: how well do you think you manage direction and structure, participation and involvement and clarity of understanding?

Direction and structure

The provision of direction and structure involves a combination of the steps I outlined in the section called 'Managing discussions' in Chapter 6 (pages 92–4) and two of the behaviours that I described in Chapter 9. These behaviours are:

☐ **Giving directions.**
☐ **Summarizing.**

Between them, *giving directions* and *summarizing* act as signposts, showing the way forward and reminding people of what has just happened. The two behaviours used together at key junctions in the meeting will have a major influence on the control of structure and direction. They are the two key 'process behaviours', and as such are key chairing skills. They encourage people to pull back from the content of a discussion momentarily in order to refocus on the process and therefore have a significant impact on the degree to which participants perceive the meeting to be well organized and controlled.

Giving directions is the behaviour that will be used at the beginning of the meeting, either by the chairperson or by the group as a whole, to establish the route of the discussion. Once established, your responsibility as process manager is to steer the group along that route, ensuring that they follow the steps identified within the agreed timescale in order to achieve the end point. Signposting by *giving directions* and *summarizing*, is the most effective way to do this, because it reminds people of the structure for the discussion and so reinforces it. People tend to be more disciplined as a result.

ACTIVITY 10.1

The next time you are responsible for managing a meeting or discussion, focus on managing the process rather than becoming involved in the content. Concentrate in particular on the two signposting behaviours – *giving directions* and *summarizing* – to ensure that you provide sufficient structure and direction to the meeting.

Controlling digressions

However well you signpost a discussion, there are always likely to be digressions when people wander off the agreed route down meandering side roads. These might be more scenic, but they tend to lead to confusion and time-wasting. This is one of the hardest jobs for the chairperson, as it involves the use of force to stop the digressor and return them to the original route.

The two signposting behaviours are the most effective way to exert control over digressors. Summarize the ground covered by the discussion so far and then suggest that it is more appropriate to follow the original route rather than pursue the digression. You may need to interrupt the digressor (more or less politely) in order to do this. For example:

'Before you go any further, Jack, let me just summarize where we are up to: we've reviewed last year's resourcing strategy and explored the likely requirement over the next two years. The next step was to identify what our priorities should be. I would like to move on to that now, and maybe we could come back to your point later, unless the group feels that we need to deal with it first.'

There are three key points to controlling digressions in this way:

☐ Do it quickly, before the digression has become established. It is much easier to get back on the main road when you can still see where it is. The longer the digression goes on, and the more people get involved, the harder it is to stop it and redirect the discussion.

☐ Offer the digressor an alternative. In the example, Jack is offered the option of returning to his digression at a more appropriate point in the discussion. It is likely that such a point won't arise (and likely that, if it has, Jack will have forgotten all about it). But it might, and having the option enables the digressor to let go of the urgency of their need to digress.

☐ Involve the rest of the group in the decision. This is especially important if the digressor is being consistently difficult or resisting your control of the meeting. Involving the group makes it harder for the digressor to focus their resistance on you and encourages the rest of the group to assert themselves. There may even be times when the group supports the digressor because they're right: the digression is valid and the structure of the discussion needs to be rearranged.

Covert management
You may sometimes participate in a meeting which is being chaired badly: possibly by someone who lacks the skills of managing process, or because the chairperson has become hopelessly entangled with the content of the discussion. In such cases, it is likely that there will be a low level of *giving directions* and *summarizing* behaviour and so the meeting will lack direction and structure.

If appropriate, you can use *giving directions* and *summarizing* yourself, even though you are not the official chairperson, to improve the management of the meeting. This will partly depend on your own ability to stay sufficiently detached from the content; and partly on the sensitivity of the chair, who may see such behaviour from a mere participant as a direct challenge to their authority as meetings manager. On the other hand, they may be relieved that other people in the group are taking responsibility for process. In some cases, they probably won't even be aware that you are doing it! But if you are frustrated with a meeting that is disorganized because it is not being chaired well, you can make a positive contribution by trying to influence the direction and structure of the discussions.

Participation and involvement

People usually want the chairperson to oversee the extent to which they are participating in discussions and are able to get involved. It is a valuable service, which if it is being well provided, allows participants in meetings to focus on content without worrying too much about whether they are taking up too much airtime or whether others aren't getting enough. If the group is aware of process and people are generally sensitive to each other's needs, overseeing the use of airtime is all that will be required. But in most cases, the chairperson will have to manage the distribution of airtime actively to ensure that it is allocated appropriately to enable the group to achieve the desired outcomes.

In order to manage participation and involvement, chairpeople have to be aware of the natural patterns of distribution of airtime within the group. To have this awareness, they have to be detached from the content of the discussion to some degree at least, so that they can observe whether someone is being dominating, whether someone is wanting to speak but is unable to 'get in', whether someone with a valuable contribution to make is, for whatever reason, not making it. With this awareness, they are able to make decisions about how to intervene with the natural distribution of airtime and reshape it more appropriately. Such intervention involves the use of two behaviours. These are:

- □ **Inviting.**
- □ **Seeking information.**

Asking questions is a key strategy for the chairperson. With questions they can control not only who is speaking, but what they are speaking about. They can shape and manage a conversation by stimulating thought and discussion without ever directly contributing to the content or disclosing their own thoughts and preferences. As we will see in the next section, they can use questions to influence debates and decisions, to steer people down particular lines of inquiry or away from others. And they can use questions to ensure that the people who need to speak are given the opportunity to do so, in the following ways:

- □ To take the airtime away from dominant people by using questions to involve members of the group who are trying to contribute but are finding it difficult to do so.
- □ To make the space available for people who are naturally quiet or shy and who are finding it difficult to claim the airtime they need.
- □ To bring into the discussion people who share their views and preferences, thus ensuring that those views are expressed without getting directly involved with the content themselves.
- □ To force people who are withholding their contribution for negative reasons to get more actively involved in the meeting and, if possible, to state their position more clearly.

When you use questions to manage participation and involvement, you will sometimes need to use *inviting* behaviour at the same time, so that you are making a deliberate attempt to bring somebody in to the discussion. The question is the invitation. Such questions might be very general:

'What do you think, Janice?'
'Have you got anything to add, Peter?'

They may need to be more specific in order to shape the contribution to achieve the effect you want. For example:

'Do you agree with Roger, Janice?'
'Didn't you have some experience with this last year, Peter?'

Questions such as these are ways in which the chairperson can influence the content of a discussion through the effective management of process (see Chapter 6).

ACTIVITY 10.2

The next time you are responsible for managing a meeting or discussion, focus on managing the process rather than becoming involved in the content. Concentrate in particular on managing involvement and participation by using *inviting* and *seeking information* in the ways described above.

Clarity of understanding

People also hope that the chairperson will manage the clarity of the discussion and make sure that all is clearly understood during the meeting. There are two behaviours which are instrumental in providing clarity, as we saw at the end of Chapter 9. These are:

□ **Testing understanding.**
□ **Summarizing.**

These behaviours need to be used regularly throughout the meeting. It may be that some of the participants use them to manage their own personal clarity, in which case this will generally be to the benefit of the whole group and can relieve the chairperson of the responsibility. But it is more likely that the chairperson will have to make sure that enough testing and summarizing take place.

We have already seen how *summarizing* is used as a signpost to manage the direction and structure of a meeting. This is its more formal usage, but not its only one. *Summarizing* can be extremely useful during a discussion in order to:

□ Restate compactly a complex contribution so that it is understood by the whole group.
□ Recap an argument in order to expose clearly any contradictions or flaws.
□ Clarify two sides of an argument in order to help people to evaluate which side they favour.

☐ Slow or calm a meeting down if the pace has become too fast or the temperature too heated.

Testing understanding can perform some of these functions too (it is often hard to tell *testing* and *summarizing* apart). But it can also be used to:

☐ Get somebody to explain further or clarify their use of language or jargon, for example: 'When you say CCT, John, do you mean Compulsive Competitive Tendering or some kind of cable television?'

☐ Help someone to clarify their own thinking when it becomes muddled, for example: 'Are you referring to the '93 or '94 figures there, Susan?'

☐ Expose and resolve possible misunderstandings in what someone is saying, for example: 'So are you suggesting we need to be more proactive or just saying that there is a lot of change in the marketplace that we need to take into account?'

Testing understanding is a versatile behaviour which can perform many functions. But even if it had just the one function of generating clarity, it would be invaluable. We take so much of what people say on face value – how many times, after a meeting or discussion, have you wished that you had checked out exactly what the person meant? It is often only when we have to implement a decision that we realize how fraught with complexity and ambiguity it is. An effective chair, who uses *testing understanding* often and well, can spare a group much of the latent confusion and frustration that meetings cause.

ACTIVITY 10.3

The next time you are responsible for managing a meeting or discussion, focus on managing the process rather than becoming involved in the content. Concentrate in particular on the two clarifying behaviours – *testing understanding* and *summarizing* – to ensure that you provide sufficient clarity to the meeting.

Summary

Figure 10.1 summarizes the three main functions required of the meetings manager or chairperson and the key behaviours used when performing these functions effectively.

Function	Behaviour
Structure and direction	Giving directions
	Summarizing
Involvement and participation	Inviting
	Seeking information
Clarity of understanding	Testing understanding
	Summarizing

Figure 10.1 Summary of key meetings management functions and behaviours.

Managing group dynamics

The skills described in the previous section will help you to manage meetings at the first three levels of process: procedural, structural and behavioural. They may also help you to control the impact of the fourth, social level. But there will be times when the group dynamics at this level of process are too powerfully disruptive – when attempts to keep the meeting on a logical and coherent track will be doomed to failure. Group dynamics can exert an enormous, distorting pressure on group interaction, under which normal procedure and behaviour buckle. In such cases, it is necessary to focus on the social level of process rather than the other three and to intervene directly in the group dynamic.

I have run countless teamwork training programmes over the years in which groups of total strangers have to work together as a team for three or four days. The strength of feeling that can be generated within a short period of time in these artificial groups doing artificial activities is mind-boggling. Sitting on the outside, I can see the dynamics forming, like clouds gathering in the sky, and they often lead to some form of crisis in the group's short life.

In the rest of this chapter, I am going to look at some of the interactive skills that can be used to intervene in the social level of process. Before I do this, I want to explore the ways in which problems arise in the group dynamic and how this affects our behaviour.

The avoidance cycle

The avoidance cycle is a model I developed some time ago to explain to a group that I was facilitating how they had arrived at their current state of

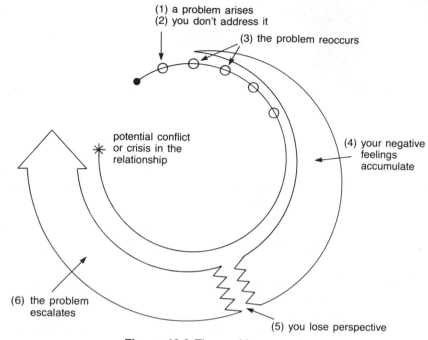

Figure 10.2 The avoidance cycle.

crisis. It is a model I have used frequently ever since! Figure 10.2 illustrates the key stages of the model, which are explained in detail below.

The avoidance cycle illustrates how conflict situations can develop when people avoid acknowledging and confronting difficult issues. And avoidance is very common, especially in groups, when there are often groundrules which encourage it, such as: 'It is not OK to rock the boat', or 'It is not OK to show your feelings'. What typically happens is this:

1. **There is a problem.** It is inevitable in all relationships that, sooner or later, someone will do something that irritates you. This might be minor: the person you share an office with is noisy. Or it may be more serious: someone turns up late for a meeting, misses a deadline, makes a mistake, ignores your instructions; a colleague is confused, or insensitive, or ungenerous, or negative, or aggressive. From the point that this happens for the first time, a new dynamic enters the relationship, and you have to decide whether to address it: 'Should I say something?'

2. **You do not address it.** You decide not to say anything. There may be several reasons why you don't, but, typically, it will be because it feels too risky. So the dynamic remains unaddressed. If the issue doesn't occur again, the matter will end here – hopefully, positive experiences

in the relationship will soon outweigh this negative one, and the problem will be forgotten.

3. **The problem does not go away.** They do it again, or something similar. It becomes apparent that it is part of who they are and the way they operate – or the way they react to you. It is no isolated incident: they are noisy, disorganized, careless; they don't evaluate how to behave very well; you make them nervous. You become aware that the issue is going to be a feature of your relationship.

4. **Your negative feelings accumulate.** The size of the problem doesn't change. It is not that they become more noisy, disorganized or careless. What changes is the extent of your feelings about the problem. Your negative feelings accumulate. The third time it happens, for example, you are more irritated by it than you were the first time. The more it happens the worse it gets.

5. **You lose perspective.** As your negative feelings accumulate, your ability to keep what is happening in perspective reduces, to the point where you lose perspective completely. Your responses to the person become irrational. You start to use words like 'always' and 'never' to describe their behaviour. You feel negative about everything they do or say, regardless of merit. You may develop a persecution complex, believing that they are deliberately trying to get at you.

6. **The problem escalates.** Once you have lost perspective, your ability to evaluate and control your own behaviour is greatly reduced. Your reactions to the person and their behaviour become more extreme and this makes the situation worse, increasing the tension between you, provoking conflict and often leading to some kind of crisis in the relationship. Typically, you will not be able to contain your feelings any more: you explode, overreacting to something which, in itself, is quite trivial. The other person is hurt and bewildered by the strength of your reaction. This can lead to conflict or some kind of crisis in the relationship.

EXERCISE 10.2

Spend a few minutes now reflecting on whether there are situations at the moment where you are 'in' the avoidance cycle; i.e. issues which you are failing to confront and about which your negative feelings are accumulating.

The avoidance cycle is a remarkably common phenomenon. I have met few people who don't have a current example of a difficult issue that they are avoiding or a situation that is likely to deteriorate unless they say something soon. And in the group setting, it is likely that several cycles are operating at the same time within the various relationships. Teams are even more pressurized environments, where the level of dependency between people can exacerbate negative feelings and accelerate the cycle: the expectations of support that are fostered by team membership are mirrored by the level of hurt and disappointment that can be felt if this support is not forthcoming, or even worse is replaced by attrition or betrayal.

CASE STUDY 10.1   The avoidance cycle

One of my favourite examples of the avoidance cycle in action was with a group of people on a training programme. They were a difficult group. They didn't want to be on the programme, didn't want to admit that they had anything to learn, didn't want to look bad in front of their peers. One man, Brian, was particularly angry and resentful. He was the longest-serving member of the group and was conscious of the status this gave him. The younger members looked up to him and were also afraid of him. He was a bully.

For the first two days of the programme, Brian behaved appallingly. He was bored and irritable; he resisted attempts to get him involved; he was aggressive both to us and to other members of the group, some of whom he constantly teased and undermined. On the third day, we did an exercise in teams – a standard exercise in which you have to rank a list of items in terms of their value to your survival. For the first time, Brian engaged with the programme. He was an expert in survival and knew what strategy should be used, which items should be at the top of the list and which firmly at the bottom.

Brian tried to persuade his team to listen to him and to follow his advice. He put forward sound logical reasons for his recommendations. He pleaded with them to accept his expertise in this area. They wouldn't have any of it. They had become so used to Brian sniping and undermining that they didn't trust him now, and even when they did start to believe that he was serious, they ignored his advice. In effect, they would rather 'die' than acknowledge Brian's contribution. They would rather punish Brian for his past behaviour than allow him finally to become a member of the team. The accumulation of negative feelings meant that the group were unable to maximize their resources when they needed to.

'Facing' things early

The key message of the avoidance cycle is that it is best to confront most difficult issues as early as possible. If you don't face the problem before your negative feelings accumulate, you are unlikely to be able to handle the confrontation effectively. Your feelings will get in the way, distorting your judgement and literally preventing you from communicating clearly – as anybody who has parented adolescent children, and disintegrated into an inarticulate heap on the floor, will know only too well!

There will be some situations, with some people, when we do face things quickly, sometimes immediately. We let them know how we are feeling and the problem is resolved. But it is likely that we only feel safe to face things in this way with a few close friends and colleagues. More often we don't say anything, hoping the problem will go away, because saying something feels like too big a risk. This might be the risk of:

☐ Appearing oversensitive and vulnerable.

☐ Appearing overcritical and negative.

☐ Communicating badly and being misunderstood.

☐ Making the other person feel bad about themselves.

☐ Provoking a defensive and hurtful response.

☐ Getting a negative response which doesn't resolve the problem.

☐ Causing a conflict that will make the situation worse.

All of these outcomes are possible. But they are less probable than you think. When we don't want to do something, we tend to create an exaggerated picture of the risks involved which justifies our inaction. I constantly get myself into a state about saying something to somebody who, when I do, responds so reasonably and positively that I am left wondering what all the fuss was about. In most cases, the actual risk will be much less than your perception of the risk.

The thing to remember is that the risk of not confronting the issue will almost always outweigh the risk of confronting it. First, because the problem is unlikely to go away of its own accord. Second, because the longer you leave it, the harder it gets to say anything. Not just because of the accumulation of negative feelings. But also because, as we lose perspective, we believe that the person will respond negatively if we say anything; in other words, our perception of the risk increases the longer we leave it. The key to confronting difficult issues is to face the problem as early as possible, when the risk involved is relatively small and your ability to manage it is relatively high.

In the group setting, tensions in relationships between some people are likely to impact on the other members of the group. It is easy to forget this, because when we get wrapped up in our own feelings we tend to lose awareness of the feelings of others. We see the problem as being 'just between me and them', but an issue between individuals is a group issue, and this is especially true in close-knit teams. Your responsibility to face things early is not just a responsibility to you and the other person/people involved, but to the group as a whole, just as it is the group's responsibility to help you to sort it out. People are often reluctant to bring their 'personal problems' into the group arena, partly for the same reasons that they avoid facing issues anyway, but also because of their discomfort with exposure to the whole group and the focus this puts them under. But in most cases, the group does have a right to know what is going on and there are several advantages to them having this understanding: one is that other members of the group may share your feelings, so that you feel less alone in the dynamic – at the least, you make it possible to get yourself some support;

and it is also likely that the group will support all the people involved to work towards a satisfactory resolution.

There are two key lessons from the avoidance cycle for groups and teams:

1. Generate a climate of openness which encourages people to express their negative feelings before they accumulate and cause serious problems.
2. Have regular reviews – using tools such as 'the round' (see Chapter 6) – which give people the opportunity to reflect on their feelings and to share them with the group as the first step towards resolution.

Although some people are naturally open and confident in expressing their feelings, most people aren't and, left to their own devices, are likely to suppress the first stirrings of negative feelings rather than acknowledge them, thus setting the avoidance cycle in motion. If people are actively encouraged to be more self-aware and more open, and feel that they can do this in a supported environment, then the group or team is in a strong position to manage its social level of process effectively.

ACTIVITY 10.4

If you suspect that there are problems in the social level of process in your group or team, use this exercise to try to interrupt the avoidance cycle. Ask your group to do a 'round' in which they have the space to clear themselves of any resentments or negative feelings about other members of the group.

Awareness and a positive momentum

Critical awareness is key to the effective management of group dynamics, because without it, the group will not have the information it needs to address the problems that arise, hopefully before they escalate. But it is also key because awareness of the issues is central to the process of resolution, and is often the only step that needs to be taken. We can be so oblivious to other people and to the impact our behaviour has on them, that, the moment we are informed of this impact, we change our behaviour, at least sufficiently for the problem to be manageable if not completely resolved. Awareness is all we need. One of my close colleagues once complained to me that he was upset by my constant low-level blasphemy, explaining that it affronted his religious beliefs. I was mortified. I had no idea that I was having this effect (I wasn't that aware of the extent to which I blasphemed!) and was immediately able to agree to his demand, much to his relief, as he had feared that I would get defensive and that his request would lead to an argument. I don't share his beliefs, but I certainly don't want to upset him and try hard now to curb my tongue.

This is an example of how awareness can sometimes lead instantly to resolution. It is not always that simple. But it is usually the case that awareness generates a positive momentum between the people involved, a momentum based on greater understanding of and sensitivity to each other's needs. When I am facilitating groups, I rarely have time to do any more than generate this positive momentum, but I firmly believe that once generated, people have the necessary goodwill and skills to move forward to a satisfactory resolution. I also know that if I try to move to resolution too quickly (and I often want to do this to satisfy my own need for admiration and feelings of accomplishment – see Chapter 4) this can threaten the positive momentum, generating a resistance which entrenches people rather than releasing their goodwill. People need to move at the speed that they feel comfortable with, and as long as the momentum is there, and it is positive, they will act.

I recently facilitated a team where the relationship between two people was clearly a long way down the avoidance cycle: the hostility between them was apparent and creating a negative climate in the team as a whole. All I had time to do was to bring the issue into the open in front of the whole group and suggest that the two people had to resolve it. Which they did. A key characteristic of the positive momentum generated by a whole group awareness of issues is that the responsibility to the group felt by the people involved fuels the momentum, as does the group's expectation that the protagonists will do something about the tension they are generating.

There are times, of course, when raising critical awareness doesn't generate a positive momentum, or that the momentum it generates is not sufficient to lead to a resolution. This is sometimes because there is not enough common ground: someone wants somebody to change their behaviour in ways that they are not prepared to do. I could have said no to my colleague, that I wasn't prepared to curb my tongue and stop blaspheming, that this was an infringement of my freedom. In effect, I would have been saying: 'I don't care that you are upset' and 'I don't care about our relationship'.

In my experience, when barriers arise which block an attempt to resolve an interpersonal problem, these barriers generally stem from deep-seated distress within one or more of the people involved. This was the situation in both of the case studies that I have used in Parts 1 and 2 (Gavin's team and Ivana's team), and severely limited my ability to work with each team at the social level of process. For each team, intervention was needed with one individual to help them work on their distress if sustained progress with the whole team was to be possible. Both people were rationally able to engage with the issues raised by the group dynamic, but their emotional undertow was so strong that it subverted their rational responses.

Objections to attempts at resolution, however plausible, need to be examined closely to see whether they are in fact smokescreens for deep-seated emotional resistance. The rational objections can be clever, and can absorb much energy and goodwill before it becomes clear that they are not the real source of the resistance.

Feedback and demands

The communication 'mechanism' which initiates and sustains the positive momentum can be described, at its most basic, as one of feedback and demand. When my colleague lets me know that my blaspheming upsets him he is giving me feedback; when he asks me not to do it again in his company, he is making a demand. These are the building-blocks of the resolution of problems in the group dynamic. Feedback initiates the momentum by raising awareness; demands take the momentum in a positive direction because they provide a framework for action and change. Here are their definitions:

☐ **Feedback** involves telling somebody how you feel about them or their behaviour, describing the impact their behaviour has on you, for example: 'It *offends* my religious beliefs when you take the Lord's name in vain', 'I am *annoyed* that you have turned up late, I've been waiting for you for twenty minutes'. When we give feedback, we use *describing feelings* behaviour (see Chapter 9).

☐ **Demands** involve asking someone to change their behaviour towards you in ways that they are likely to be able to achieve and respond positively to, for example: 'Could you try not to blaspheme when we are together', 'Next time, please let us know how late you are going to be so that we can decide whether to start without you'. When we make demands, we use *suggesting* or *proposing* behaviour (see Chapter 9).

The mechanism of feedback and demands is straightforward but often requires great courage and skill. The main values of the mechanism are that it generates a manageable level of awareness and a positive structure for action. Feedback should be regarded, both by the giver and the receiver, as invaluable information, for it is the only way that the receiver will know for sure what impact they have on someone else. Our self-awareness can never extend that far – we can never know for certain how people feel about us unless they tell us. We depend on feedback to learn how to be in the world, how to manage ourselves and our relationships more effectively. Without it, we are denied the opportunity to gain insight and make changes. If my colleague had not told me how he felt about my blaspheming, he would have been denying me the opportunity to do something to improve the situation.

Feedback has another value, in that it communicates key information about how you are defining the problem, which in turn significantly affects the receptivity of the person you are giving the feedback to. Feedback signals that you are defining the problem as one that is shared between you. My colleague wasn't saying that I was wrong to blaspheme, but that my blaspheming offended him. I could have argued with the former. I can't argue with the latter. I might think that he shouldn't be offended, but I have to accept the fact that he is. He was letting me know that *we* had a problem, not that I was at fault. He wasn't blaming me. If he had, it is likely that my response would have been far more defensive, as, like most people, I tend not to react to blame positively.

Demands provide a structure in which the awareness that comes from feedback can be turned into action. It is important that the action demanded should be directed at sustaining the positive momentum rather than at trying to solve the whole problem, for it is unlikely that a realistic demand could be made which would resolve everything. Demands should be focused on achieving the next step forward together, even if that is not as big as you would like. Feedback is an indicator of your positive momentum towards the other person. The demand is your invitation to them to indicate their preparedness to make a positive move towards you. The invitation should be one that they are likely to accept. My colleague asked me only to stop blaspheming in his presence, even though he may have wanted me never to blaspheme again.

One way that as a manager or team-leader you can help members of your team to resolve tensions or issues in the group dynamic, is to suggest feedback and demands as a communication exercise. I use it frequently when I am working with teams as a kind of clearing-house in which the unsaid can be safely said and unfinished business can be safely finished. This can be incorporated with 'the round' (see Chapter 6) so that people use their space in the round to give feedback to and then make demands of each other. You can support this by ensuring that the feedback is not blaming and that the demands are realistic. I sometimes use an extended version: resentments, appreciations and demands.

ACTIVITY 10.5

Practise using feedback and demands as a mechanism to generate awareness and positive momentum either by:

☐ Facing an issue that exists between you and another member of your team, in which you feel you are in the avoidance cycle and that this is damaging the relationship.

☐ Organizing a round in which all members of the team have the opportunity to give feedback and make a demand of another member.

The limitations of feedback and demands

The process of turning awareness into action is also the limitation of this mechanism, as it characterizes its underlying principle, which is behaviour modification: seeking to encourage change in the way a person behaves in relation to you. The limitation is that behaviour is usually only the surface representation of a dynamic between people. It is likely that the forces below the surface, generated by the personalities and psychologies of the people involved and the interconnections between them, will overpower any attempts to tamper with the visible symptoms.

There are times when feedback and demands won't work because the undertow of the dynamic is too fierce, either because an individual's psychology is too distressed or the connection between psychologies is too entangled. A more rigorous analysis of the causes of the problems is required in such circumstances and a more intensive approach to resolution – one that I usually don't have the time or the skills to engage in.

But it is rare for the group to suffer dynamics that can't be addressed in part by the mechanism of feedback and demands. Even if the behaviour modification only addresses the surface representation of a problem, it can relax the tensions in a relationship in the short term and by so doing have a benign effect on the deeper forces at work. People often invest much emotional energy in developing a sophisticated analysis of problems in group dynamics, in understanding and explaining the deep forces at work in people's personalities and the chemistry between them. Such analysis can be helpful in promoting understanding of the issues involved. The problem is that analysis alone doesn't sustain positive momentum, and often can be a distraction which impedes the development of momentum: there are times when the deeper the understanding, the harder it becomes to extract yourself from it as the complexities of the problem seem to require impossibly complex solutions.

Managing crisis

There will be times when the group dynamics are so complex and entrenched that they lead to crisis: the breakdown of relationships within the team, either through withdrawal or open conflict. In such conditions, the mechanism of feedback and demands will not be enough to manage the force of the feelings unleashed. The crisis has to be diffused before awareness and positive momentum can be generated. Unfortunately, our initial responses to such crises tend to have the opposite effect, fuelling the strength of feeling and exacerbating the misperceptions that are flying around.

There are three processes to bear in mind when caught up in crises in group dynamics. These are:

□ The emotional pendulum.

□ Process v content.

□ Staying separate.

Managing the pendulum
I introduced the emotional pendulum in Chapter 7. It is one of the tools that I have learnt through my involvement with the Pellin Institute. If you haven't already done so, you should read the section on the pendulum in Chapter 7 before continuing to read this section.

One of the applications of the pendulum is to help us understand and manage our responses when confronted with crises in group dynamics. In particular, it helps us to manage the timing of our responses. For when we are confronted with crisis, our natural response is to swing into a high. This can be helpful in that it can give us the courage to take risks in challenging people or defending ourselves and the value of this should not be underestimated. There are times when the crisis needs to be worked through cathartically, in which case people need to commit themselves to expressing their feelings in order to 'bottom out' the causes of conflict. The reckless disregard that we experience when we are high helps us to overcome the inhibitions that normally prevent us from doing this. The cathartic effect of such draining of emotion is in effect a climactic feedback session. It is high risk, for such cathartic expression is volatile and hard to control. Irrevocable hurt can be caused and relationships may never recover.

When we are high we are, by definition, not calm. When we are not calm, we find it harder to evaluate rationally and to control our behaviour accordingly. If we want to diffuse the crisis rather than exacerbate it, we need to be in the calm of our emotional pendulum, where we are more likely to keep things in perspective, to understand other people's positions and to behave calmly. Because the impact of a crisis is to swing us into the high, we need to manage our pendulum in order to bring it back into the calm, and to do this ideally before responding to the provocation or invitation to join in. There are three steps you can take to bring your penduum back into the calm:

□ Go somewhere else – literally remove yourself from the scene of the conflict at the earliest opportunity. Go and get a coffee or go for a walk. The physical movement itself will help you to control the swing of the pendulum, as will being in a different environment, away from the sources of stimuli that are triggering the swing to the high.

☐ Reflect on your feelings – focus on how you feel in response to the crisis rather than on the behaviour of the other people involved. It is tempting to focus only on them and their behaviour, blaming them for the crisis and allowing this to distort our perceptions of them as people. This tends to fuel the strength of our feelings, our anger and resentment. Ironically, focusing on our feelings and trying to understand why we have responded in the way we have, helps to keep them under control. Ask yourself: 'Why do I feel so angry? Why do I resent that so much?'

☐ Get feedback – ask someone who is not directly involved in the dynamic to give you feedback about the crisis and the events leading up to it. It is important to choose someone who will not collude with you and who will give you straight and honest feedback, even if that challenges your own perceptions and behaviour (we tend to seek out people who we know will support our view).

These three steps will help you to retain a more objective and detached perspective on events. They won't of their own accord bring you back into the calm – you can get high telling the story to the person you have gone to for feedback, for instance. You need to take these steps with the intention of managing your pendulum and finding your calm. If you do that, they are likely to help.

Focusing on process
When groups reach crisis, this represents a breakdown in their process. If the group is to emerge from the crisis and function effectively again, it must acknowledge this, recognize that the issues are process issues and address them accordingly. In my experience, however, the tendency is to get locked into the content of the crisis – arguing furiously over specifics: what people said or did exactly, or didn't do or say. These facts are not irrelevant, but in less stressed circumstances, they would not of themselves generate such strength of feeling in people. There is something else going on, underlying the actual, factual events. The words and actions may have triggered the crisis, but they are not the underlying cause. This lies in the social level of process: in the relationships between people and the dynamics that these relationships generate.

Argument over content will not lead to resolution. The content is the battleground. People will slug it out until they are exhausted trying to prove that they are right and the other person wrong, trying to allocate blame and to exact punishment. It is unlikely that this will help. Only when it is recognized that the content is reflecting more substantial, deeper issues, when people agree to set the content aside in order to address the process, will the downward spiral be halted. This can be very hard to do. It is hard to let go of the desire to be proved right, to demonstrate that the other person is in the wrong, to punish them for their wrong-doing, expose them to the world for what they 'really are', to turn others against them as well as gathering support for yourself. It is hard to put the specifics to one side and to review the relationships: to understand why people are feeling as strongly as they are. It is difficult to know sometimes why you feel so angry and even harder to find the words to express these reasons. But if the crisis is to be managed effectively, this is exactly what needs to happen.

Staying separate
Finally, there is a simple principle that is worth iterating here. I am grateful to have learnt it early in my working life, when it was referred to by the phrase: 'stay separate!' and this is how I refer to it still. To *stay separate* means to:

☐ Hear what people are saying about you without immediately taking it on board: to stay separate from their perceptions of you which, after all, are only their perceptions.

☐ Not confuse fact with opinion, to recognize that feedback says as much about the giver as it does the receiver, that they are never entirely detached from their own emotions, that their feedback is not the truth about you, it is simply useful information.

☐ Hear the feedback without becoming defensive, to reflect on it from the calm of the pendulum, and to extract from it what feels useful to you.

When group dynamics start to break down and move towards crisis, people become hurtful. They are distressed by the worsening dynamic, may feel hurt themselves, angry and resentful. They say things to each other, about each other, which, consciously or not, are likely to cause hurt. They will blame others and they will want to punish them. The punishment often takes the form of criticism and personal attack, moving from the specifics of events and behaviour to the broader canvas of generalization and personality. In these circumstances, staying separate is crucial, in the same way that it is crucial to focus on process rather than content. It is impossible not to feel hurt by these personal attacks, but it is important to see that they are an expression of the dysfunction of the group process and to hear them without taking them on board. There is likely to be something within what is being said that will be worth reflecting on, but you don't have to internalize it and can choose to reject it.

When we fail to stay separate, we are prey to two impulses: one is to lash back, trying to cancel out people's words with words of our own, and thus escalating the conflict so that it spirals into a painful attempt at mutual annihilation; the other is to reject what they are saying completely, seeing it as a manifestation of their own distorted perspective and inadequate personality, and thus in effect ignoring them and withdrawing from the relationships. These are understandable responses when confronted with behaviour which threatens our sense of self. But they are likely to worsen the crisis, to generate a negative rather than positive momentum, and to cause irreparable damage to the relationships.

EXERCISE 10.3

Spend a few minutes now reflecting on times when you have been in a relationship at work which has reached some form of crisis. Use the three concepts explored above – managing the pendulum, focusing on process and staying separate – to review how you behaved during the crisis and whether there are ways in which you could have managed it more effectively.

Summary

In the first section of this chapter, I explored the key skills required to manage the procedural level of process: chairing skills. I have summarized these in Figure 10.1. They are a particular application of some of the core interactive skills I described in Chapter 9. These chairing skills will help you to manage formal meetings and informal group discussions effectively. They will also help you to manage any interaction – even one-to-one interactions – because the same requirements and the same solutions usually apply. They are the baseline process management skills and thus a good shopping-list for the development of your interactive skills generally.

In the second section, I focused on the more complex skills involved in the management of the issues occurring at the social level of process. I used the avoidance cycle to illustrate the internal processes that interfere with our behaviour and self-control when confronted with these issues. And I explained the key behavioural mechanism that can be used to generate awareness and positive momentum: feedback and demands. This mechanism and these behaviours are the baseline relationship management skills. They are worth practising as they will help you to manage all your relationships more effectively.

ACTIVITY 10.6

Before moving on to the next chapter, consider whether there are particular behaviours that have been covered in this chapter that you feel it would be useful for you to practise. If so, plan how you intend to practise them. It is best to identify specific meetings or discussions where it would be appropriate for you to practise the management of procedural process. Great care needs to be taken in identifying appropriate opportunities to practise the management of the social level of process.

11

Influencing skills

In Chapter 3, we looked at the two principal leadership styles: being directive and being consultative. These styles describe your overall approach to leadership. They have many forms of expression: the extent to which you communicate with your people; the degree to which you involve them in decision making; the amount of time you spend with them; how you spend time with them. But the clearest form of expression is the way that you influence them. Your leadership has most impact on your people when you try to get them to do what you want them to do. And your skills as a leader are brought into sharpest relief when they don't want to do it, when their resistance has to be overcome and their commitment gained. Influencing skills are a key requirement of effective leadership.

EXERCISE 11.1

Spend a few minutes now reflecting on your influencing skills: How effective are you at persuading people to do what you want? Do you gain their commitment? How do you go about persuading people?

In this chapter, we are going to look in detail at three aspects of influencing:

☐ Styles.
☐ Strategies.
☐ Skills.

Persuasion styles

The directive and consultative styles of leadership are full-blown versions of two styles of persuasion. These are:

☐ **Push:** When you tell people what you want them to do, tell them why and tell them how. You have made all the decisions. You don't invite much discussion, except to ensure that they understand what is expected of them.

☐ **Pull:** When you involve people in a process whereby together you identify what needs to be done and how it should be done. A process of joint problem-solving, decision-making and action-planning in which you act primarily as an enabler, using questions to help your people understand and resolve the issues for themselves.

I am going to illustrate the difference between the two styles by returning to a simple domestic scenario that I used in the section on 'Ideas' in Chapter 9 – going to see a film one evening. Imagine that you want to go and see a specific film and you want to persuade a partner or friend to go with you. Here is how the two styles might operate:

Push style

You: They're showing *Brief Encounter* at the Arts Cinema tonight. Let's go and see it. It starts at 8.00 pm.

Friend: Oh, not tonight. I don't want to go out tonight.

You: Oh, come on! It will do you good to get out. And we can go for a drink afterwards, meet Linda and Barry. You've been saying you want to see *Brief Encounter* for ages!

Friend: I know, but I'm exhausted. Isn't there anything on telly?

You: There's absolutely nothing on. That's why I looked to see what was on at the cinema. We don't have to stay late. I'll do all the driving. Once you get out you'll perk up. It'll do you good. And it's *Brief Encounter* – it's brilliant – you'll love it – you'll cry – it'll be great!

Pull style

You: Have you got anything planned for tonight?

Friend: No. I'm exhausted. I just want to watch TV.

You: Is there anything on?

Friend: I don't know, I'll have a look. . . . No. Nothing.

You: Are you too tired to go out?

Friend: I don't want to have to get changed or anything.

You: If you fancy just sitting in front of a screen, why don't we see
            if there is anything on at the Arts?
Friend: OK. As long as we come straight back. I need an early
            night.

There is no guarantee that in this situation either style will have worked.
The lure of *Brief Encounter* may not have been enough to overcome the
friend's exhaustion. But it shows how different the styles are.

EXERCISE 11.2

Spend a few minutes now reflecting on your persuasion style: Which of the two
styles illustrated above do you tend to use? Do you mainly use a 'push' style?
Do you ever use a 'pull' style? Are you able to use both with equal facility?

For most people, **push** is their natural style. We use it all the time, in
the numerous small persuasions we engage in during a normal day. I shout
down to my wife as I write this: 'Make me a cup of tea, please!' – I am using
a push style. I suggest some changes to a letter that a colleague is sending
to a client – I am using a push style. For many people, **push** is not only
their natural style but their only style. They are either unaware of other
options or unable to implement them. And when they become managers
this fact alone means that they will almost certainly be a directive leader.
Effective communicators are able to use both **push** and **pull**, and they know
when to use which style.

We are now going to look at how they make this choice, first by
understanding the different impacts of the two styles, and then by
exploring the circumstances in which one is more appropriate than the
other.

Impact

There are four key areas where the styles differ in impact.

Exposure
When you use a **push** style, you reveal your desired outcome early in the
interaction. In the above example, it was clear that you wanted to go and
see the film. The friend's responses were conditioned by this knowledge.
When we look at persuasion strategy later in this section, we will see that
such exposure can weaken your position – when the other person is in no
doubt what it is they are resisting, this makes it a lot easier for them to
resist.

When you use a **pull** style, you do not have to disclose your desired outcome. At no point in the example above did you declare what you wanted to do. This means that you are more able to adapt your preferences or your argument according to the information you receive. If your friend is so tired, it might not be a smart idea to suggest going out for a drink after the film.

So a **push** style is less flexible than a **pull** style. It is also riskier, because when you expose your desired outcome, it is clear to both parties whether you were successful in achieving it or not. There may be times when you would prefer the other person not to know.

Outcome

When the other person does not want to do what you want them to do, a **push** style tends to lead to a battle of wills which somebody has to win, and therefore somebody has to lose. In other words, unless there is common ground to start with, a **push** style can lead to a win/lose outcome. And nobody likes losing. If your friend digs their heels in and you don't go to the cinema – you are likely to feel some disappointment or resentment. If you get your way, your friend is also likely to feel aggrieved.

When you use a **pull** style, you are better able to take the other person's position into account and therefore to fashion a solution that meets the needs of both of you. A **pull** style is more likely to lead to a win/win outcome which both of you feel good about.

Commitment

A natural consequence of the different character of outcome that can be achieved is the level of commitment that is generated. If someone is on the losing end of a **push** style persuasion, their commitment is often quite low. There have been times, for example, when I have allowed myself to be pushed into going out but have been determined not to enjoy myself as a way of getting my own back! Our natural inclination when we lose a persuasion is often to sabotage the outcome and/or to make sure that we win next time.

Because a **pull** style tends to generate a win/win outcome which both parties have been involved in developing and so feel some ownership over, people generally feel committed to making sure that outcome is implemented successfully.

Quality

As we have seen throughout Chapter 9, an asking style tends to lead to better-quality solutions for two reasons: you get more input on the issues and the possible options; and people feel more committed to solutions when they have contributed to their development. For these reasons, it is likely that a **pull** style will generate better-quality solutions than a **push** style.

We can see this in the example: the **push** style applies pressure on the friend which is likely to interfere with the quality of the outcome in one of two ways: they may dig their heels in, determined not to lose the argument; or they may agree to do things that they don't really want to do, just to shut you up. This pressure can in fact create a lose/lose outcome: you stay at home in an atmosphere of frustration and resentment; you go out and the friend sabotages your enjoyment of the film. The information gathered by the initial questioning of the **pull** style enables you to lead the discussion towards a more appropriate outcome.

EXERCISE 11.3

Spend a few minutes now reflecting on instances recently when you have had to persuade somebody to do something. Which style did you use: push or pull? Bearing in mind the points above, do you feel now that it was the appropriate style to use in the circumstances?

I am not suggesting that you should use a **pull** style every time you try to persuade a friend to go to the pictures with you! Most of the time a **push** style will be appropriate and effective. And it will be in a majority of the situations where you need to be persuasive at work too. Which is just as well, because **pushing** is a lot easier than **pulling**. This will become clearer when we have looked at persuasion strategy, but you might already be appreciating that a **pull** style can be hard work. You are having to process information and frame questions at the same time, and behaviourally this is far more difficult than coming straight out and telling them what you want them to do. However, there will be times when a **push** style won't be appropriate and unfortunately these tend to be the times when it is important for you to be successful.

Conditions of use

There are certain conditions when a **push** style is not going to get you the quality and commitment that you want, when you will need to use a **pull** style instead. The following four factors will help you to decide which style to use.

The degree of importance

A **push** style works well with issues that are not urgent, critical or complex. Luckily, most of the persuasions we undertake fall into this category. They are minor interactions whose outcome is not hugely important to us because, if we do not get our way, the consequences will not be that significant. It's not the end of the world if we don't go and see *Brief Encounter* tonight. The situation does not warrant the amount of thought, effort and care required by a **pull** style persuasion. We push, we hope for the best, we win some, we lose some.

But if it is important to us, if it is urgent, if the issues are complex, if the consequences are significant – then we need to take more care. The pay-off justifies the effort involved and it is possible that we should use a **pull** style as this represents the safest and most careful approach. It will depend on the other factors listed below, but it is wise, before each major persuasion, to get into the habit of considering which style you should be using.

The balance of power
When you are using a **push** style, your success to a large extent will depend on the balance of power between you and the other person. This power may derive from your position in the organization or from the force of your personality, or both. If you are more powerful than the other person, then it is more likely that a **push** style will be effective. It doesn't mean that it will necessarily be appropriate. This will depend on other factors, as we will see. But **push** works best when accompanied by power – which is one of the reasons why managers and leaders resort to it so easily.

The reverse is also true. If you have less power than the other person, it is less likely that a **push** style will be effective. They will use their power to resist you and they are likely to win. For this reason, it is often unwise to use a **push** style with people senior to you in the organization. Unless your expertise is seen to give you greater power and authority, they may object to you pushing them around. It is often safer to use a **pull** style, particularly because of the lower level of exposure involved and the greater flexibility that **pull** gives you.

The room for manoeuvre
One of the key factors in deciding which style to use concerns the amount of room for manoeuvre that you have available, by which I mean the extent to which you are committed to achieving one specific solution. If there are other options that would be acceptable to you, if there is scope for adjustment or compromise, then you are clearly in a much more flexible position. A **pull** style is ideal when you have room for manoeuvre in that it creates the climate and the process required to generate and explore options with the other person. You don't need to **push** one solution when it is possible to explore a range of them.

A **pull** style is much harder to use without room for manoeuvre. It still might be appropriate, but it will require careful application to direct the person towards your desired outcome. If there is a risk that they will reject

;ing a consultative approach to gain their commitment to implement
)utcome in the least problematic way.

ERCISE 11.4

pend a few minutes now reflecting on a situation in the near future when you
are having to persuade someone to do something. Bearing in mind the conditions
outlined above, which style do you think you should use: push or pull?

It is usually only when the level of resistance is high that persuasions
become complicated and you have to consider actively the impacts and
conditions described above. Most people I work with have had the
experience of failing to get their way in the face of strong and often
unexpected resistance. Hopefully you will be working with groups who
have a high level of goodwill both towards you and the objectives you are
leading them to achieve and who therefore are not going to resist you often.
But if the dynamics within the group are poor, the morale low, the activity
unrewarding, the organization uncaring or inefficient, your leadership
style inappropriate – then every time you need to get them to do something
can feel like an uphill battle, a battle of wills.

Persuasion strategy

Resistance to change is a complex process, which reflects people's
personality as much as any rational considerations about the rights and
wrongs of the change in question. However, at the root of this process there
is usually a simple calculation which goes as follows:

☐ What is this change going to cost me?
☐ How am I going to benefit from it?
☐ Do the costs outweigh the benefits?

For most people, this calculation will be their instinctive response to any
demand you make of them which requires them to change the way they
do things. Your attempts to persuade them and get their commitment to
what you want are, in essence, attempts to influence the way they make
that calculation. The two key components are:

☐ **Cost:** This might be financial cost, or time, effort, hassle, risk of failure,
loss of status and so on.

your solution, however, a **pull** style will not b
be counter-productive for two reasons: it can e.
they have more influence over the outcome tha.
can give them the opportunity to rehearse all thei.
your solution.

In other words, it is not wise to use a **pull** style when
that you will have to revert to **push** if you are not successi
has been through a consultation exercise only to find that t.
been completely ignored will understand why. The disillusic
greater than if **push** was used from the beginning.

The level of resistance

The final key factor in deciding which style to use is the level of resista.
you are likely to encounter from the person or people you are persuadin,
A **push** style works well when the resistance is low, and this will be the
case most of the time, which is why **push** is the style we use most
regularly. If you know your friend has been dying to see *Brief Encounter*
for years, has got nothing else planned for the evening and wants to go
out, then you don't need to embark on a **pull** style persuasion to convince
them to go and see the film with you. A quick and incisive **push** will
do the trick.

But if you know that the person is likely to resist – whatever the reason:
rational or emotional – then you know it is going to be hard work to
persuade them and it is likely that a **pull** style will be more effective. This
is mainly because, with a **pull** style, you don't expose your desired outcome
early, and therefore are not giving the other person anything tangible to
reject or resist until later in the interaction, by which time, as we will see,
you may have been able to influence the basis of their resistance.

The problem is that you often won't know what the level of resistance
is going to be. If this is the case, you need to establish the level of resistance
quickly, and the safest way to do this is to ask questions, which tends to
lead you into a **pull** style. This is illustrated by the two examples above:
the **push** style encountered unexpected resistance which, once articulated,
becomes even harder to overcome. The **pull** style, by starting with the
question: 'Have you got anything planned for tonight?', uncovered both
the level and the causes of the resistance. This makes it possible to evaluate
whether and how best to overcome it.

There will be times when the level of resistance is so strong, so deeply
entrenched, so immovable, that a **pull** style, however skilfully and
persistently executed, will fail. This is especially true if there is no benefit
to the other person or people in doing what you want them to do and when
you have no room for manoeuvre. These are the most difficult scenarios
and there is no easy answer: in my experience, the best strategy is usually
to **push** and to **push** hard, making it clear that there is no alternative, and

☐ **Benefit:** This might be financial gain, savings in time and effort, improvements to working conditions, increased job satisfaction, greater opportunities to develop, greater recognition and so on.

If the perceived cost of change is greater than the perceived benefit, the change is likely to be resisted. The cost to your friend of going to see *Brief Encounter* was having to find the energy to rouse themselves after a long day. If this outweighs any pleasure they will get from seeing the film, they will resist your attempts to get them to go and see it. To understand why this is the case, we must break benefit down into its two component parts: value and need.

Value and need: Our perception of the benefit of change is made up of two parts:

☐ The value we think the change will have for us in the future.

☐ The need we have to change what we are doing now.

These may sound similar but are quite different, and their difference is at the heart of effective persuasion. It is not just that the effort involved in going out when we are exhausted and low outweighs the pleasure we will get from seeing *Brief Encounter*. It is that it cuts across what we want to do: spend a quiet evening in watching the telly eating a take-away delivered to the door! There may be some value in seeing the film, but if we have no desire to let go of how we are already planning to spend the evening, we will be difficult to shift out of the armchair.

EXERCISE 11.5

Spend a few minutes now reflecting on times when someone has tried to persuade you to change the way you do something. To what extent did your perception of the need to change differ from their perception of value?

The mistake we often make when we are persuading people is to confuse need with value, and to assume that our perception of the value of change will be the same as their perception of the need to change. We assume that because we know they will enjoy seeing *Brief Encounter* that they will automatically want to go and see it when it is on. To understand the causes of someone's resistance, **we must first assess their perception of the need to change**.

The development of need: Our need to change is based on how we feel about our present situation and our awareness of the problems we have in that situation. Imagine that the roles are changed: you are exhausted after a long day; you have decided that you are going to spend the evening in, get a take-away, watch the telly, go to bed early, take it easy. A friend phones to see if you want to go to see *Brief Encounter*. Your response will depend entirely on how satisfied you are with your plan for the evening. If you are convinced that it is what you need to do, you will decline the offer. If you have any doubts, you are open to persuasion. There may be all sorts of reasons for your doubts:

☐ There is nothing on telly.

☐ You're so tired that you feel restless and you can't relax.

☐ You're starting to feel lonely.

☐ When you've done this before it just makes you feel worse.

☐ You don't like the idea of missing out on anything.

☐ If you order a take-away you'll break your diet.

It depends when your friend phones. Early in the evening and these misgivings may not have entered your consciousness. Two hours later, you may be crying out for somebody to rescue you from your self-imposed exile. This development of need over time is typical, as illustrated in Figure 11.1.

Our need to change usually starts as a small dissatisfaction with how things are in the present, or concern about what will happen in the future. We don't do anything at this stage, because the need isn't big enough. If the dissatisfaction grows, so too does our need to change. If the dissatisfaction grows big enough, we will start to contemplate action.

But that is all we do. The call from the friend has got us thinking: what do I really want to do? It has focused our dissatisfaction with our original plan. But we are not ready to ditch it quite yet. We now need to consider what the **value** will be of going to see the film. We are still exhausted. We need to be convinced that going out is the better solution (see Figure 11.2).

Here are some of the benefits that we could get:

☐ We could get to see the film at last.

☐ We would be with other people.

☐ We wouldn't get bored.

☐ We could get a kebab on the way back and not eat too much.

☐ Our friend would be pleased.

☐ Our friend would be more likely to phone us up again.

When we think about the value in this way, our motivation to do something increases yet further. These thoughts mill around in our heads, causing confusion as they rub up against our earlier analysis of need. Maybe going

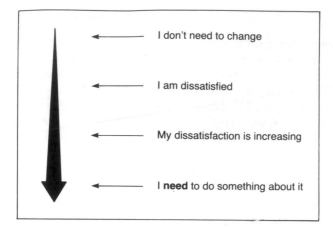

Figure 11.1 The development of need.

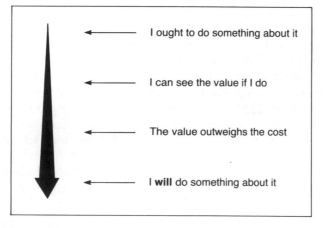

Figure 11.2 The development of the awareness of value.

to see the film would be better for us after all. And suddenly we feel less tired than we thought we did!

EXERCISE 11.6

Spend a few minutes now reflecting on times when you have decided to change some aspect of your life (e.g. buy a new car, take more exercise, organize your work better, give up smoking). Think about the process that you went through to reach the decision to change, focusing on:

☐ The increase of your dissatisfaction with the present.
☐ Your growing awareness of the value of change.

Strategies for overcoming resistance

Our success at persuading our friend to go to the film depends partly on when we phoned – where they were up to in their internal process of need development. This will determine the level of resistance we encounter and therefore how hard we have to work to overcome it. If we phone at the right moment, they might fall, sobbing pathetically, into our arms. But we can't rely on getting the timing right. Usually, when we are persuading people, we are having to accelerate the process of need development. We can't wait for them to become aware of the need to change for themselves. It would take too long. You'd miss the beginning of the film!

The key point is that it is *their* perception of need that we are having to influence. We may know that the worst thing our friend could do is stay in on their own. The trouble is, that knowing we are right can actively get in the way. Because something to us seems blindingly, obviously, unarguably right, this does not mean that the other person will see things in the same way. There is one central premise behind effective persuasion: **being right isn't persuasive**. This is absolutely critical. When we know we are right, we tend to underestimate the possible level of resistance. We can't conceive how anybody could object, and so we are unprepared for resistance. And when we encounter it, we tend to focus on value. Look back to the **push** style example on page 222: 'Oh, come on! It will do you good to get out. And we can go for a drink afterwards, meet Linda and Barry. You've been saying you want to see *Brief Encounter* for ages!'

These are statements of value. You are telling your friend why they should want to go out. But because this is not based on an understanding of their actual need (as opposed to what you think they should need), you can only talk about value in terms of the benefits as *you* see them. Only when you know what the friend's needs are, can you focus your description of value by relating the benefits specifically to them. If you know your friend is tired, for example, you might not suggest going for a drink afterwards as this weakens your argument.

The tendency to focus on our solutions and on the value we see in them is at the heart of what goes wrong in countless persuasions. We try to prove to the person that we are right – and whether we are right or wrong is immaterial. What is important is whether the person **needs** what we want them to do. Because we believe that all we have to be is right, we make the mistake of trying to develop their perception of the *value* of the change when we should be focusing on developing their *need* for it.

EXERCISE 11.7

Spend a few minutes now reflecting on times when you have tried to persuade someone to do something they were reluctant to do. To what extent did you try to convince them that you were right about the value of the change? To what extent did you try to develop their need to change?

In order to overcome resistance and generate commitment, we need to use a strategy that is based on the following four steps.

Develop the need for change
The first step is to develop the other person's awareness of the need to change by focusing on their dissatisfactions with the present and their concerns about the future. These may be dissatisfactions and concerns that they already feel, for example, the fact that there is nothing worth watching on TV. Or they may be ones that they *should* feel but are not aware of, for example, your frustration with them for never wanting to go out.

Develop awareness of the value of change
Dissatisfaction alone won't be enough to convince people that they need to act. Sometimes the dissatisfaction isn't big enough; sometimes the cost still outweighs the value. So the second step in the persuasion strategy is to develop the other person's awareness of the value of change. Most of the value will lie in the resolution of the dissatisfactions and problems experienced in the present. But there are likely to be other values that they may not be aware of.

Develop ownership of the solution
Whenever possible, you should involve the person you are persuading in developing a specific solution for achieving what you want them to do. If you help your friend to plan how best to spend the evening, you will be increasing their commitment to the solution that is agreed, because they will feel that:

☐ They have some power in the situation.
☐ You respect their ability to solve their own problems.
☐ They have some ownership of the eventual solution.
☐ Their concerns have been taken into account.

As we have seen, a **pull** style, using *seeking proposals* behaviour, tends to generate more commitment and better quality.

Develop solutions that minimize cost
So far, we have addressed two of the three elements of resistance: need and value. The persuasion strategy has been to develop an awareness of value that outweighs the perception of cost. But even when this is done successfully, the cost element doesn't go away and still needs to be handled.

It is best to address cost at the solution stage, partly because it will be balanced by the perception of value, and partly because you can deal with it at a practical level. If you clarify what the cost concerns are, you can develop a solution which will resolve as many of them as possible. For example, given that your friend is exhausted, you could go and pick them up rather than meet them at the cinema.

It is unlikely that you will be able to resolve all the costs in this way – there is usually a price to be paid for change. But by getting the concerns on to the table, and exploring ways of resolving them, you will be signalling your desire to help the person manage the costs, and this will have a positive impact on their commitment to what is finally agreed.

The sequence of these four steps is important, and is based on two underlying principles:

☐ It is better to develop the need before you develop the solution. If people feel they need the solution, they are more likely to be positive when you engage them in developing it.

☐ It is better to increase the awareness of value before trying to reduce the perception of cost. If people feel there is value in changing, their perception of cost is likely to reduce. And people are more likely to engage constructively on how to manage the cost if they feel that there is sufficient value.

ACTIVITY 11.1

Identify an interaction you have had recently when you have tried to persuade someone to do something they have been resistant to. It should be an interaction which you feel you could have managed more effectively. Use the four-stage structure for developing need and generating commitment to help you assess the causes of difficulty you experienced in the interaction and to plan ways in which you could manage it more effectively if you were to tackle the issue again.

Persuasion skills

I am now going to look at the skills involved in executing a persuasion strategy based on developing need. I am going to cover three skill areas. These are:

☐ Identifying outcomes.

☐ Persuasion scenarios.

☐ Persuasive questions.

The other key skill involved in pull style persuasions is the way in which you generate solutions. As I have covered this in general in the section on 'Ideas' in Chapter 9, I will not be revisiting this here. If you haven't read this section, you should do so after you have finished this chapter.

Identifying outcomes

In my experience, many of the problems that managers experience when they are persuading others are caused by the identification of inappropriate outcomes. Sometimes this is because managers don't spend enough time rigorously clarifying what their outcomes are. Sometimes it is because they simply get it wrong, and that is because it can be hard to get right. Here are the three most common mistakes I come across:

Outcomes and solutions

Many managers cause themselves no end of trouble by not making the distinction between outcomes and solutions. This is a crucial distinction, which relates back to the earlier passage on room for manoeuvre. The difference between the two can be defined as follows:

☐ The **outcome** is the change that you want to take place as a result of the persuasion.

☐ The **solution** is the way that this change is going to be achieved.

The mistake that is often made is that rather than focus on the desired outcome, we 'lock into' a specific solution and try to persuade the person to agree to it. We try to persuade our friend to go and see *Brief Encounter*, for example, when our desired outcome is to spend the evening with them. The confusion of outcomes with solutions causes two problems:

☐ There is probably more than one solution which could achieve the desired outcome – the one we have identified may not be the most appropriate or effective.

☐ We are more likely to generate resistance to a specific solution than a desired outcome. And once the solution has been resisted, it is much harder to get agreement to the outcome.

Here are some real-life examples of times when managers have suffered from confusing outcomes and solutions.

A senior technician was given the task of improving the relationship between a group of engineers and the laboratory technicians on a factory site. He decided that the way to do this was to arrange fortnightly meetings. After two meetings, people stopped coming. The relationship between the two groups deteriorated as a result. The inappropriate solution defeats the desired outcome.

- ☐ **Inappropriate outcome:** Get the two groups to meet together regularly.
- ☐ **Appropriate outcome:** Get better collaboration between the engineers and technicians.

A senior manager wants to improve the ability of one of his people to work in a team. She sends him on a groupworking skills programme. He resents this hugely, hates training, hates interpersonal skills training in particular, is shy, and awkward, doesn't want to be part of a team. He refuses to gain anything from the programme, goes back to work more stubbornly resistant than ever, and the relationship with his manager has deteriorated.

- ☐ **Inappropriate outcome:** Get him to go on the groupworking skills programme.
- ☐ **Appropriate outcome:** Get him to contribute more in team meetings.

In both of these examples, there are several possible solutions that would be more effective ways of achieving the desired outcome.

EXERCISE 11.8

Spend a few minutes now reflecting on examples from your own experience when you have caused yourself problems by locking into a specific solution rather than focusing on your desired outcome. If you can't think of examples from your own experience, think about some of the people you work with.

Focusing on the desired outcome before thinking about solutions will help you to:

- ☐ Clarify the change you want to see.
- ☐ Think of a range of possible solutions.
- ☐ Consider the preferences of the other person.

Ideas and action
I once observed a manager attempting to persuade an engineer during his appraisal that the safety procedures on the chemical plant where they worked were essential. He got nowhere. The engineer thought that *safety*

was essential, indeed he had the best safety record on the site, but he thought that the procedures were an overelaborate waste of time and he had more important things to do than jump through hoops for the bureaucrats in head office. They argued about this for a long time.

The manager told me afterwards that this was not the first time he had had that conversation, almost word for word, and he never got anywhere. And the sad thing was that although this was his best engineer he couldn't recommend him for promotion because he didn't follow the safety procedures. As a result, the engineer was getting increasingly bitter and disillusioned and it was getting harder to manage him.

The manager's problem was that by choosing to persuade the engineer that the safety procedures were essential, he had made his desired outcome focus on *ideas* not action. He wanted the engineer to agree to the principle of safety procedures, and got nowhere (wasting a lot of time getting there). The outcome he actually wanted was for the engineer to follow the procedures, and he doesn't have to agree with them to do that; it would be nice if he did, but it isn't a necessity. If the manager had made his desired outcome focus on the **action** he wanted the engineer to take, he could then get him to weigh the advantages of taking that action (promotion) against the cost (hassle).

☐ **Appropriate outcome:** Get him to use the safety procedures rigorously for the next month.

EXERCISE 11.9

Spend a few minutes now reflecting on examples from your own experience when you have caused yourself problems by focusing your desired outcomes on ideas rather than action. If you can't think of examples from your own experience, think about some of the people you work with.

If you anticipate that the other person is going to be resistant to the changes you want to see, you will almost always need to focus your desired outcome on actions rather than ideas. This will help you to:

☐ Avoid fruitless and repetitive arguments.

☐ Control the scope and focus of the discussion.

☐ Devise an effective strategy for persuading the other person.

Consultation and implementation
A variation on the need to persuade on ideas and action can be illustrated by a conversation I had with the project manager of a project I was facilitating. This was a major construction project and the client wanted to

develop a partnership with the contractor: to set up one project team made up of people from both organizations. At the time, this was a radical initiative in the construction industry, and the contractors particularly were not happy with the idea. Although there were potentially considerable benefits, it involved a substantial shift in attitude and behaviour.

The project manager had been successful in persuading his engineers to set up a combined engineering team. The procurement people were working together, albeit uneasily because of the personalities involved. But the contractor's construction manager was violently opposed to this way of working. The project manager had spent several sessions consulting with him to persuade him to make the decision to merge the two teams. Not surprisingly, he was getting nowhere.

In fact, the construction manager had no choice. The client was insisting on a joint team and nothing the construction manager could say was going to make any difference. The project manager, in his attempts to win him round, was embarking on a bogus consultation exercise which was masking the real nature of the situation. Better for him to establish that the decision was a given than to live in hope that the construction manager was going to make the decision for him. The project manager's time would be better spent working with him on how best to implement the decision to minimize the very real problems that it presented and to maximize the benefits that could be gained.

☐ **Appropriate outcome:** Develop an implementation plan for effectively merging the two construction teams.

EXERCISE 11.10

Spend a few minutes now reflecting on examples from your own experience when you have caused yourself problems by focusing on consultation rather than implementation. If you can't think of examples from your own experience, think about some of the people you work with.

Persuasion scenarios

So far, we have focused on a persuasive scenario in which you are trying to persuade someone to do something, the key variable being their level of resistance to your desired outcome. This is not the only persuasive scenario, however, and as a preface to looking at persuasive questions, I want to discuss briefly different kinds of persuasion, or rather the two key dynamics that determine the nature of the persuasive scenario. These dynamics revolve around outcomes and can be identified by answering these two questions:

☐ Do you have an outcome and if so how much room for manoeuvre do you have?

☐ Do they have an outcome and if so how different is it from yours?

The existence of outcomes creates the two key dynamics of persuasion: **movement** and **distance**. The movement we have looked at so far is one in which you are trying to move someone *towards* your desired outcome. The level of difficulty will be determined by the distance you have to move them – how resistant they are. Their resistance may be based on a rejection of your desired outcome, or on a preference for their own. This introduces a second persuasive movement: *away* from their desired outcome. The level of difficulty will be determined by the distance you have to move them – how acceptable their desired outcome is to you.

In other words, there will be *positive* persuasion scenarios when you are moving people towards your desired outcome; and there will be *negative* persuasion scenarios when you are moving people away from their desired outcome. This depends partly on who initiates the interaction, and partly on who is clear about what their desired outcome is. Figure 11.3 illustrates the two dynamics.

The dynamics of movement and distance are helpful in clarifying what kind of interaction we are engaged in, as follows:

☐ When you both have clear outcomes which are quite close together, then the amount of persuasive movement required will be low. This is the most straightforward persuasion scenario, which often quickly turns into a problem-solving discussion.

☐ When you have a clear desired outcome and they don't, the movement you are trying to achieve is positive, i.e. towards your outcome. This movement is created, as we have seen, by developing their need for your solution.

☐ When they have a clear outcome which they are trying to move you towards, and you don't have a clear outcome of your own, then the movement you are trying to achieve is negative, i.e. moving them away from their desired outcome. As we will see in the next section, this movement is created by creating doubt in their mind about the effectiveness of their solution.

☐ When you both have clear but different outcomes, the movement you are trying to achieve is both negative and positive. This is the most difficult scenario, especially when the distance is great. It is not just a persuasion, it is a full-blown negotiation, in which you are likely to have to make concessions if agreement is to be reached. Persuasion will be a key stage in this process and you will have to decide whether to concentrate on positive or negative movement.

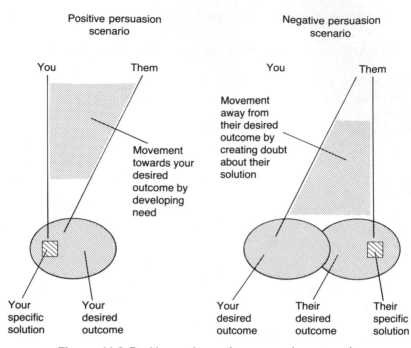

Figure 11.3 Positive and negative persuasion scenarios.

EXERCISE 11.11

Spend a few minutes now reflecting on recent persuasive interactions. Use the four options outlined above to clarify the nature of these interactions and then assess whether your strategic choices were appropriate.

Persuasive questions

There are three types of question that create movement in persuasions. The first two are necessary when you are trying to generate positive movement towards your desired outcome. The third is necessary when you are trying to generate negative movement away from the other person's desired solution.

Positive movement

The two questions which generate positive movement focus on developing the other person's need for your desired outcome or specific solution are:

The problem-focused question

Problem-focused questions make the person you are persuading recognize the dissatisfactions they are experiencing in the present or are likely to experience in the future if things don't change. They help to develop the first level of need to change. For example, to use a current issue in my life:

'Are you **worried** about having too much work at the moment?'
'How big a **problem** is it that you are overloaded?'
'Are you **concerned** that it's going to get worse in the future?'

The words in bold are the key words: they probe directly for dissatisfaction. If I answer any of those questions positively ('Yes, I'm worried. It's a big problem. I think it will get worse') then you have helped me to acknowledge an issue which, although I know it exists, I tend to ignore. If I answer the questions negatively ('No, things are fine, thanks'), the questions are still problem-focused ones – they just didn't uncover a problem.

If the questions above seem too direct, you can probe more gently. For example:

'Are you **happy** with your current workload?'
'How **confident** are you that you are managing it well?'
'Do you feel **positive** about things being easier in the future?'

These are still problem-focused questions. If I answer negatively ('Not very, I'm overloaded and I can't see a way out!'), I am acknowledging the same problems and dissatisfactions. The same process of need development has been initiated.

I know there is a problem with working too hard at the moment (caused mainly by adding the writing of this book to my workload!). But this is not a new problem for me; it is in fact one that I have come to accept as a constant in my life. If you were trying to develop my need to change the way I manage my work, you would need to do more than just get me to acknowledge that it was an issue. You would need to help me to see the price I paid for being so overworked. You would need to ask problem-focused questions which uncovered the *consequences* of the problem. For example:

'Don't you get more tired **as a result**?'
'Does that have **implications** for the quality of your work?'
'How does that **affect** your social life?'
'Does that **mean** you can never plan beyond the short term?'

The words in bold are the key words: they probe directly for the knock-on effects of the original dissatisfactions, thus forcing me to consider the full size and nature of the problem and its impact on my life. In other words, they influence the way I perceive cost – in this case, the cost of staying as I am.

ACTIVITY 11.2

Identify an interaction you have had recently when you have tried to persuade someone to do something they have been resistant to. It should be an interaction which required positive persuasion. Write down the problem-focused questions you could have asked the other person to develop their need to change. Alternatively plan a similar interaction that you know you will be having in the near future.

The value-focused question
Value-focused questions help the person you are persuading to recognize the need to change and the payoff to be gained if they do. They help to develop the second level of need to change: the perception of value. For example, continuing with my issue of working too hard:

> 'Would you **like** it if you had less work?'
> 'Would you **prefer** to spend more time at home?'
> 'Would you **feel happier** if you were under less pressure?'

The words in bold are the key words: they are seeking to establish initially that I do want to change. They establish the basis from which the value of change can be more fully explored. To raise my perception of the value of doing something about my current workload, you need to ask value-focused questions which help me to imagine the benefits of change. For example:

> 'What could you do with the extra time if you were working less?'
> 'Why would you like to spend more time at home?'
> 'How would reducing the level of pressure actually help?'

Questions such as these attempt to influence my perception so that in my mind the value of change outweighs the costs involved. I don't know what solution you are leading me to here to help me manage my workload better, but it is likely to involve me in some kind of effort, plus a requirement to let go of whatever emotional needs are being met by working too hard. These are considerable costs which will underpin my resistance to change. If you are to be successful, you will have to convince me that the gain is greater than the cost.

ACTIVITY 11.3

Identify an interaction you have had recently when you have tried to persuade someone to do something they have been resistant to. It should be an interaction which required positive persuasion. Write down the value-focused questions you asked or could have asked the other person to develop their perception of the value of change. Alternatively plan a similar interaction that you know you will be having in the near future.

Negative movement

The third type of persuasive question is used to generate negative movement away from the other person's preferred outcome.

The flaw-focused question

Flaw-focused questions expose weaknesses in the other person's preferred solution and so demonstrate that it is not appropriate. Without openly disagreeing, you can use such questions to drive wedges between the person and their solution, so that they conclude for themselves that it is unworkable. For example, if I proposed that the best way to help me manage my workload was to employ an administrator, you might ask questions such as these:

'But how much of your time is spent doing the kind of work an administrator would do?'
'Do you have the volume of administrative work to justify employing somebody?'
'Are you ever going to have the time to train an administrator so that they are able to provide you with the kind of support you need?'
'Will having an administrator stop you from taking on more work than you can handle?'
'To what extent would having an administrator address the root causes of your problems with overwork?'

Such questions force me to evaluate my proposal thoroughly. It may be that after such evaluation, I convince you that my proposal is valid – in which case the process has still been valuable for me. But it is possible that your questions will help me to recognize that my proposal will incur unacceptable costs or that it is not addressing the underlying issues, or both. If they do, they have the effect of moving me away from my proposal and will create a willingness on my part to propose alternatives or to consider your suggestions.

In effect, flaw-focused questions prepare the ground for defining need and therefore of moving back up the need development continuum. This is the essence of negative persuasion, when the other person presents you with a solution which you do not accept. The process is as follows:

☐ First, create distance between them and their solution by exposing its weaknesses.

☐ Second, use value-focused questions to define the need more clearly. For example:

'So is controlling the amount of client work you do at any one time the only way you are going significantly to reduce your workload?'

☐ Third, use problem-focused questions to move further back up the continuum to explore problems and develop dissatisfactions. For example:

'Why is it that you end up taking on more work than you can sensibly handle?'

At which point, sensing that this case study is getting a bit near the bone, I think I will stop!

ACTIVITY 11.4

Identify an interaction you have had recently when someone has tried to persuade you to do something that you have not wanted to do. Write down the flaw-focused questions that you asked or could have asked the other person to create distance between them and their preferred solution. Alternatively plan a similar interaction that you know you will be having in the near future.

Summary

In this chapter, we have looked at three aspects of managing persuasive interactions: style, strategy and skills. This has returned us to the issue of leadership style that we addressed in Chapter 3. The ways in which we choose to persuade and influence people are one of the most direct indicators of the kind of leader we are. The two principal persuasion styles – push and pull – are reflections of and expressions of the two principal leadership styles – directive and consultative. As with effective leaders, effective persuaders are able to use both styles effectively and appropriately.

Whatever style is appropriate, the principal underpinning persuasion strategy is the same: being right isn't persuasive. Whether you are pushing or pulling, it is advisable to see things from the other person's point of view and assess the level of need they do or should have for your desired outcome. Unless there is no benefit to them whatsoever, your approach should be to develop their need before exploring or proposing ways in which those needs could be met.

Whereas the push style is behaviourally straightforward – giving information and proposing – the pull style requires sophisticated questions which are focused on developing awareness of need and value. Although these questions are not alien to us, when we are using them consciously to persuade, they are a difficult skill to master. To use a pull style effectively, you not only have to ask smart questions, but you have to listen intently to what the other person is saying, to process the information they give and quickly formulate questions which create movement or doubt. This is a skill that needs to be practised – and one that is worth practising.

ACTIVITY 11.5

Before finishing, consider whether there are particular skills or behaviours that have been covered in this chapter that you feel it would be useful for you to practise. If so, plan how you intend to practise them. It is best to identify specific meetings or interactions where you know in advance that you are going to have to persuade people.

Index